Jefferson's Declaration of Independence

Jefferson's Declaration of Independence

Origins, Philosophy and Theology

Allen Jayne

THE UNIVERSITY PRESS OF KENTUCKY

Publication of this volume was made possible in part
by a grant from the National Endowment for the Humanities.

Scholarly publisher for the Commonwealth,
serving Bellarmine College, Berea College, Centre
College of Kentucky, Eastern Kentucky University,
The Filson Club Historical Society, Georgetown College,
Kentucky Historical Society, Kentucky State University,
Morehead State University, Murray State University,
Northern Kentucky University, Transylvania University,
University of Kentucky, University of Louisville,
and Western Kentucky University.

Editorial and Sales Offices: The University Press of Kentucky
663 South Limestone Street, Lexington, Kentucky 40508-4008

98 99 00 01 02   5 4 3 2 1

Frontispiece: Thomas Jefferson, a photogravure
made from the original painting by Mather Brown.

Library of Congress Cataloging-in-Publication Data
Jayne, Allen.
Jefferson's Declaration of independence : origins, philosophy, and
theology / Allen Jayne.
p.   cm.
Includes bibliographical references (p.   ) and index.
ISBN 0–8131–2017–9 (cloth : acid-free recycled paper)
1. United States. Declaration of Independence. I. Title.
KF4506.J39   1998   97–33157
973.3'13—dc21

This book is printed on acid-free recycled paper meeting
the requirements of the American National Standard
for Permanence of Paper for Printed Library Materials.

Manufactured in the United States of America

To Linda, Andrew, and Catherine

Contents

A recollection of our former vassalage in religion and civil government, will unite the zeal of every heart, and the energy of every hand, to preserve that independence in both which, under the favor of Heaven, a disinterested devotion to the public cause first achieved, and a disinterested sacrifice of private interests will now maintain.

—Thomas Jeferson, 17 October 1808

Preface

This book is based on my work in the history of ideas at Cambridge University. Some of the research, however, was done earlier, when I did not consider its relevance to practical life or intend to pursue graduate studies. At that time, my love for the study of ideas was particularly keen if they were abstract. Now, I find the material in this book relevant to current life in the United States, and perhaps other places, especially where it concerns the question of whether the political power of a government should be used to impose religion on its people. This was a burning issue in Jefferson's time, as it is today. Since there are many in the United States who fervently believe we should use governmental power in support of religious values, and many who just as fervently believe we should not, the heat from this issue is likely to be felt for some time.

If he were here today, Jefferson would support the latter group; he was instrumental in the passage of both state and federal laws that kept religion out of politics and politics out of religion. This book explains why he acted as he did and why he believed that all people in the United States, including those who support the use of political power in matters of religion, would benefit from the separation of state and church. I find Jefferson's thinking in this respect fundamentally sound. Indeed, I cannot help speculating—given the religious authoritarianism and sectarian bigotry that existed in the colonies in 1776 and have not been altogether eradicated today—that without the efforts of Jefferson and others, especially Madison, to establish the First Amendment to the Constitution, we could have become another Bosnia, Northern Ireland, or Middle East. In the eighteenth century, as a keen student of history, Jefferson saw law as a means to prevent sectarian disputes from erupting into persecution, strife, and war as they had done on a massive scale in sixteenth- and seventeenth-century France and seventeenth-century Germany, where Catholics and Protestants killed masses of people during their sectarian wars.

Since Jefferson did more than any other Founding Father to shape
and articulate the ideas and ideals upon which American civilization
is based, it seems logical to judge him by the positive or negative impact of those ideas and ideals. Yet there are those who argue that we
should judge him by his character as a man and by twentieth-century
standards of what is good despite the fact that others have written on
the injustice and absurdity of judging historical figures by today's standards. Indeed, there are those who even suggest that we should ignore
his ideas or scorn him because he allegedly took his slave Sally Hemings
as a mistress, had several children by her, and was, to a great extent,
isolated in his racist views. Such *ad hominem* and *ad tu quoque* arguments have often been politically motivated, not only during Jefferson's
life but even in the twentieth century. Douglass Adair in effect stated
this as respects the Hemings allegation and gave a scholarly analysis
of evidence indicating that it was not Jefferson but his nephew Peter
Carr who was Sally's lover and father of her children ("The Jefferson
Scandals," 1974). As to the allegation that Jefferson was isolated in
his racist views, Joyce Appleby cites evidence to the contrary: as an
abolitionist he inspired the Northwest Ordinance, which permanently
eliminated slavery from half of the United States, and the fact that his
racist idea of freeing slaves but having them live in separate territory
was not confined to him or a few like him but was popular among
abolitionists in the late eighteenth and most of the nineteenth centuries (*Los Angeles Times,* 10 November 1996).

Yet even if the allegations of these arguments were true, they have
no relation to the truth or goodness of Jefferson's legacy of ideas and
ideals. Socrates pointed out this principle of logic with a rebuke in
Phaedrus: "The men of old . . . deemed that if they heard the truth
even from 'oak or rock,' it was enough for them; whereas you seem to
consider not whether a thing is or is not true, but who the speaker is
and from what country the tale comes."

I am deeply indebted to three persons in connection with this book.
First among these is Bhek Pati Sinha, who has been a close friend of
my family for many years. During that time his generosity in sharing
his vast knowledge of ideas kindled and sustained my interest in this
subject. In fact, it was he who, during a visit to Monticello, when I
expressed an interest in the ideas and ideals of the third president of
the United States, suggested that I do research on Jefferson. Second
among these three is my wife, Linda. She gave me continuous support
during this endeavor, which on many occasions meant sacrificing her

own pleasure and convenience. The third member of this trinity is Richard Tuck, my Ph.D. supervisor at Cambridge. His suggestions and criticism helped me avoid many errors. I am also indebted to J.R. Pole of Oxford and Mark Goldie of Cambridge for their helpful comments and criticisms. And to the staff of the rare books reading room of the excellent University Library of Cambridge—where I sometimes found myself reading books by those who influenced Jefferson in the same editions as he owned or recommended—I express my gratitude for their courtesy and efficiency.

Introduction

Ralph Barton Perry's comment "The history of American democracy is a gradual realization, too slow for some and too rapid for others, of the implications of the Declaration of Independence" illustrates the importance America has ascribed to the Declaration's succinctly expressed ideals.[1] Given that importance, the question arises, What are those ideals, especially as Thomas Jefferson, the principal author of the Declaration, intended them to be? Answering this question has proved difficult for scholars, partly because Jefferson, by his own admission, neither originated the ideas and ideals contained in the first American document nor clearly explained where he got them.[2]

Since knowledge of the source of the ideas Jefferson placed in the Declaration is important to understanding its ideals, much has been written on this subject. Yet the images of the Declaration's principles remain confused and blurred, for there have been diverse opinions as to who the thinkers and philosophers were who contributed to the Declaration via Jefferson, not to mention different interpretations of particular contributors. So diverse are the opinions of scholars who have written on the political theory of Thomas Jefferson and the Declaration of Independence over much of this century that support can be found for virtually every contemporary political ideology within this vast array of literature, as a few samples will show.

Despite its diversity, this literature can be divided into two general categories. The first is dominated by what is called the liberal or Lockean orthodox interpretation, according to which government is formed to protect the natural rights of the individual. C.B. Macpherson's possessive individualism interpretation of Locke (the dominance of individual self-interest over the well-being of the community) has come to be associated with this category,[3] even though many scholars maintain that it distorts Locke, who emphasized morality as a restraint on actions that would damage the community.[4] The second category comprises a variety of revisionary interpretations that minimize or exclude the influence of Locke, most of which are communitarian as a result of subordinating individual rights and interests to the overall well-being of the community. The communitarian revisionists as Thomas Spragens perceives them, however, are not opposed to liberalism. Rather, they have attempted "to recapture some of the . . . moral depth" that liberalism "lost as a result of the philosophical shifts and political divisions" it "encountered during its several hundred year history."[5]

The pillar of the first category is Carl Becker's seminal work *The Declaration of Independence: A Study in the History of Ideas*, published in 1922. There Becker stated of "the political philosophy of Nature and natural rights" promulgated in the Declaration, "The lineage is direct: Jefferson copied Locke, and Locke quoted Hooker."[6] For almost fifty years no one challenged Becker's Lockean perspective; his ideas were more or less confirmed by succeeding generations of scholars.[7]

The late 1950s, however, marked the beginning of the second category. This was the inception of the "classical republican" movement within the revisionist school, culminating in a different conclusion as to the source of the political theory of the Declaration of Independence. In republicanism the state is based on "virtue," which consists in individuals subordinating their personal interests to the overall public good of the commonwealth. This communitarian element of republicanism, with its "lament for a lost golden age,"[8] is, of course, different from Lockean liberalism based on governmental protection of individual rights, including the right to property acquired through labor. Caroline Robbins's *Eighteenth-Century Commonwealthman*, published in 1959, laid the foundation for classical republican revisionists. She maintained that the political thought of Aristotle, Machiavelli, Harrington, and Sidney, among others, provided the basis as well as the extension of classical republicanism.[9] It was Bernard Bailyn, however, who provided the basis for interpreting Jefferson's political ideology as classical republican. His contention in *The Ideological Origins of the American Revolution*, published in 1967, that Jefferson was a thorough reader of the Greek and Roman classics and that classical republicanism was present in the colonies led other scholars to wonder whether Jefferson and the Declaration might be interpreted in terms of republicanism rather than Lockean liberalism.[10]

J.G.A. Pocock, one of the most prominent explicators of classical republicanism, did perceive this ideology in the Declaration. In his extensive writings Pocock defined the type of person who would form the foundation of the ideal republican state as one who was economically independent through property ownership. Such independence gave an individual the ability to liberate himself from his self-interests, thereby enabling him to concern himself with the public good or over-all well-being of the commonwealth. Pocock called such economic in-dependence "virtue" and its lack or loss "corruption." If an individual lost his economic independence, his moral health would be undermined by a dependence on "government or social superiors." His concern for the public good would then give way to concern for his own eco-nomic survival, which would be contingent upon abiding by the po-litical concerns or even the political dictates of those upon whom he was dependent. Such "demoralization" of individuals could also arise from exclusive concern with "private or group satisfactions" for purely selfish reasons. Once deterioration of the moral health of individuals started, it was "likely to prove uncheckable," since "men could not be born with new natures." This view of the moral nature of man was described by Pocock as "at once post-Christian and prehistoric."[11]

What wrought havoc with civic "virtue" and brought about "cor-ruption," according to Pocock, was "patronage": one branch of gov-ernment making others, and individuals too, dependent upon it through credit, national debt, or the army. Factions attempting to effect such dependency he called "Court," and those in favor of classical republi-canism he called "Country." The Country ideology, which emphasized "mixed government and personal independence," "belonged to a tra-dition of classical republicanism and civic humanism, anchored in the Florentine Renaissance [Machiavelli], Anglicized by James Harrington, Algernon Sidney, and Henry St. John, Viscount Bolingbroke, but look-ing unmistakably back to antiquity and to Aristotle, Polybius, and Cicero." This ideology was widely disseminated and accepted in the eighteenth century, according to Pocock, accounting "for much of the classicism" of that period, which was characterized by a "civic and patriotic" disposition.[12]

Pocock maintained in *The Machiavellian Moment* (1975) that the American revolution was a manifestation of a Renaissance humanist, classical republican "Machaivellian moment," since the colonists claimed they were resisting a corrupt British imperial Parliament. He also maintained that liberalism of a Lockean natural rights variety in colonial America was a myth.[13] It is hardly any wonder, then, that when speaking of the role of the Declaration of Independence in the American Revolution, he said it was

a quasi-Lockean rhetoric that enumerated the wrongful acts by which the government of that state [Great Britain] had lost its lawful authority over the American people. . . . The result, however, was less the dissolution of all government over that people than the exaltation of their existing governments into states; rather, it was contended—by arguments that made use of Locke's doctrine of a right to emigrate—that these governments already existed in history and by right of their historic origins enjoyed a contractual autonomy. The chain of arguments to this point was juristic; it deployed the concept of right rather than the republican concept of virtue.[14]

Pocock's conclusion that the Declaration was "quasi-Lockean rhetoric" suggests that he saw a different aspect of the Declaration's "rhetoric" than its Lockean part. He mentioned such an aspect, one that was classical republican, when he said of the content of the first American document: "King and Parliament must be represented as totally corrupt and aiming at total corruption; the new states must establish sovereignty in the only form that aimed at the systematic institutionalization of virtue. For the reason that they must become states, they must become republics. The rhetoric of right as the precondition of independence merged with the rhetoric of liberty and virtue as the preconditions of one another."[15] This view of the Declaration tends to reduce its Lockean aspect to one that was immediately useful to the colonies in separating themselves from their mother country but not one that would have the lasting significance of its classical republicanism. Other scholars, among them Gordon Wood, Lance Banning, Forrest McDonald, and John Murrin, largely if not completely support this view.[16]

A nonclassical republican, communitarian revisionary interpretation of the source of Jefferson's ideas in the Declaration, one that excludes Lockean influence, is Garry Wills's *Inventing America: Jefferson's Declaration of Independence* (1978). Wills maintained that virtually all the ideology of the Declaration came from the Scottish Enlightenment thinkers, especially the moral sense philosopher Francis Hutcheson.[17] Hutcheson's moral sense, as Wills described it, "was directed to others—it was the principle of sociability, of benevolence, not selfishness." Wills went on to state that "no politics built upon the moral sense could make self-interest the foundation of the social contract." Hutcheson's ideas on rights were consistent with the moral sense, and Wills described a Hutchesonean right as "a power over others." Such a power, however, was legitimate only "so long as benevolence or innocence are directing" it, and the criterion or "test" of a rightful power was its contribution to the public good.[18] To put it another way, a Hutchesonean right is a power to compel others to perform benevolent acts that enhance the well-being of the community—which makes Hutcheson a communitarian.

Wills then elaborated on Jefferson's phrasing in the Declaration and that of some Hutchesonean passages and concluded that Jefferson placed Hutcheson's ideas in the Declaration, even though he was careful not to argue that Jefferson borrowed directly from Hutcheson. This interpretation gives the Declaration a communitarian rather than an individualistic emphasis born of Lockean ideas on rights. Wills, it should be mentioned, minimized the impact of the Scottish philosopher Henry Home, Lord Kames on Jefferson's moral sense ideas. Kames, as Wills pointed out, made a distinction between justice, which he defined as refraining from doing harm to others, and benevolence, which he defined as performing acts that benefit others.[19]

Still another nonclassical republican revisionary interpretation of Jefferson's political ideas, one with a Marxist cast, is found in Richard Mathews, *The Radical Politics of Thomas Jefferson* (1984). Mathews maintained that Jefferson did not subscribe to either classical republicanism or possessive individualism. The retrospective aspect of the classical republican and civic humanist ideology was alien to Jefferson's thinking, since the author of the Declaration, as Mathews stated, "argued the necessity for every generation to exercise its natural right to create anew its political life." Jefferson's idea of "freedom," continued Mathews, "requires that each generation must have a chance to begin society over again every twenty years," at which time "all the laws would automatically become void." This would entail a revisionary approach to law to make it correspond with the "human and social evolution" Jefferson saw continuously taking place. Such a change of law could be accomplished through revolution, and Jefferson, said Mathews, "was America's first and foremost advocate of permanent revolution."[20]

As respects Lockean possessive individualism, Mathews is of the opinion that Jefferson argued against a capitalistic economy by urging men to live in rural communities with the "small farm" as the means of supporting their families: "This pastoral life style," said Mathews, "is based, not on profit, but on science, moderation, and beauty," a way of life that would give men "leisure" and thereby time "to think." It would produce the type of unspecialized man whom, Mathews stated, "Marx described in *The German Ideology*" and "hoped to restore to his universality." Mathews, like many of the revisionist scholars, made Jefferson a communitarian. He found evidence for what he described as "communitarian anarchism" in his study of the American Indians, "which resulted in a deep admiration of these tribal communities" and "helped to convince Jefferson that man was a social, harmonious, cooperative, and just creature who, under the appropriate socioeconomic conditions, could happily live in a community that did not need the presence of the Leviathan."[21]

Another extremist interpretation is Conor Cruise O'Brien's *Long Affair* (1996). O'Brien, however, sees Jefferson's ideas as in accord with those of the Ku Klux Klan and terrorist Timothy McVeigh instead of Marx, as Mathews does, even though he goes along with Mathews's view that Jefferson was an advocate of perpetual revolution. Apparently, neither O'Brien nor Mathews seriously considered Jefferson's idea that when a democratic constitution, agreed upon by the people or their representatives, needs amendment or is not adhered to, "we can assemble with all the coolness of philosophers, and set it to rights, while every other nation on earth must have recourse to arms to amend or restore their constitutions."[22]

Certainly there are critics of the view that classical republicanism or indeed any ideology with a communitarian thrust was the predominating ideology of the American revolutionary and postrevolutionary periods. Joyce Appleby and Isaac Kramnick are prominent among such critics; so are John Diggins, Thomas Pangle, Steven Dworetz, and Garret Ward Sheldon, all of whom have reasserted a Lockean influence on the Declaration.[23] Yet the communitarian side of what has now become an ongoing debate among scholars has not been inactive. Barry Alan Shain, for example, in *The Myth of American Individualism* (1994), gives what he calls a "majoritarian" communitarian interpretation of the Declaration and perceives no Lockean influence on that document at all.[24]

Considering the diversity of opinion as to the source of the ideas Jefferson incorporated in the Declaration, one of the twofold purposes of this work is to trace where he got those ideas by examining the writings of some of the authors he read before he drafted that document. Comparing statements in these works with some Jefferson wrote in the Declaration and others scattered throughout his extensive writings will show their impact on his thinking and how they shaped his worldview as succinctly expressed in the Declaration. The second purpose of this work is to demonstrate that Jefferson's worldview was promulgated in the Declaration not only as political theory that justified political independence from Great Britain but also as heterodox theology, which Jefferson believed was inextricably linked to the efficacy of the Declaration's democratic polity. I argue that this succinctly stated theology, with its heterodox concepts of God and man, was among the primary truths of the democratic polity institutionalized in the Declaration. In addition, I argue that Jefferson saw the concepts of God and man upheld by orthodox theological circles in the colonies as antithetical to the Declaration's theological and political ideals. Scholars such as Paul Conkin have argued that it is impossible to determine Jefferson's worldview because he "always ended up with such an eclectic mix of ideas as to defy systematic ordering. He was a creature of mood and sentiment much more than a rigorous thinker."[25] There is some truth in this, yet to say that Jefferson's ideas "defy systematic ordering" seems extreme. And even if Conkin is right, some would argue that it is the business of scholars to try to bring coherence to Jefferson's thought, however unsuccessful such attempts may be.

The first chapter describes some of the principal beliefs held in the predominant orthodox theological circles of the colonies at the time of the Declaration. The second chapter deals with the sources of Jefferson's heterodox theology, emphasizing its deistic, universal, and impartial God. The third chapter explains the premises and principles of Jefferson's politics. The fourth, fifth, and sixth chapters discuss the nature and significance of Jefferson's concept of man as an essentially moral being (not tainted by original sin) endowed with reason and rights. They show why Jefferson adopted ideas, philosophies, and theologies that affirmed and upheld the morality, reason, and rights of man and why he rejected those that denied these three attributes of human nature or claimed authority over them. These chapters also emphasize Jefferson's epistemic views, including those contained in the Declaration, and their relation to his concept of a democratic polity, as well as his reasons for rejecting philosophical skepticism. The seventh chapter documents Jefferson's defense of the Declaration's political theory and heterodox theology against the orthodox religious views of the time. The conclusion discusses his hope and trust that the natural rights of man underlying the Declaration would finally prevail the world over.

I believe that my interpretations of Jefferson's ideas and ideals as stated in the Declaration are original in two ways: first, they demonstrate that a succinctly stated heterodox theology is institutionalized in the Declaration as a primary truth and necessary corollary of its political theory; second, they demonstrate through analysis the vital function of Jefferson's and the Declaration's epistemic views in Jefferson's and the Declaration's concept of democracy. I think these interpretations are important because without them the ideas and ideals of the Declaration of Independence cannot be understood as Jefferson intended them to be understood. Writing on early modern political thought, Mark Goldie stated that "philosophical theology is not properly recognized in modern histories of political thought written from a secular standpoint."[26] Certainly Jefferson's and the Declaration's political thought in the eighteenth century have been written about, for the most part, from a secular perspective that offers at best a limited account of theology. This work is intended to demonstrate in a comprehensive way the interdependence of political thought and philosophical theology (including epistemology) in Jefferson's worldview as expressed in the Declaration of Independence.

1

The Theological Context

It is important to an understanding of Jefferson's views to note the antiegalitarian, antidemocratic implications of Judeo-Christian orthodoxy in the colonies at the time of the American Revolution. It is not easy, however, to determine what colonial religious orthodoxy was because religious pluralism was rampant in the latter half of the eighteenth century in the British Atlantic colonies of North America. Prominent among religious groups from the beginning of the war with Great Britain in 1775 to the adoption of the Declaration of Independence on 4 July 1776 were Calvinist or Calvinist-related sects. According to Ralph Barton Perry, they included 575,000 Congregationalists, the majority of whom were New England Puritans; 410,000 Presbyterians; 75,000 Dutch Reformed; 25,000 Baptists; and 50,000 German Reformed, who were also influenced by Zwingli. Of the remaining colonial population, Anglicans probably exceeded 1,000,000, but there were also many nominal Anglicans among the 476,000 slaves in the South who followed the faith of their masters. Methodists and Lutherans were few, and Jews numbered about 2,000.[1] James McGregor Burns adds that there were in addition 25,000 Catholics and 200,000 members of German churches apart from Reformed.[2] As John Locke said of such different religious groups, each believed that it alone was orthodox and others erroneous and heretical, and as Ian Harris says, "he denied that there was any judge of orthodoxy on earth."[3] Jefferson agreed and indeed sounded much like Locke when he said the various sectarian groups of the world were "all different, yet every one confident it is the only true one," and added with a touch of sarcasm, "A man must be very clear-sighted who can see the impression of the finger of God on any particular one of them."[4]

Knowledge of the differences among these various religious groups at the time of the Revolution, however, is less important to this work than knowledge of their similarities: the orthodox theological beliefs shared by the colonial religious groups that were antithetical to the heterodox theology and political theory of Jefferson's worldview as reflected in the Declaration of Independence. Among these shared beliefs were an aspect of God common to Judaism and the theologians who founded or contributed to the theologies of the colonial Christian denominations, and an aspect of man held by those theologians.

One general aspect of orthodoxy common to Judaism and Christianity in the colonies was the claim of having been chosen by God to the exclusion of other religions, denominations, and sects. This claim began with the founding of Judaism and Christianity, both of which are based on revelation—specifically, exclusive revelations made by an eternal, transcendental God who is above and beyond human understanding. These revelations are exclusive because they are closed to the vast majority of human beings and cannot be attained by virtue of any human effort. They come only from God and in only two ways: either God grants them to one or a very few human beings—prophets—chosen by Him to the exclusion of all others, or He gives them through the incarnation of God in human form on earth. What God reveals in these two ways is truth: the truth of God, the truth of creation, the truth of humanity, and the true morality. Once made, these divine revelations are set forth in writing and thereby become the word of God, or scripture. They are considered final and conclusive—good, true, and complete for all eternity.

The dispute between Judaism and Christianity is not over the concept of exclusive revelation common to both religions but over the authenticity of the recipients, the authenticity of their claimed revelations, and, when they conflict, which revelations are truly final and conclusive. Judaism claims that the revelations God gave to Moses are final and conclusive and that they contain the whole of religious truth; nothing, therefore, can be added. As Maimonides described Judaism, "Remember that ours is the true and authentic Divine religion, revealed to us through Moses, the master of the former as well as the later prophets."[5] This is, of course, the reason Judaism rejects the revelations of Jesus. Christians, however, claim that Jesus' revelations are later and greater than those of Moses and, as set forth in the New Testament, are final and conclusive and contain the whole of religious truth because they come from God in the form of the Son, the second person of the Trinity. Jesus' words "I am the way, the truth, and the life: no man cometh unto the Father, but by me" (John 14:6)[6] make this clear, according to Christians. Each religion thus believes itself chosen by God to be the only recipient of the complete version of God's truth and holds that anyone who wants religious truth or salvation must come to them.

As a result of exclusive revelation, Judaism and Christianity both establish a hierarchy of authority from God above to a prophet or incarnation, thence down to scripture or church or temple, and thence to the rabbis or priests or ministers. Beneath this hierarchy are the people, subject to its authority, thereby having no choice but to believe and obey what is contained in God's exclusive revelations and the instructions and interpretations of them provided by the intermediaries or agents of God (the rabbis, priests, or ministers). Therefore, individuals who align themselves with predominating versions of Judaism and Christianity are not allowed to remain a part of that religion if they use their reason to deny the truth claims of God or His hierarchy of authorities. Rational conclusions must agree with these authorities, which do not give reason the freedom to reject their truth claims.[7] Exclusive revelation in this manner restrains and constrains the use of individual reason in religion and thereby claims authority over the people in the name of God.

Putting man under the authority of God's chosen agents or intermediaries gives rise to the belief by each religion, denomination, or sect that it alone has been given the true version of exclusive revelation and is thereby chosen by God, which in turn gives rise to sectarian bigotry and persecution. In addition, exclusive revelation makes scripture infallible. Scripture is God's exclusive revelation in written form, and since it came from an all-wise, all-knowing, all-powerful, and benevolent God, it cannot be erroneous. This is precisely how the vast majority of colonial Americans, as well as most of the world's Christians and Jews at that time, regarded the Old and/or New Testament.[8] As a result, men who followed these religions were subject to an infallible, inerrant, God-given, authoritative epistemology. To them the revealed word of God in the Bible was the source of knowledge of the truth not only of God, man, and morality but also of science, since creation as described in Genesis was part of the Bible and was therefore regarded as literally true. Miracles too, a vital part of both the Old and the New Testament, were regarded as true. The miracles described in scripture established proof of the authenticity of the prophets and the incarnation, who were the recipients and disseminators of God's revealed word or truth.

Predestinator God

One aspect of truth believed to have been revealed through exclusive revelation was the nature of God, a part of which was His predestinator function, which gave rise to the doctrine of predestination. This doctrine is part of Judaism as a result of God's choosing through his grace the "seed" of certain individuals to become the chosen people and nation of Jewish religion.[9] It is also part of both Catholic and Protestant theology. In Christianity, predestination is grace or a special favor from God, but instead of being granted to a people, as in Judaism, it is granted only to certain individuals at the time of creation. Christian predestinating grace directs or destines individuals to the state of salvation in the future, a state they cannot attain by moral actions alone, according to predominating versions of Christianity.

As Saint Thomas Aquinas wrote in *Summa Theologica:* "It is fitting that God should predestine men. For all things are subject to His providence. . . . Now if a thing cannot attain to something by the power of its nature, it must be directed thereto by another; thus, an arrow is directed by the archer towards a mark. . . . For to destine is to direct or send. . . . Thus it is clear that predestination, as regards its objects, is a part of providence." Aquinas emphasized that not all are predestined to salvation: "It is clear that predestination is a kind of exemplar of the ordering of *some* persons towards eternal salvation, existing in the divine mind" (emphasis added). This "ordering of *some* persons" is an election or choosing by God of certain individuals for salvation and the exclusion of others. Aquinas specified that the reason for God's choice of some over others was love: "Predestination logically presupposes election; and election presupposes love. . . . Whence the predestination of some to eternal salvation logically presupposes that God wills their salvation; and to this belongs both election and love:—love, inasmuch as He wills them to this particular good of eternal salvation; since love is to wish well to anyone, . . .—election, inasmuch as He wills this good to some in preference to others; since He reprobates some. . . . For by His will, by which in loving He wishes good to someone, is the cause of that good possessed by some in preference to others."[10] In short, God loves and prefers some persons and not others from the very beginning. God is motivated by this loving preference to grant predestinating grace to those He loves and to withhold such grace from those He does not love.

Some theologians, it is true, maintained that predestination was antithetical to the performance of good works by an individual, based on free will, as a contributing factor to salvation. Catholics, however, established a delicate and somewhat precarious balance between predestinating grace and good works, both of which they deemed necessary for salvation. St. Ignatius of Loyola, even though he said, "It must be true that no one is saved except he who is predestinated," expressed apprehension about the negative impact an emphasis on predestination might have upon the performance of good works. Yet he did not wish to emphasize good works without grace, for such works alone would not guarantee salvation. To avoid these extremes, he advised caution in stressing either predestination or good works in connection with salvation: "We must speak with circumspection concerning this matter, lest perchance stretching too far the grace of predestination of God, we should seem to wish to shut out the force of free will and the merits of good works, or on the other hand, attributing to the latter more than belongs to them." Loyola maintained that persons who thought they were predestined by God for salvation or damnation would very likely neglect good works, or even indulge in sin, and then rationalize their actions by arguing, "If my salvation or damnation is already determined regardless of whether I do ill or well, it cannot happen differently." Therefore Loyola advised not only caution but moderation when talking of predestination by stating, "We should not speak on the subject of predestination frequently."[11]

Martin Luther also promulgated the doctrine of predestination, finding a scriptural basis for it in both Old and New Testaments. He maintained that the difference between Isaac and Rebecca's twin sons Jacob and Esau was election or predestination by God: Jacob was predestined; Esau was not. He quoted Jesus' words in John 13:18 and 6:44 in support of predestination: "I speak not of you all: I know whom I have chosen" and "No man can come to me, except the Father which hath sent me draw him." Luther maintained further that good works born of the free will of individuals could not be reconciled with predestination, and yet the elect would overcome the inclination to sin— born of Adam and Eve's original sin—and would indulge in good works. This effect of predestination, however, was *not* because of the moral redemption and free will of the elect. Election did not change their inclination to sin; their good works were due to the intervention of God in their lives, not their free will. It was God's righteousness, God's guidance, and God's strength, said Luther, that enabled those elected to refrain from sin and perform good works.[12]

Predestination was part of Huldreich Zwingli's theology, as well. He pushed the doctrine to its extreme implications by maintaining that those predestined, whether born before or after the advent of Jesus, could not be damned by original sin or the lack of Christian sacraments; election saved them: "Jacob was beloved by God before he was born; original sin, therefore, cannot have damned him. So Jeremiah, John and others. . . . This . . . concerns election and predestination. . . . Therefore, blessedness and grace are from election, so also is rejection, not from the participation in signs or sacraments."[13]

John Calvin emphasized the doctrine of predestination more than any other Christian theologian. In his *Institutes of the Christian Religion* he specified: "We call predestination God's eternal decree, by which he determined with himself what he willed to become of each man. For all are not created in equal condition; rather, eternal life is foreordained for some, eternal damnation for others. Therefore, as any man has been created to one or the other of these ends, we speak of him as predestined to life or death." Calvin developed his exegesis on predestination with a discussion of God's election or choosing of some peoples or nations whom He favored over others for a magnificent destiny, citing the Jewish people and nation as an example: God chose the "whole offspring of Abraham, to make it clear that in his choice rests the future condition of each nation." He cited Deuteronomy 32:8–9 in support of this claim: "When the Most High divided the nations, and separated the sons of Adam . . . the people of Israel were his portion, . . . the cord of his inheritance." Calvin emphasized that according to Moses, God chose the Jewish people and their nation as His own because of His preferential love for the patriarchs, not because of any merit in the Jews. He again quoted scripture to support this position (Deuteronomy 4:37), which specified that God, because of this love of the patriarchs, "chose their seed after them."[14]

Maimonedes too maintained that the Jews' favored position with God was based not on merit but on God's loving grace: God's choice of the Jewish people and nation "did not happen because of our merits but rather as an act of Divine grace."[15] Calvin, by emphasizing lack of merit and even demerit on the part of the Jews, made it clear that God granted grace of His own free will and that no meritorious action or even law could bind Him to grant it. If God could be bound in any way, He would not be free, according to Calvin, who said: "In the election of a whole nation God has already shown that in his mere generosity he has not been bound by any laws but is free, so that equal apportionment of grace is not to be required of him. The very inequality of his grace proves that it is free."[16] Like individuals, nations were treated unequally by God, according to Calvin. God in an arbitrary fashion favored and disfavored whomever and whatever he pleased.

Calvin applied to individuals his arguments in support of God's freely given grace to peoples and nations. He maintained that no person could by the merit of good works put God in his or her debt and thereby compel Him to grant the reward of salvation: "God of his mere good pleasure preserves whom he will, and moreover . . . he pays no reward, since he can owe none." Calvin cited Paul (Romans 11:5–6) to substantiate his position that salvation by God's freely given predestinating grace was opposed to salvation earned by individual good works: "If it [salvation] is by grace, it is no more of works; otherwise grace would no more be grace. But if it is of works, it is no more of grace; otherwise work would not be work."[17]

Calvin completely ruled out an individual's good works as a means to attain salvation. Eternal life or death was determined solely by God's freely given grace at the time each individual was created, before he had a chance to perform any works, good or bad. Calvin even denied that God's foreknowledge of an individual's future good or bad works determined whether or not God would grant salvation or impose damnation: if God granted grace or condemned men to damnation based on foreknowledge, that grace or condemnation would not be freely given; it would be the result of an individual's (future) merit or demerit. In addition, Calvin believed, as did Luther, that all virtue in any individual was the result of election, which brought divine righteousness, guidance, and the strength to be moral despite the elect's inborn inclination to sin or moral taint, the effect of original sin. Election or predestinating grace did not change an elect's tainted nature. It merely provided divine help to overcome that nature. As Calvin put it, some individuals were "elected to be holy, not because already holy." He again quoted Paul (2 Timothy 1:9) to support his position: God "called us with a holy calling, not according to our works, but according to his own purpose, and the grace that was given to us by Christ before time began."[18]

The predestinating God of the New Testament who granted loving grace to some, as Aquinas pointed out, was also a practitioner of hate, according to Calvin, who used both the Old and the New Testament to support his view.[19] In Malachi 1:2–3, God said of the twin sons of Isaac and Rebecca, "Yet I loved Jacob, And I hated Esau." In Romans 9:11–13, Paul not only repeated the message from Malachi but put it in the context of predestination, for God's statement of Jacob's election was made to Rebecca preceding the birth of her twins: "(For the children being not yet born, neither having done any good or evil, that the purpose of God according to election might stand, not of works, but of him that calleth;) It was said unto her, The elder [Esau] shall serve the younger [Jacob]. As it is written, Jacob have I loved, but Esau have I hated."

Saint Augustine, one of the early advocates of predestination who influenced later theologians, including Calvin, also quoted Romans 9:11–13. In his *Enchiridion* the Bishop of Hippo perceived that the Apostle Paul's account of what God said in these verses, as well as the Old Testament's similar statements in Malachi, would very likely cast God in an unjust light. This was because God professed love and hatred for Jacob and Esau respectively before either had committed any actions that could be the basis of these feelings or judgments. "For it seems unjust," said Augustine, "that, in the absence of any merit or demerit from good or evil works, God should love the one and hate the other." He justified God's opposite treatment of Jacob and Esau, however, first by stating that both were born under God's wrath and condemnation as a result of the effects of original sin—"Thus both the twins were born children of wrath, not on account of any works of their own, but because they were bound in the fetters of that original condemnation which came through Adam"—and then by maintaining that God could freely grant or deny his love and grace as He pleased, despite the fact that both Jacob and Esau deserved condemnation. Therefore, God "loved Jacob of His undeserved grace, and hated Esau of His deserved judgement." Thus God was just in His unequal treatment of Jacob and Esau, in Augustine's opinion, but was nonetheless a God of hate for all mankind as a result of the effects of original sin in the absence of His freely given grace.[20]

The doctrine of predestination, then, was a pervasive aspect of orthodox Judeo-Christian theology. It was in Catholicism as well as Protestantism, since Paul, Augustine, Aquinas, Loyola, Luther, Zwingli, and Calvin all believed in it.

Tainted Humanity

According to orthodox versions of Christianity both Catholic and Protestant, the inability of men and women to save themselves by their own moral acts was due to the inherited effects of the original sin of Adam and Eve. Unlike predestination, the fall is not a part of Judaic belief but is fundamental to the doctrine of virtually every Christian denomination. Paul, Augustine, Aquinas, Loyola, Luther, Calvin, and Zwingli all described it as an affliction of moral taint or propensity to commit sin to which no human being is immune.[21] As a result of this taint, human nature is not to be trusted for moral determinations or moral behavior. "For cursed be the one that trusteth in man," said Saint Augustine, quoting Jeremiah 17:5.[22] Trust should be in God, not man. God's revelation or scripture, with emphasis on His law, became the principal object of trust in God for Protestantism, whereas God's agents in the form of the Church and its priests assumed that position in Catholicism.[23] The difference was not absolute but a question of emphasis, since the Reformers did not exclude the church nor the Catholic hierarchy the word of God as an object of trust in God.

One of the effects of the doctrine of original sin was that it deprived people of moral authority both individually and collectively. The source of moral authority in Catholicism was found in the "tradition and the teaching of the Church" and its priests, who, as intermediaries between God and man, administered that authority.[24] Protestants were subject to the moral authority of scripture as administered by the clergy. For example, Puritans in New England elected a pastor, but this democratic element then stopped abruptly because it was his duty to instruct the congregation on moral ordinances, and he would talk down to the congregation from the authority of his office and scripture.[25] Despite the Protestant emphasis on the authority of scripture over that of church and priests, Lutherans and most Calvinist denominations maintained an ecclesiastical authority to interpret the scriptures according to their particular theological perspectives, and that authority applied to revealed moral law as well as doctrine. This scriptural and ecclesiastical authority, or Protestant scholasticism, granted that men had the use of reason but only if its conclusions agreed with the teachings and precepts of scripture as interpreted by ecclesiastical authority; Protestant scholasticism in this respect paralleled medieval scholasticism. Its authoritarian approach vitiated Luther's concept of the priesthood of all believers and the Reformation's original emphasis on direct individual access to God's revelations in scripture and freedom to interpret those revelations.[26] There was de facto authority of church and clergy even in liberal sects that allowed individual interpretation of God's revealed word, for their clergy were the individuals who usually had the greatest knowledge of scripture; hence, their congregations in most instances yielded to their views of moral law as well. Regardless of denomination, Forrest Wood maintains, by virtue of their position in the church or the community, the colonial clergy all made some claim to moral infallibility and thereby authority over their congregations.[27] Such was the moral authority of orthodox Christian leaders at the time of the American Revolution, Adolph Koch argued, that it kept the laity in their place and provided them with a "slave's morality."[28]

Nor was the authority of the colonial clergy confined to doctrine and morality. It extended to politics. In 1780 Joseph Galloway wrote of the political influence of the ecclesiastical authorities of various sects on their followers before the Revolutionary War, especially the Presbyterians. He said that in the synods of that denomination, "all their general affairs, political as well as religious, are debated and decided" and "from hence their orders and decrees are issued throughout America; and to them as ready and implicit obedience is paid as is due the authority of any sovereign power whatever."[29] Discussing the New England clergy's political authority and preachments in colonial America, Richard Buel Jr. and Edmund S. Morgan wrote that the clergy of all colonial sects never stopped giving instruction in political thought in the 1760s and 1770s.[30] It seems clear, therefore, that colonial American religions stultified individual determinations of morality, religious opinion, and politics on the part of their own members and followers.

The concepts of God, man, and the source of religious truth common to the theologies of colonial Christian groups at the time of the Declaration of Independence, and their resultant authority over the individual, were not only antithetical to the political theory but also the heterodox theology of that document. Jefferson's ideas, therefore, would conflict with those concepts, as well as with Judaism's theology of a chosen people and nation, before 1776. Among those who would shape his thinking during this period was Lord Bolingbroke, who was instrumental in his abandonment of orthodox theological views. As a result of Bolingbroke's influence, and that of the Enlightenment as well, Jefferson emerged with a critical disposition toward Judeo-Christian theology and a commitment to the universal God of nature or natural theology.

2

Bolingbroke and the Enlightenment

Jefferson's heterodox religious views were founded on an Enlightenment outlook in general and the writings of Henry St. John, Lord Viscount Bolingbroke, in particular. It is the God of his heterodoxy that appears in the Declaration of Independence rather than the God of the Bible.

Jefferson's introduction to the Enlightenment by William Small marked the beginning of a thought process that led to his rejection of the doctrines of the Anglican faith in which he had been raised.[1] A product of the Scottish Enlightenment, Small received a master's degree from Marichal College in Aberdeen in 1755. In 1758 he moved to Virginia to teach mathematics and natural philosophy at William and Mary College in Williamsburg—a unique appointment since professorships were generally filled by clergymen of the Church of England.[2] Small was well qualified for his position, however, since he was extraordinarily knowledgeable. As John Dos Passos wrote, he "knew what the first rate men of England and Scotland were writing and thinking" and no doubt passed much of that knowledge to Jefferson, who began his studies at William and Mary in 1760.[3] Jefferson's acknowledgment of the impact of Small on his life is found in his *Autobiography*:

> It was my great good fortune; and what probably fixed the destinies of my life that Dr. William Small of Scotland was the[n] professor of Mathematics, a man profound in most of the useful branches of science, with a happy talent of communication, correct and gentlemanly manners, & an enlarged & liberal mind. He, most happily for me, became soon attached to me & made me his daily companion when not engaged in the school; and from his conversation I got my first views of the expansion of science & of the system of things in which we are placed. Fortunately the Philosophical chair became vacant soon after my arrival at college, and he was appointed to fill it

per interim: and he was the first who ever gave in that college regular lectures in Ethics, Rhetoric & Belles lettres.[4]

Unfortunately, little else is known of William Small.[5] He left William and Mary in 1764, approximately two years after Jefferson's studies under his direction were completed and after he had, as Jefferson stated, "filled up the measure of his goodness to me, by procuring for me, from . . . G. Wythe, a reception as a student of law."[6] The fact that Small was a talented man, however, is substantiated by his subsequent activities in Birmingham's Lunar Society, where he became "an intimate friend of [Erasmus] Darwin, [Mathew] Boulton, and [James] Watt."[7]

When Jefferson said that Small gave him his "first views on the expansion of science & of the system of things in which we are placed," he was no doubt referring to the system of the cosmos described by Copernicus and Newton and derived from human sensory perceptions and reason, not the heaven-and-earth system of Genesis based on God's revelation. Although Jefferson did not elaborate on Small's science, a system he described in one of his commonplace books is based on science and therefore along the line of Small's. This commonplace book consists of Jefferson's notes on various authors he studied as a young man.[8] Among the longest entries are extracts from criticism of biblical religion that he had copied by 1775 from Bolingbroke's five-volume *Philosophical Works*.[9] It is in these extracts that a scientific description of the "system of things in which we are placed" is found.

Bolingbroke's background and studies reveal how he cultivated his critical Enlightenment disposition toward religion. He began a brilliant political career when he entered Parliament in 1700 and subsequently became one of Queen Anne's secretaries of state. He negotiated the Treaty of Utrecht in 1713, but his future in politics collapsed when the Tory government ended in 1714 and the Whigs gained power. Anticipating Whig reprisals, Bolingbroke went to France. During his ten-year exile he met and became friends with Voltaire and Montesquieu and studied philosophy and history. Among those who influenced his thinking were Samuel Pufendorf, Benedict Spinoza, Pierre Bayle, Nicolas Malebranche, Francis Bacon, John Locke, and Anthony Ashley Cooper, Earl of Shaftesbury; deists John Toland, Anthony Collins, and Lord Herbert of Cherbury; and various Renaissance humanist and classical writers.[10]

The Enlightenment definition of philosophy, according to Peter Gay, was "the organised habit of criticism."[11] The instrument of that criticism was human reason. According to Ernst Cassirer, the practitioners of Enlightenment values used their critical reason to oppose the "power of convention, tradition, and authority in all fields of knowledge." Cassirer believed that the French Enlightenment especially used this approach in the fields of theological and religious knowledge.[12] The philosophes' examination of these fields often led them to conclude, as Bolingbroke did, that there was little or no truth content in some of the most important Christian doctrines. The philosophes thereby challenged orthodox Christian epistemic authorities—the incarnation, prophets, revelation, church, and clergy—and affirmed the critical reason of each human being as the principal truth authority in theology and religion. Bolingbroke, who had intimate contact with the French Enlightenment and contributed to it, wrote on religion in a way that represents what Gay and Cassirer said about the Enlightenment. His criticism stirred a great deal of controversy after the posthumous publication of his work in 1754.[13] It prompted Dr. Samuel Johnson to comment that Bolingbroke was "a scoundrel for charging a blunderbuss against religion and morality; [and] a coward because he had not the resolution to fire it off himself [while he was alive]."[14]

Bolingbroke's contribution to Jefferson's religious ideas was profound. Gilbert Chinard wrote that the religious views in Jefferson's extracts from Bolingbroke were responsible for those Jefferson "held in common with the philosophes" in his earlier years, indeed the principal source of Jefferson's religious views throughout his life: "No single influence was stronger on Jefferson's formation and none was more continuous. He followed Bolingbroke in his distrust of metaphysical disquisitions. . . . He accepted his belief in some sort of a universal religion not limited to the Jews. Most, if not all of the ideas he expressed in his correspondence with John Adams during the last twelve years of his life, could be illustrated with quotations taken from the abstracts of Bolingbroke in his commonplace book."[15]

A statement Jefferson made in 1821 demonstrates this lasting impact. His comments in response to an inquiry on his views of Thomas Paine and Bolingbroke were steeped in admiration. Bolingbroke, he said, "was called a tory, but his writings prove him a stronger advocate for liberty than . . . the whigs of the present day." Both men "were alike in making bitter enemies of the priests and pharisees of their day. Both were honest men; both advocates for human liberty. . . . Lord Bolingbroke's [writing] . . . is a style of the highest order. . . . His conceptions, too, are bold and strong. . . . His political tracts are safe reading for the most timid religionist, his philosophical, for those who are not afraid to trust their reason with discussions of right and wrong."[16]

✳   Jefferson was among those who were "not afraid to trust their reason," as he carefully read Bolingbroke's philosophical tracts. Indeed, Bolingbroke was a major contributor to his idea that there should be no authority over or restraints upon individual reason in any field, including religion. Jefferson put this idea into practice during his years of study prior to writing the Declaration of Independence, a period he recalled in 1814 as one when he was "bold in the pursuit of knowledge, never fearing to follow truth and reason whatever results they led and bearding every authority which stood in their way."[17] John Locke also contributed to this disposition. In chapter 21 of his *Essay concerning Human Understanding*, "Of Power," Locke stated, "I with an unbiased indifferency followed Truth, whither I thought she led me."[18] The similarity of this statement to Jefferson's may well have been due to Jefferson's early knowledge of chapter 21 of Locke's *Essay* (see chapter 6).

Science, Genesis, Deism, and Natural Law

The way Bolingbroke wrote on the "system of things in which we are placed" would have appealed to Jefferson for its religious as well as its scientific content, for Jefferson developed an early interest in both heterodox religion and science.[19] Bolingbroke began his description of the "system of things" with an attack on Moses' primitive account of it (Genesis 1:3). Light and darkness, day and night, earth and sea, heaven and earth, and stars as mere lights was Genesis's simplistic description of the system. This contrasts sharply with what Copernicus described as a universe with an endless number of stars, many of which were like the sun with systems of planets. Indeed, the Genesis version undermined the veracity of the Old Testament, according to Bolingbroke: Moses was supposed to be divinely inspired, and no one so inspired could mislead men with such blatant falsity. To the contention of some that Moses was merely conforming himself to the ignorance of the people, since his purpose was to instruct them not in natural philosophy or science but in the true doctrine of the one God, Bolingbroke responded: "Was it necessary to that purpose that he should explain to them the Copernican system? No, most certainly. But it was not necessary to this purpose neither, that he should, give them an absurd account, since he thought fit to give them one, of the creation of our physical, and we may say, of our moral system."[20] The implication of this argument was that either Moses was not divinely inspired and was therefore a fraud, or God misled him and the people with the "absurd account" in Genesis of the "system of things in which we are placed."

Bolingbroke went on to attack the biblical view that the world and all that is in it were created for man and under his dominion (Genesis 1:26–30) and that the earth and man were the center of creation. These ideas, he said, were not in accord with scientific knowledge. He emphasized that the universe was not made for any particular creature or any particular part of that universe: "The system of the universe must necessarily be the best of all possible systems," and this could not be the case "unless the whole was the final cause of every part, and no one nor more parts the final causes of the whole."[21] Neither were the parts made for the whole: "The celestial phenomena were no more made for us than we were for them." Rather, he believed, a reciprocity between the parts and the whole was established by the creator at the time of creation; each was made for the other. He concluded that in the universal system man is just one among many creatures, which implies that the creator is a God who does not favor any creature over another. "That noble scene of the universe, which modern philosophy has opened," he said, "gives ample room for all the planetary inhabitants."[22]

The substratum of Bolingbroke's conception of the universe and his biblical criticism was Lockean sensory-based epistemology. Bolingbroke emphasized the empiricism of *An Essay concerning Human Understanding*.[23] Consistent with that emphasis he believed that the miracles depicted in the Bible, frequently offered as proof that its revelations were authentic, were themselves not authenticated by objectively verifiable sources, and therefore it was ridiculous to accept them. Moreover, from a theological perspective, Bolingbroke believed that miracles performed by God in order to direct and sustain His creation undermined the concept of God as an all-perfect and all-wise being who established law in His creation to govern it. As Bolingbroke put it, "Nothing can be less reconcileable to the notion of an all-perfect being, than the imagination that he undoes by his power in particular cases [miracles] what his wisdom [and law born of wisdom], to whom nothing is future, once thought sufficient to be established for all cases."[24] This was an argument that simultaneously attacked the biblical God of miracles and upheld the God of deism and natural theology. If God found it necessary to intervene in the world with miracles, it was tantamount to an admission that He was not all-wise and all-perfect. If He were, He would have established at the time of creation a system of nature with perfect laws that would govern it for all time and under all circumstances. A system with such laws would make miraculous intervention unnecessary. Bolingbroke's reasoning here seems indebted to Spinoza's similar argument that miracles, which go against God's laws, go against the God who made those laws and that it is absurd to think God would go against Himself in this way.[25]

The alternative to the God of revelation who intervened in the world with miracles was the watchmaker God of deism, natural theology, and natural religion, one who established the laws of nature in the material universe at the time of creation and then left it alone. Bolingbroke believed in such a God. He was, however, of the opinion that each law and each manifestation or effect of events governed by that law was itself a miracle, for without that law there would be no governing of events and no order in creation. In short, in the absence of law there would be chaos. Further, God's orderly creation of the universe was the result of not just one law of nature but an aggregate of many laws that did not change but governed the motion of objects in a manner which, under similar conditions, was always the same. Hence, the entire universe was an aggregate of the effect of laws or miracles, as Bolingbroke described the laws of nature. The laws that governed the universe could be empirically detected by the human sensory intellectual faculty or empirical reason. The miraculous order they established in the universe was what proved the existence of God, who placed them there, according to Bolingbroke, and not the unproved miracles of revealed scripture, which were known only by hearsay. Affirming the miraculous laws of nature, natural theology, and natural religion and dismissing the questionable miraculous events of the Bible, Bolingbroke said:

> The missionary of supernatural religion [revelation] appeals to the testimony of men he never knew, and of whom the infidel he labors to convert never heard, for the truth of those extraordinary events which prove the revelation he preaches: and it is said that this objection was made at first to Austin the monk by Ethereld the saxon king. But the missionary of natural religion can appeal at all times, and every where, to present and immediate evidence, to the testimony of sense and intellect, for the truth of those miracles which he brings in proof: the constitution of the mundane system [laws of nature] being in a very proper sense an aggregate of miracles.[26]

Here again he sounded like Spinoza, who argued that we gain knowledge of God by gaining knowledge and understanding of His laws, which govern the world, and not through miracles such as those described in revelation, which leave us in ignorance.[27]

One problem with the biblical God who constantly intervened in the course of nature or natural events with His miracles was that He made science and scientific law, which depend upon predictability to be viable, unpredictable. His very intervention in the process of nature was a cause of that unpredictability. The God of deism or natural theology, on the other hand, who established His laws of nature in the universe at the time of its creation and then left it alone, was a God whose predictability could be depended on, once those laws were discovered. Deism was therefore conducive to science, and it would seem this was among the factors that influenced Jefferson, who was an advocate of science, to adopt a deistic theology.[28]

Related to Bolingbroke's empiricism was his distaste for metaphysical speculation. He maintained that metaphysics was the presumption or assumption of something beyond the scope of what can be empirically proved and was therefore unreliable. "I combat," he said, "the pride and presumption of metaphysicians."[29] Mysteries he ranked even lower than metaphysical speculations; they could not even be known, for a mystery by definition is not known. Echoing John Toland, Bolingbroke stated: "No man can believe he knoweth not what nor why. And therefore he, who truly believeth, must apprehend the proposition, and must discern it's connection with some principle of truth. . . . Now let me ask again, can any man be said to apprehend a proposition which contains a mystery, that is, something unintelligible; or any thing more than the sound of words?"[30]

Jefferson, under the influence of Bolingbroke, also abhorred metaphysicians and mysteries. He referred to what metaphysicians "fabricated" as "metaphysical insanities."[31] When commenting on the Trinity—which he rejected, as did Bolingbroke[32]—he echoed the sense of the foregoing statement: "Men of sincerity," he said, could not "pretend they believe" in the unknowable "mysticisms that three are one, and one is three; and yet that the one is not three, and the three are not one."[33] He expressed the same ideas when he stated, "I had never sense enough to comprehend the trinity and it has always appeared to me that comprehension must precede assent."[34] As Chinard points out, although these comments were made after the writing of the Declaration, they seem to reflect the early influence of the Bolingbroke extracts he copied as a young man. (See chapter 7 for further evidence of Jefferson's early reflection on and rejection of the Trinity.)

✳Jefferson's own belief in God, like Bolingbroke's, was based on empirical observations of nature and the conclusions derived from them, along with the knowledge of the laws of nature he obtained through the study of science. In a letter to John Adams he depicted this natural theology approach to gaining knowledge of God as confirmation of a deistic divine being, using teleological and cosmological arguments:

I hold, (without appeal to revelation) that when we take a view of the universe, in its parts, general or particular, it is impossible for the human mind not to perceive and feel a conviction of design, consummate skill, and indefinite power in every atom of its composition. The movements of the heavenly bodies, so exactly held in their course by the balance of centrifugal and centripetal forces; the structure of our earth itself, with its distribution of lands, waters and atmosphere; animal and vegetable bodies, examined in all their minutest particles; insects, mere atoms of life, yet as perfectly organized as man or mammoth; . . . it is impossible, I say, for the human mind not to believe, that there is in all this, design, cause and effect, up to an ultimate cause, a Fabricator of all things from matter and motion.[35]

These comments did not refer to the God of miracles found in scripture or revelation. Jefferson specifically stated that he did not appeal to revelation. The God he described was a "Fabricator of all things," one whose "consummate skill" was evidenced by His creation. Laws made by that God for the universe were the laws of nature or scientific laws, such as those that held the "heavenly bodies so exactly in their courses." These comments describe a God who constituted perfect laws to direct and govern His creation at the time He created it. By making these comments and by not appealing to what Bolingbroke described as the imperfect God of revelation and scripture, whose laws were so defective that He had to use miracles to govern the universe, Jefferson demonstrated that he had adopted the deism, natural theology, and natural religion of Bolingbroke.

Revelation and Law

Bolingbroke also attacked the scriptural laws governing humankind as well as the God of the Bible who revealed those laws, by questioning whether the God of the Bible was just. He believed that punishments and rewards, as a vital part of law, should be meted out "in a due proportion" to the degree of badness or goodness of human actions. The God of the New Testament, according to Bolingbroke, failed to pass this test of justice; was it just, he asked, "to reward the greatest and the least degr[ee] of virtue, and to punish the greatest and the least degree of vice, alike?" Yet the God of the New Testament granted salvation to saintly individuals as well as those who were moderately good; for persons of either category the state of bliss in heaven would be the same. In like manner, that God condemned to hell, a place that tormented everyone equally, both depraved individuals and those who were moderately bad. Bolingbroke ridiculed those who believed that the God who rewarded such extremes equally was just: "I ask what these persons would say if they beheld a man, who had done some trifling good to society, recompensed like one who had saved his country or if they, who were convicted of petty larceny, should be delivered over to the hangman, at one of our sessions, with those who had been found guilty of assassination and robbery."[36]

Bolingbroke continued his attack with an analogy depicting two individuals of equal virtue in this life but of "very opposite fortunes": one "extremely happy," the other "unhappy." If both are equally rewarded after death, reasoned Bolingbroke, then "there arises such a disproportion of happiness in favor of one of these virtuous men, as must appear inconsistent with justice." Such injustice on the part of the New Testament God "can be imputed to nothing but partiality, which theism will never impute to the supreme being, whatever artificial theology may do, and does in many instances."[37] The "theism" or theology that Bolingbroke mentions here as an alternative to the "artificial theology" of revelation was that of natural religion or natural theology, and the God of that "theism" was a deistic, impartial God, the antithesis of the partial God of revelation.

As for the specific biblical laws that govern people, Bolingbroke concentrated his attack on those of the Old Testament, denying the justice both of those laws and of the God that revealed them. He began by stating that manmade laws are imperfect because the passage of time eventually renders them obsolete due to the gradual changes in conditions that time inevitably brings. As Bolingbroke put it, manmade laws are often rendered "useless and even hurtful" in the "natural course of things." He argued that since human legislators cannot foresee the natural changes that would eventually make their laws inappropriate or unjust, they certainly cannot foresee the accidental or extraordinary conditions that would occasionally render their laws obsolete. He then defined a perfect law as one "made with such a foresight of all possible accidents, and with such provisions for the due execution of it in all cases, that the law may be effectual to govern and direct these accidents instead of lying at the mercy of them," adding that another measure of a perfect law was the "clearness and precision of it's terms."[38]

From this definition he argued that if God truly made the laws of the Old Testament, they would, since He was perfect, manifest both these characteristics of perfection—but in fact they manifested neither: "We cannot read the bible," he said in regard to the first test of perfection, "without being convinced that no law ever operated so weak and so uncertain in effect as the law of Moses did." And since the least of "accidents and conjunctures" was enough to "interrupt the course, and defeat the designs, of it," such accidents would cause the people "not only [to] neglect the law, but [to] cease to acknowledge the legislator." Moreover, it was absurd to blame this ineffectiveness of Mosaic law on the stubbornness of the people in order to rescue "the honor of the law" and the idea that God made it. God's perfect law, Bolingbroke maintained, would overcome these and similar difficulties: "We speak here of a law supposed to be dictated by divine wisdom, which ought, and which would have been able, if it had been such, to keep in a state of submission to it, and of national prosperity, even a people rebellious and obstinate enough to break through any other." As to the "clearness and perfection of its terms," the second measure of the perfection of law, Bolingbroke was blunt in his criticism. To him the language of the Old Testament laws was even worse than that used in many manmade laws: "The language in which this law was given is, the learned say, of any languages, the most loose and equivocal, and the style and manner of writing of the sacred authors, whoever they were, or wherever they lived, increased the uncertainly and obscurity [of the law]."[39]

By contrast, the laws of nature as placed in creation by God provided not only scientific laws governing the material objects of the universe but also laws governing human behavior. These laws, like those that govern the universe, could be detected by reason. Bolingbroke compared them with the laws of the Old Testament, especially those in Deuteronomy 13.[40] There men were instructed to kill anyone who tried to influence or entice them to follow another God and thereby practice idolatry: "And thou shalt stone him with stones, that he die; because he hath sought to thrust thee away from the Lord thy God" (Deuteronomy 13:10). This rule applied even to "thy brother, the son of thy mother, or thy son, or thy daughter, or the wife of thy bosom, or thy friend" (Deuteronomy 13:6). That there was no room for mercy in dealing with such persons was made clear by the command "Neither shall thine eye pity him, neither shalt thou spare, neither shalt thou conceal him: But thou shalt surely kill him" (Deuteronomy 13:8–9). Idolatrous cities were to be dealt with in the same manner: "Thou shalt surely smite the inhabitants of that city with the edge of the sword, destroying it utterly, and all that is therein and the cattle thereof . . . and [thou] shalt burn with fire the city, and all the spoil thereof every whit, for the Lord thy God" (Deuteronomy 13:15-16). All this carnage and destruction was to be done "for the Lord thy God" and at His command.

Bolingbroke rejected such laws and the God of the Old Testament who made them. Simultaneously he accepted the God of natural theology and that God's laws of nature, which would not allow murderous acts. To Bolingbroke the God of natural theology was all-perfect because of the nature of His laws whereas the Old Testament laws were an example of the imperfection and lack of justice of the biblical God. As he put it:

> I say that the law of nature is the law of god. Of this I have the same demonstrative knowledge, that I have of the existence of god, the all-perfect being [of natural theology]. I say that the all-perfect being cannot contradict himself; that he would contradict himself if the laws contained in the thirteenth chapter of Deuteronomy, to mention no others here, were his laws, since they contradict those of nature; and therefore that they are not his laws. Of all this I have as certain, as intuitive [knowledge], as I have that two and two are equal to four, or that the whole is bigger than a part.[41]

Here Bolingbroke not only stated that "demonstrative knowledge" of God and the law of nature were obtainable with reason, via the empiricism described by Locke, but he also used "intuitive knowledge" as Locke did in *An Essay concerning Human Understanding*.[42]

While Jefferson was practicing law, his citation of Deuteronomy during a case in 1771 indicated his knowledge of that book of the Old Testament.[43] Considering this citation and Bolingbroke's influence on him, it becomes understandable why he objected to government based on the law of the Bible and preferred the law of nature. Consistent with those objections and preferences was a legal opinion he wrote as to why Christianity and the laws of the Old Testament were not part of the English common law, a system he praised as "the glory and protection to that country" in *A Summary View of the Rights of British America* (1774).[44] Jefferson did not specifically mention a reason for that praise, but it could well have been due to a theory of some common law jurists and legal thinkers—William Blackstone, Thomas Wood, Edward Wynne, Richard Woodson—that English common law had a nonbiblical ethical source and foundation: the law of nature. Lord Mansfield also subscribed to this theory as did Sir Richard Aston.[45] Jefferson would have been aware of this theory, since he had, according to Robert Ferguson, extraordinary knowledge of the "English legal tradition."[46]

The legal opinion is undated but was placed in Jefferson's second commonplace book in the latter half of 1776.[47] In it Jefferson maintained that the Saxons brought the common law to England, free from any Christian influence, in the fifth century, because the introduction of Christianity into Saxon England did not take place until the seventh century, after the conversion of the Saxon king "about the year 598." The subsequent admission of Christianity as part of the common law occurred, in Jefferson's opinion, because of fraudulent judicial decisions resulting from "the alliance between Church and State in England," which "has ever made their judges accomplices in the frauds of the clergy."[48]

Jefferson cited the decisions of various judges, including those of Sir Mathew Hale and Lord Mansfield that led to this "fraud," as linked to a change of the word "ancient" used to describe "scripture" by Chief Justice John Prisot in a 1458 Year Book case.[49] Jefferson maintained that "ancient scripture" referred to the ancient written law of the Christian church and observed that "Finch's law Book published in 1613" changed Prisot's "ancient scripture" to "Holy scripture." The words "ancient scripture," argued Jefferson, would not have been much use to those who wished Christianity to be a part of the common law because they could only have referred to the Old Testament if they did not refer to the ancient laws of the church: hence the alteration.[50] The change to "Holy scripture" precipitated a series of judicial decisions which, with absolutely no legal foundation, included Christianity in the common law, according to Jefferson.[51] They culminated in Judge Mathew Hale's taking the "whole leap" when he "declared at once, that the whole bible [Old Testament] and [New], testament, in a lump make part of the Common law." Jefferson concluded his opinion with the statement: "Thus they [the Judges] incorporate into the English code, laws made for the Jews alone, and the precepts of the gospel, intended by their benevolent author as obligatory only *in foro conscientiae;* and they arm the whole with the coercions of Municipal law."[52]

Jefferson wrote later of this sequence of events as "the most remarkable instance of Judicial legislation, that has ever occurred in English jurisprudence, or perhaps in any other"; it was "the adoption in mass of the whole code of another nation."[53] Most Christians would have greeted such an adoption as a blessing, but not anyone who had read and assimilated Bolingbroke's ideas on the imperfection and injustice of biblical law, as Jefferson's extracts indicate he had done.

Historical Methodology

The most substantial of Bolingbroke's challenges to the authenticity and veracity of both Old and New Testament theology came from the strict empiricism he applied to the verification of religious historical events recounted in scripture, beginning with the authentication of the character of those who witnessed them. "History to be authentic," he said, "must give us not only the means of knowing the number but of knowing the character of witnesses."[54] Unless witnesses were objective and honest, the facts they presented were, according to Bolingbroke, a proof that "would not be admitted in judicature, as Mr. Locke observes." He added that a court of law would not admit "any thing less than an attested copy of the record." He believed that such strict legal authentication and verification of testimony should apply to all history, indeed that the verification of historical religious events was even more important than the verification of legal matters such as property. In legal matters if facts must be attested to when even "the sum of ten pounds may not be at stake," was it not more important, he asked, that similar measures "be taken, to assure ourselves that we receive nothing for the word of God, which is not sufficiently attested to be so?"[55]

Bolingbroke took religion seriously, as he thought everyone should, and he did not think people should be duped out of religious truth—any more than they should be duped out of property—by false testimony. He was therefore highly critical of the veracity not only of scriptural claims but of those of the Catholic Church, which, he said, "established many maxims and claims of right, by affirming them constantly and boldly against evident existent proofs of the contrary." In addition he stated that the Church's reliance on tradition for religious truth often led to untruth: "A story circumstantially related, ought not to be received on the faith of tradition; since the least reflection on human nature is sufficient to shew how unsafely a system of facts and circumstances can be trusted for it's preservation to memory alone, and for it's conveiance to oral report alone; how liable it must be to all those alterations, which the weakness of the human mind must cause necessarily, and which the corruption of the human heart will be sure to suggest." To make sure that people were not duped or misled about the truth of historical religious events, Bolingbroke established four criteria as a method of authentication, attestation, and verification:

> To constitute the authenticity of any history, these are some of the conditions necessary. 1. It must be writ by a contemporary author, or by one who had contemporary materials in his hands. 2. It must have been published among men who are able to judge of the capacity of the author, and of the authenticity of the memorials on which he writ. 3. Nothing repugnant to the universal experience of mankind must be contained in it. 4. The principal facts at least, which it contains, must be confirmed by collateral testimony, that is, by the testimony of those who had no common interest of country, of religion, or of profession, to disguise or falsify the truth.[56]

Much of the history in the Pentateuch could not be verified by any of these four criteria, according to Bolingbroke. First, Moses was not a contemporary of a great deal of it—creation, for example: even "Adam himself" would not have known "what passed on the first five days" of creation. Moses did not fulfill the second criterion either: "Were the writings of Moses published among people able to judge of them and of their author? . . . I believe not." As for the third criterion, Bolingbroke said, if occasionally things "repugnant to the experience of mankind" are found in human histories such as Livy's, these are isolated by readers who accept the rest. But this was "not the case" with the Old Testament, where "incredible anecdotes" were so frequent that "the whole history is founded on such[;] it consists of little else, . . . and if it were not a history of them, it would be a history of nothing." Finally, there was no collateral verification of the Old Testament writings by objective or disinterested witnesses, as the fourth criterion required. The witnesses to Moses' history, he said, "are in truth but one, the testimony of Moses himself."[57] The combined effect of these statements is a sweeping rejection of the authenticity of historical events recorded in the Old Testament, including its accounts of miracles. Bolingbroke specifically rejected some of these: "That the Israelites had a leader and legislator called Moses, is proved by the consent of foreign[ers] whom I call collateral witnesses. Be it so. But surely it will not follow that this man conversed with the supreme being face to face; which these collateral witnesses do not affirm. The Israelites were an egyptian colony, and conquered Palestine. Be it so. It will not follow that the red sea opened a passage to them, and drowned the Egyptians who pursued them."[58]

New Testament miracles were also attacked by Bolingbroke, although not in the same way. He pondered why it was that "the miracles wrought to propagate Christianity had greater effect out of Judea than in it." He also reflected on the "glorious purposes of this [New Testament] revelation," which was made by "the son of god himself" and concluded that "the stupendous miracles in the heavens, and on the earth, that were wrought to confirm it . . . must have left reason nothing to do, but have forced conviction, and have taken away even the possibility of doubt." Yet this did not happen among the Jews who would have been the closest witnesses "of the signs and wonders that accompanied the publication of the gospel," since within the Jewish community neither "the learned" nor "the scribes" nor "the pharisees" nor "the rulers of the people" nor the people themselves, for the most part, accepted the revelation of the gospel. On the contrary, the Jews by and large not only rejected that revelation but became the "persecutors of Christianity." This rejection made Bolingbroke suspect that the miracles of the gospel were not authentic: "If we suppose ourselves transported back to that time, and inquiring into the truth of this revelation on the very spot where it was made, we shall find that, far from being determined by authority in favor of it, our reason would have had much to do in comparing the various and contradictory testimonies, and in balancing the degrees of probability that resulted from them."[59]

Without completely denying the gospel events, then, Bolingbroke asserted here that they were shrouded with doubt. Jefferson, in a letter to his nephew Peter Carr challenging the accuracy of the revealed word of the gospel, sounded much like the Bolingbroke of his extracts: "When speaking of the New Testament, . . . you should read all the histories of Christ, as well as those whom a council of ecclesiastics have decided for us, to be Pseudo-evangelists, as those they named Evangelists. Because these Pseudo-evangelists pretended to inspiration, as much as the others, and you are to judge their pretensions by your own reason, and not by the reason of those ecclesiastics."[60] Here Jefferson, like Bolingbroke, expressed doubt about the orthodox view of gospel events but did not make any outright denial of them; he wanted his nephew to make his own judgment with his own reason. He affirmed here, as had Bolingbroke, that individual reason rather than scriptural or ecclesiastical authority should be the sole authority to determine what was true in matters of religion.

In rejecting the scriptural accounts of miracles, Jefferson often used Bolingbroke's third criterion for determining authentic history: that is, to disregard any event "repugnant to the universal experience of mankind." To William Short in 1820, Jefferson mentioned Livy in this way in a manner virtually identical to that of the Bolingbroke extracts: "When Livy and Siculus, for example, tell us things which coincide with our experience of the order of nature, we credit them on their word, and place their narrations among the records of credible history. But when they tell us of calves speaking, of statues sweating blood, and other things against the course of nature, we reject these as fables not belonging to history."[61]

Writing to John Adams, Jefferson again used the third criterion in his rejection of miracles. He was milder than Bolingbroke in his denunciation of some miracles described in the Old Testament but vehement about one in the New Testament. The Decalogue, the Old Testament says, was miraculously "written by the finger of God," but Jefferson asked:

Where did we get the ten commandments? The book indeed gives them to us verbatim, but where did it get them? For itself tells us they were written by the finger of God on tables of stone, which were destroyed by Moses; it specifies those on the second set of tables in different form and substance, but still without saying how the others were recovered. But the whole history of these books is so defective and doubtful, that it seems vain to attempt minute inquiry into it; and such tricks have been played with their text, and with the other texts of other books relating to them, that we have a right from that cause to entertain much doubt what parts of them are genuine.

But Jefferson gave no such benefit of the doubt to the New Testament's account of the miraculous Virgin Birth:

And the day will come, when the mystical generation of Jesus, by the Supreme Being as His Father, in the womb of a virgin, will be classed with the fable of the generation of Minerva in the brain of Jupiter. But we may hope that the dawn of reason and freedom of thought in these United States, will do away [with] all this artificial scaffolding, and restore to us the primitive and genuine doctrines of this the most venerated Reformer of human errors.[62]

Jefferson in the last part of this statement made reference to restoring "the primitive and genuine doctrines" of Jesus by getting rid of miracles, which he regarded as imposture. Bolingbroke was no doubt one of Jefferson's first contacts with the idea that much of orthodox Christian doctrine was "artificial theology" or imposture.[63]

Biblical versus Natural Religion

In Christianity Paul was a major source of imposture, according to Bolingbroke. It was Paul, not Jesus, who formulated the fundamental orthodox Christian doctrines of original sin, atonement, and salvation by faith and the grace of God.[64] Belief in most or all of these doctrines was necessary for salvation, according to orthodox Christians. Therefore, said Bolingbroke, orthodox Christians must believe that Jesus died without giving his followers "sufficient knowledge of the terms of salvation" and that Paul remedied this deficiency with his formulation of Christian doctrines. But Paul's remedy could only be "the grossest absurdity" and "little more than blasphemy," since it was also the view of orthodoxy that it was the Son of God who was sent by his Father "to make a new covenant with mankind." To believe that the work of the Son and the Father needed to be supplemented by a man such as Paul, then, was to take the position that the work of God was done "imperfectly." In short, according to Boling-broke, orthodox Christianity, if carried to its logical conclusion, re-sulted in the absurdity that persons "who were converted to Chris-tianity by Christ himself, and who died before the supposed imperfection of his revelation had been supplied by the apostles, by Paul particularly, lived and died without a sufficient knowledge of the terms of salvation."[65]

Bolingbroke maintained that "a religion, revealed by God himself immediately, must have been complete and perfect, from the first pro-mulgation in the mind of every convert to it." If Christianity was a new covenant with humankind, the result of God's grace in sending his own Son—who was God in the second person of the Trinity—to establish that covenant, then any supplementations or alterations to the teachings of the Son, such as those promulgated by Paul, were not part of that covenant. If they were, then, as Bolingbroke put it, "How often, I say it with horror, might not god change his mind?"[66] Jefferson, like Bolingbroke, rejected Paul's teachings, and this rejection (see chap-ter 4) can be traced to his extracts from Bolingbroke's writings.

Bolingbroke's critical rejection of Christian doctrine was severe, especially with respect to the fall of man, which he maintained was the foundation of orthodox Christianity: "If redemption be the main and fundamental article of the Christian faith," then "the fall of man is the foundation of this fundamental article." But the doctrine of the fall, he believed, was incompatible with the nature of God. For God to create a being so defective that it would fall, and then condemn it to damnation unless He intervened with His grace, was "absolutely ir-reconcilable to every idea we can frame of wisdom, justice, and good-ness, to say nothing of the dignity of the supreme being."[67] Bolingbroke rejected the doctrine of atonement on similar grounds. He pointed out the absurdity as well as the lack of goodness and justice of a God who would sacrifice the blood of His innocent Son to atone or give satis-faction for men, all of whom offended Him as a result of the fall:

God sent his only begotten son, who had not offended him, to be sacrificed by men, who had offended him, that he might expiate their sins, and satisfy his own anger. Surely our ideas of moral attributes will lead us to think that god would have been satisfied, more agreeably to his mercy and goodness, without any expiation, upon the repentance of the offenders, and more agreeably to his justice with any other expiation rather than this. . . . Let us suppose a great prince governing a wicked and rebellious people. He had it in his power to punish, he thinks fit to pardon them. But he orders his only and beloved son to be put to death to expiate their sins, and to satisfy his royal vengeance.[68]

These ideas on atonement are strikingly similar to those of the sixteenth-century theologian Faustus Socinus, and Jefferson mentioned Socinians in the notes on religion he made in 1776 just after the adoption of the Declaration of Independence.[69] Like Socinus, Bolingbroke was unable to reconcile the Christian doctrine of atonement with his concept of a just God and therefore rejected this doctrine "in all its circumstances," which included the fall—as did Jefferson.[70]

Bolingbroke maintained that this imperfect or defective God of biblical revelation was partial, unjust, cruel, capricious, immoral, and unmerciful. As a result, He was not a fit object of love and worship, whether as the Jehovah of the Old Testament or the Predestinator of the New Testament. As an alternative to the biblical God of revelation, Bolingbroke offered the all-perfect God of natural theology, who could be discovered by human reason and was worthy of adoration:

> Natural religion represents an all perfect being to our adoration and to our love; and the precept "thou shalt love the lord thy god with all thy heart["]; will be effectual in this system. Can any man now presume to say that the god of Moses, or the god of Paul, is this amiable being? The god of the first is partial, unjust, and cruel; delights in blood, commends assassinations, massacres and even exterminations of people. The god of the second elects some of his creatures to salvation, and predestines others to damnation, even in the womb of their mothers.[71]

As Bolingbroke remedied the imperfect science and law contained in revelation by replacing them with science and law born of reason, he remedied the imperfect God of scripture by replacing Him with the rationally discovered all-perfect God of natural religion.

Jefferson too believed in the God of natural religion, and his criticisms of the Old and New Testament God sound much like Bolingbroke's. "Cruel" and "remorseless" were the terms Jefferson applied to the partial or "family God of Abraham, of Isaac and of Jacob, and the local God of Israel." In a similar vein, he said that the Jewish faith "had presented for the object of their worship, a Being of terrific character, cruel, vindictive, capricious and unjust."[72] He saw the New Testament God as the same sort of being. He abhorred the Predestinator God of Calvin and Paul who, as Bolingbroke stated, "elects some of his creatures to salvation . . . and others to damnation even in the womb of their mothers."[73]

Calvin included the doctrine of predestination among his five points, which Jefferson considered as "blasphemies" against God.[74] But Jeffer- ✳ son knew long before he drafted the Declaration of Independence that predestination extended beyond Calvinism to other predominating theologies and denominations of Christianity; predestination was a part of the Thirty-Nine Articles, article 17, of the Anglican faith, in which he was raised.[75] Nevertheless, it was Calvin's theology emphasizing predestination that bore the brunt of Jefferson's scorn for the Predestinator God of the New Testament, as reflected in a letter to John Adams: "I can never join Calvin in addressing *his god*. He was indeed an atheist, which I can never be; or rather his religion was one of daemonism. If ever man worshipped a false god, he did. The Being described in his 5 points, is not the God whom you and I acknowledge and adore, the Creator and benevolent Governor of the world; but a daemon of malignant spirit. It would be more pardonable to believe in no god at all, than to blaspheme Him by the atrocious attributes of Calvin."[76] Apart from condemning and denying the Predestinator God of Calvin and the New Testament in this statement, Jefferson affirmed the existence of another God, "the Creator and benevolent Governor of the world," whose attributes both he and John Adams acknowledged and adored. That God was the God of natural theology since Jefferson affirmed that God. His praise of that God as adorable echoed that of Bolingbroke.

Bolingbroke consistently maintained that it was inconceivable to him, and Jefferson certainly agreed, that God would show partiality to any religion, denomination, sect, or individual. This was no doubt the reason that, as Chinard stated, Jefferson accepted Bolingbroke's "belief in some sort of a universal religion not limited to the Jews."[77] Chinard could have continued that neither would that religion be limited to Christians or the people of any religion. A truly universal religion would be all-inclusive and therefore have a truly impartial God, since partiality would be contradictory to universality or all-inclusiveness. Bolingbroke described such a deistic, impartial, universal, all-inclusive God in his theology of natural religion, which (as noted above) he called "theism." After denouncing the biblical God for His partiality, Bolingbroke said that this was an attribute "theism will never impute to the supreme being."[78]

This message, with all its tolerance and political implications, took root in Jefferson's mind, as the very first paragraph of the Declaration of Independence reveals:

> When in the Course of human events, it becomes necessary for one
> People to dissolve the Political Bands which have connected them
> with another, and to assume among the Powers of the Earth, the
> separate and equal Station to which the Laws of Nature and of
> *Nature's God* [emphasis added] entitle them, a decent Respect to the
> Opinions of Mankind requires that they should declare the causes
> which impel them to the Separation.[79]

This passage does not refer to the God of revelation or the Bible but to
"Nature's God," or Bolingbroke's deistic God of natural religion. The
impartiality of this God to all nations and peoples can be seen in
Jefferson's reference to "one People," the colonists, who were under
the "Laws of Nature." According to these "Laws" and "Nature's God"
who established them, a people or a nation was not chosen by God
over other peoples and nations of the earth. Rather they were all given
a "separate and equal Station" by those "Laws of Nature" and "Nature's God." Jefferson's God of the Declaration is, therefore, antithetical to any God who would manifest partiality by choosing one people
or nation over others, as did the God of the Old Testament. The God
of the Declaration repudiates such partial choosing, for all peoples
and all nations are equal in His eyes.

This impartial Bolingbrokean God was not only antithetical to a
God who would grant grace to one people over others, but also antithetical to the Christian God who would grant some individuals saving grace while denying such grace to others. Saving grace, therefore,
was no part of the "Nature's God" of the Declaration. It was also
alien to persons who were the product of "Nature's God." Such persons were very different beings from those created by the God of the
predominating versions of Christianity. They were not, according to
Jefferson, abject, helpless, depraved victims of original sin, dependent
upon God's grace for salvation and under His hierarchy of religious
authority. Rather, they were independent moral agents who could themselves know and perform good works according to the moral laws of
nature and thereby earn their salvation. Such persons by their very
nature made saving grace unnecessary. Jefferson had adopted this concept of humanity before writing the Declaration (see chapter 4).[80] The
idea that men were not dependent on God's grace for salvation but
could earn it by good works was contained in one of the books that
Jefferson recommended for purchase in a letter to his brother-in-law
Robert Skipwith in 1771.[81] Titled *The Oeconomy of Human Life,* it
was a short book of fifty-eight pages alleged to have been "translated
from an *Indian Manuscript* written by an antient Bramini."[82] Millicent

Sowerby has written that some believe it to be the work of Robert Dodsley, an "English poet, dramatist and bookseller," and "Philip Dormer Stanhope, fourth Earl of Chesterfield."[83]

The book was essentially a moral treatise, and though Jefferson seemed familiar with all the books he recommended to Skipwith,[84] this one was especially important to him. Desbordes sent him a French translation of *Oeconomy* long after Jefferson's first contact with it, and in writing to thank Desbordes in July 1807, Jefferson stated that "this elegant little morsel of morality has always been a great favorite of mine."[85] In it, the concept that salvation is not granted by God's grace but earned by good works is poetically expressed: "Virtue is a race which God hath sent him [man] to run, and happiness the goal; which none can arrive at until he hath finished his course, and receiveth his crown in the mansions of eternity."[86]

Jefferson was extremely critical of a God who, like the God of the New Testament, created men who would fall and thereby become incapable of independent moral agency, unable to earn their own salvation through the performance of good works. He called such a God "a bungling artist."[87] Jefferson's early rejection of the grace made necessary by such a "bungling artist" was manifest in the Declaration's allusion to an impartial "Nature's God," a God who was antithetical to partial grace. That rejection continued in his later years. "Were I to be the founder of a new sect," he wrote in 1819, "I would call them the Apiarians, and after the example of the bee, advise them to extract the honey of every sect. My fundamental principle would be the reverse of Calvin's, that we are to be saved by our good works which are within our power, and not by our faith which is not within our power."[88] Calvin believed that not only salvation but also faith and good works were the result of God's grace;[89] by rejecting grace, Jefferson in this statement comes down firmly on the side of good works by individual human beings as the means of attaining salvation.

"Nature's God" of the Declaration, like the laws of nature, was not made known to humanity by God's exclusive revelation or the custodians of such revelation, whether church or priestcraft. "Nature's God" could be detected with the reason of each individual human being. Jefferson, by referring to "Nature's God," thereby departed from the Old and New Testament in giving reason precedence over revelation as a means of gaining knowledge of God. In addition, he remedied three deficiencies of the biblical God and biblical religion that Bolingbroke had pointed out. First, he avoided being under the authority of revelation, which was alien to science. Second, he avoided being subject to the laws of revelation as regulators of human behavior, laws that were not only imperfect but inferior to human laws derived from reason. Third, he avoided being under the authority of a God who was unjust and partial, cruel and vindictive, whimsical and capricious. By contrast, "Nature's God," or the God of natural theology, natural religion, and deism, was a God whose natural laws could be discovered by reason and science, who left men free to make their own laws with their reason, and who was worthy of adoration, since He was a perfect God with sublime attributes.

Although Bolingbroke was not the only influence on Jefferson's theology of equality as expressed in the Declaration (John Locke was another and a great influence on the political ideology of the document as well), the extracts from Bolingbrokes's writings provided the basis for Jefferson's reference to "Nature's God" and his rejection of orthodox Christian doctrine. Adrienne Koch called it more than rejection; Jefferson, she said, before and during the time he drafted the Declaration of Independence, manifested a concealed "hatred for ceremonial institutionalized Christianity."[90] Hatred seems too strong a term to describe Jefferson's reaction against New Testament religion, but there was a bitterness there that extended also to Old Testament religion and theology. One principal reason for that bitterness, apparently, was that he thought the partiality of biblical theology could not provide appropriate organizing principles for an egalitarian democratic society.

3

Locke and the Declaration

That John Locke's *Second Treatise of Government* made a profound influence on Jefferson can be seen in the ideas expressed in the Declaration of Independence. This view has long been held by many scholars, including Carl Becker and Morton White.[1] Yet, there have been challenges to the idea of Locke's influence; Richard Mathews, for example, argued that Jefferson's political theory was devoid of both Lockean possessive individualism and classical republicanism.[2] It was Garry Wills, however, who made the most publicized challenge to the view that Locke influenced Jefferson and the Declaration. In his *Inventing America*, Wills said, "There is no indication [that] Jefferson read the *Second Treatise* carefully or with profit." He went on to state, "There is no conclusive proof that he read it at all (though I assume he did at some point)." Wills gives three reasons for his opinion. First, there is no evidence that Jefferson owned a copy of the *Treatise* except for the brief period of a few months between late 1769, when he received one from a bookseller, and 1 February 1770, when a fire destroyed his home at Shadwell—including his library with the exception of a very few items such as his commonplace books.[3] Second, he never copied a single passage of the *Treatise* in either his literary or his government commonplace book. Third, though he did paraphrase a portion of chapter 11 of the *Second Treatise* before the Declaration of Independence in his government commonplace book,[4] Wills alleged that this citation was erroneously and inappropriately used. He described this error by stating that Jefferson, when gathering historical evidence that kings were elected, appended "a reference to the eleventh chapter of the *Treatise* on legislative supremacy—which is not the same matter at all."[5]

By examining the context in which the Lockean paraphrase was commonplaced, however, along with the contents of the chapter cited, it can be shown that Jefferson did cite Locke correctly and appropriately and in a manner that indicates considerable knowledge of the

Second Treatise. Jefferson's government commonplace book demonstrates that he had done considerable historical research on the governments of Denmark, Sweden, Norway, Poland, and Great Britain by studying the writings of Robert Molesworth, Rene Aubert de Vertot, Thomas Salmon, and William Robertson.[6] The people of Denmark, he said, endeavored to elect a king who was "valiant, just, merciful, affable, a maintainer of the laws, a lover of the people, prudent and adorned with all other virtues fit for government." If they made a wrong choice and the king proved a tyrant, however, the people frequently "deposed him, often times banished, sometimes destroyed him." They did so by calling the king before the representative body of the people, or if he was too powerful for this, "they dispatched him" and then chose a new king. At the death of a king who had served the people well, preference would be given to his family in choosing a successor, especially his eldest son "when all other virtues were equal" among those considered for his replacement. Jefferson concluded that this process of selecting a king "was the antient [*sic*] and is the present constitution of Sweden, . . . and it may certainly be deemed the present constitution of Great Britain."[7]

Jefferson's research notations enumerated several historical precedents for nonhereditary and nontestamentary successors to the throne of England, some of which were accomplished by election.[8] He prefaced these precedents with the statement "The following instances of the right of electing a king by the people of England prove such a right reserved to them." He maintained that the constitution of Great Britain, in its pure unaltered state, gave the people the right to elect their king and that Parliament had usurped this right by passing unlawful acts that established succession without election. He argued that England's legislative body, as originally established in the constitution by the people, consisted of an elected king in addition to Parliament. Therefore, acts of Parliament to establish successors to the throne without an elected king's approval were made by a legislative power altered from the way the people originally established it. Such acts, concluded Jefferson, were not binding. It was in support of this conclusion that he paraphrased chapter 11 of Locke's *Second Treatise:*

> Acts of parl. have indeed been passed for settling succession; but they
> are void in their nature; because a king, elected by the people, is one
> of the branches to whom the people have deputed the power of
> making laws; and they have never bound themselves to submit to any
> laws but such as have received the approbation of the Commons, the
> Lords, and a king so elected, and his being merely a delegated power,

cannot be deputed to others by the whole delegates, much less by two branches of them only, to wit the Lords and Commons. Locke. Gov. 2. 11.[9]

Apart from the question of whether Jefferson's historical references were accurate and his interpretation of them correct, he was correct and appropriate in his use of Locke as an authority for his argument. Substantiation of this is found by reference to that part of Locke's chapter "Of the Extent of the Legislative Power" which he paraphrased: "The *Legislative cannot transfer the Power of Making Laws* to any other hands. For it being but a delegated Power from the People, they, who have it, cannot pass it over to others. The People alone can appoint the Form of the Commonwealth, which is by Constituting the Legislative, and appointing in whose hands that shall be. And when the People have said, We will submit to rules, and be govern'd by *Laws* made by such Men, and in such Forms, no Body else can say other Men shall make *Laws* for them."[10]

What Jefferson proved, at least to his satisfaction, in his historical research and paraphrased citation of the *Second Treatise* was the basic authority of the people over the legislative body, including an elected king. He believed this was a fundamental part of the ancient constitution of England and the present one too, if the usurpation of Parliament were remedied. That ancient constitution, as he interpreted it, was what he referred to in his *Notes on the State of Virginia* as having the "freest principles," which, "with others derived from natural right and natural reason," formed the basis of government in America.[11] What Locke's chapter 11 stressed and Jefferson made use of in his paraphrase was that to alter the legislative power without the consent of the people who established it, and then to make laws with that altered legislative body, was to violate the sacred principle of government by consent of the people. Laws made in such a way were not laws and did not need to be obeyed, said Locke:

> This *Legislative* is not *only the supreme power* of the Commonwealth, but sacred and unalterable in the hands where the Community have once placed it; nor can any Edict of any Body else, in what Form soever conceived; or by what Power soever backed, have the force and obligation of a *Law*, which has not its *Sanction from* that *Legislative*, which the publick has chosen and appointed. For without this the Law could not have that, which is absolutely necessary to its being a *Law, the consent of the Society,* over whom no Body can have a power to make Laws, but by their own consent, and by Authority received from them.[12]

The combination of these ideas with Jefferson's conclusion that kings were an elected part of the legislative power under the legitimate constitution of England had obvious implications for the colonies, which resented laws passed by Parliament that they deemed oppressive. It rendered all laws made by Parliament illegal until sanctioned by an elected king. It would seem, therefore, that Jefferson was applying his interpretation of English history and knowledge of Lockean political theory to the colonies before he drafted the Declaration of Independence. It would also seem that since he knew chapter 11 of the *Second Treatise* well enough to paraphrase provisions that applied to the legality of legislation relative to the successors of elected kings, his knowledge of that chapter extended beyond those provisions and indeed to the entire work. Evidence of this may be seen in the similarity of many of the provisions of the *Second Treatise* with those of the Declaration, which clearly shows that Jefferson not only had extensive knowledge of Locke's work but put it to use in drafting the Declaration. These similarities can be shown by comparing passages from the first printing of the Declaration as approved by the Continental Congress (see the appendix) with some from the *Second Treatise*. There were, of course, alterations in Jefferson's rough draft before the approved copy was printed. In order to demonstrate that the ideas conveyed in the first printed copy were Jefferson's, I annotate each passage quoted to show that either the passage was not altered, or that the alterations were made by Jefferson himself, or that they did not change the meaning of his rough draft language.

General Similarities

In chapter 19 of the *Second Treatise,* titled "Of the Dissolution of Government," a provision similar to those paraphrased by Jefferson from chapter 11 as respects the authenticity of law passed by an altered legislative body goes even further. It not only states that laws passed by an altered legislative are not laws and need not be obeyed but adds that legislative alteration dissolves the government and gives the people the freedom to form a new one. As Locke put it:

> The *Constitution of the Legislative* is the first and fundamental Act of Society, whereby provision is made for the *Continuation of their Union,* under the Direction of Persons, and Bonds of Laws made by persons authorized thereunto, by the Consent and Appointment of the People, without which no one Man, or number of Men, amongst them, can have Authority of making Laws, that shall be binding to the rest. When any one, or more, shall take upon them to make Laws,

whom the People have not appointed so to do, they make Laws without Authority, which the People are not therefore bound to obey; by which means they come again to be out of subjection, and may constitute to themselves a *new Legislative,* as they think best, being in full liberty to resist the force of those, who without Authority would impose any thing upon them. Every one is at the disposure of his own Will, when those who had by the delegation of the Society, the declaring of the publick Will, are excluded from it, and others usurp the place who have no such Authority or Delegation.[13]

The basic purpose of the Declaration of Independence of 4 July 1776 was to make a formal statement that the authority of the British government over the former colonies had been dissolved.[14] It listed as the just causes of that dissolution the "repeated Injuries and Usurpations" inflicted on the colonies by the "King of Great-Britain."[15] Many of the specific "Injuries and Usurpations" (enumerated below) were alleged to be the result of altering the legislative power appointed by the colonial people. In short, the dissolution of government as the effect of legislative usurpations or alterations—the core concept of the foregoing Lockean passage—became a principal thrust of the Declaration. Legislative alterations or usurpations caused the people, as Locke put it, to "come again to be out of subjection," allowing them to "constitute to themselves a *new Legislative.*" The Declaration followed this Lockean premise by stating that the colonial people had the right as respects their government "to alter or to abolish it, and to institute new Government"[16] as a result of legislative usurpations or alterations as well as some other abuses which, Locke maintained, dissolved a government.

Other provisions of the *Second Treatise* are also strikingly similiar to general ideas contained in the Declaration. One that supplied the format Jefferson used is found in the last paragraph of chapter 18, "Of Tyranny." It urged men to observe the actions of a prince because those actions, not his pretensions or protestations, were what revealed his true intentions and purposes:

But if all the World shall observe Pretenses of one kind, and Actions of another; Arts used to elude the Law, and the Trust of Prerogative (which is an Arbitrary Power in some things left in the Prince's hand to do good, not harm to the People) employed contrary to the end, for which it was given: if the People shall find the Ministers, and subordinate Magistrates chosen suitable to such ends, and favoured, or laid by proportionably, as they promote, or oppose them: If they see several Experiments made of Arbitrary Power, and . . . a *long*

Train of Actings shew the Councils all tending that way, how can a Man any more hinder himself from being perswaded in his own Mind, which way things are going.[17]

At the beginning of the Declaration, in the "all the World" manner of Locke, Jefferson made an explicit appeal to world public opinion when he stated that "a decent Respect to the Opinions of Mankind" requires that when "it becomes necessary for one People to dissolve" their government, "they should declare the causes which impel them" to such action.[18] The causes that led to the Declaration of Independence were alleged in that document to be offenses committed by the king against the colonies. These were described as "a long Train of Abuses and Usurpations, pursuing invariably the same Object"— abuses, that is, revealing the king's true purpose to be "a Design to reduce them [the colonists] under absolute Despotism."[19] Here, as in Locke, attention is directed to actions. Even the terminology is similar. In addition to "a *long Train of Actings*" in chapter 18, Peter Laslett has pointed out that "a long Train of Abuses" in the Declaration is identical with language in chapter 19 of the *Treatise*. Locke speaks there of "*a long train of Abuses* [emphasis added], Prevarications, and Artifices, all tending the same way, make the design visible to the People."[20] Notice that in addition to the "abuses" phrase, Jefferson used "Design" in describing the king's purposes or objects in the same way Locke did. "Despotism," however, was not the only design or object of the king's actions. A second one mentioned in the Declaration was "the Establishment of an absolute Tyranny" over the colonies.[21] Then, after citing despotism and tyranny as the king's general objects or designs, Jefferson alleged that the king committed specific actions or abuses for the attainment of those objects or designs, quite "a long train" of them. Finally, toward the end of the Declaration, Jefferson wrote a conclusion about the king that he believed any reader would deem justified as a result of having read the enumerated specific abuses: "A Prince whose Character is thus marked by every act which may define a Tyrant, is unfit to be the Ruler of a free People."[22] In this manner, Jefferson's format in the Declaration conformed to the one Locke specified in his chapter 18, which instructed men to observe the actions of their prince in order to determine his "design" or object.

The idea of despotism or despotic power also shows a similarity between the *Second Treatise* and the Declaration. Locke defined such power as "Absolute, Arbitrary Power" which, being absolute and arbitrary, can be used "to take away" the lives of individuals subject to it. Such power came in conflict with "the *fundamental Law of Nature*," which was, according to Locke, "*the preservation of Mankind.*" Because this law was "the Will of God," Locke stated that each man was "*bound to preserve himself,* and not to quit his Station wilfully." In other words, each individual had the obligation to protect himself or herself from despotic power in the state of nature which continued to apply after a government was formed. Therefore, if the government had absolute arbitrary power with its potential to do harm to an individual by exercising it in a despotic way, individuals could and should resist it since they were obligated to preserve themselves. As Locke expressed this point when he wrote of governmental power: "It being out of a Man's power so to submit himself to another, as to give him a liberty to destroy him; God and Nature never allowing a Man so to abandon himself, as to neglect his own preservation: And since a man cannot take away his own Life, neither can he give another power to take it."[23] Jefferson in the Declaration approached the problem of despotic power from the perspective of the unalienable rights of man rather than an obligation to God. Nonetheless, the thrust of his argument is similar to Locke's, as is seen in this statement: "But when a long Train of Abuses and Usurpations . . . evinces a Design to reduce them [the people] under absolute Despotism, it is their Right, it is their Duty, to throw off such Government, and to provide new Guards for their future Security."[24]

Still another similiarity between the *Second Treatise* and the Declaration is the contention that the people had the power to judge whether or not the government's power had become absolute or arbitrary and whether the government was doing them harm. They did this, according to Locke, by appealing to God for His judgment on government, and only they could judge when the circumstances of government warranted such an appeal.[25] The people would, of course, not ask God for His judgment unless they deemed the circumstances of government adverse to them and it would be expected that God's judgment would be favorable to their interests as they perceived those interests. Realistically, this would be the way the people could be expected to perceive God's judgment. Indeed, realists would say that it was the people, not God, making the judgment as to whether or not the power of their government was absolute or despotic or was doing them harm. Therein lay a problem: if used whimsically and capriciously by the people, such judicial power would lead to a constant dissolution of government and cause what Locke described as "a perpetual foundation for Disorder." To assuage the fears of those who believed the people would thus abuse their judicial power if they had it, Locke argued that they would not "throw off" a government "till the Inconvenience is so great, that the Majority feel it, and are weary of it, and find a necessity to have it amended." As he stressed in chapter 19: "People are not so easily got out of their old Forms, as some are apt to suggest. They are hardly to be prevailed with to amend the acknowledg'd Faults, in the Frame they have been accustom'd to. And if there be any Original defects, or adventitious ones introduced by time, or corruption; 'tis not an easie thing to get them changed, even when all the World sees there is an opportunity for it. This slowness and aversion in the People . . . have been seen in this kingdom."[26]

Jefferson made the same point in the Declaration. He too sought to allay the fears of those who thought that giving the people the power to judge their government would be disruptive to political stability. To the historical argument of Locke, he added a prudential one: "Prudence, indeed, will dictate that Governments long established should not be changed for light and transient Causes; and accordingly all experience hath shewn, that Mankind are more disposed to suffer, while Evils are sufferable, than to right themselves by abolishing the Forms to which they are accustomed."[27]

Specific Similarities

Perhaps the most striking similarities between the *Second Treatise* and the Declaration may be seen in the specific abuses alleged against the king in that document.[28] According to the first of those allegations, the king "has refused his Assent to Laws, the most wholesome and necessary for the public Good."[29] According to Locke, the "public good" is an end or purpose of government.[30] Moreover, when governors neglect or oppose laws that are necessary to achieve an end of government, the power of government, which is derived from the people, is dissolved and reverts back to the people, who are free to form a new government. As Locke put it: "For all *Power given with trust* for the attaining of an *end,* being limited by that *end,* whenever that *end* is manifestly neglected, or opposed, the *trust* must necessarily be *forfeited,* and the Power devolve into the hands of those that gave it, who may place it anew where they shall think best for their safety and security."[31] In the context of this comment, the first specific abuse alleged by the Declaration was a serious one, since by refusing to assent to laws "necessary for the public Good" the king opposed an end of government. This alone, according to a Lockean criterion, provided grounds for the dissolution of government.

The second abuse alleged by Jefferson was the king's refusal to allow the governors of the colonies "to pass Laws of immediate and pressing Importance, unless suspended in their Operation till his Assent should be obtained."[32] Laws "of immediate and pressing Importance" were conducive to the public good and thus an end of government. Then Jefferson mentioned neglect, the second of Locke's two reasons for dissolving the government when that neglect vitiated one of government's ends. He did this by stating as respects laws passed by colonial legislatures held in suspense pending the king's assent, "And when so suspended, he has utterly *neglected* to attend to them" (emphasis added).[33]

The third abuse alleged that the king had "refused to pass other Laws for the Accommodation of large Districts of People, unless those People would relinquish the Right of Representation in the Legislature."[34] Such arbitrariness on the part of the king is one of the specific ways in which the legislative is altered, according to Locke in chapter 19, which states generally that the alteration of legislative power from the way the people have established it dissolves the government. It states specifically of an executive who becomes arbitrary, "When . . . a single Person, or Prince, sets up his own Arbitrary Will in place of the Laws, which are the Will of the Society, declared by the Legislative, then the *Legislative is changed*."[35] In this passage Locke described a prince who, after gaining arbitrary power, nullified laws made by past legislative bodies that reflected the will of society. The result of relinquishing "the Right of Representation in the Legislature," stated in the Declaration, even though it does not mention such nullification and might not immediately have this effect, would be to subject the people to the arbitrary power of a king over which they had no control. That power could be used to nullify the will and the well-being of the people at any time and thereby result in despotism or tyranny. Locke defined tyranny as "*the exercise of Power beyond Right,* which nobody can have a Right to," utilized by an individual not for "the good of those, who are under it" but rather for "the satisfaction of his own Ambition, Revenge, Covetousness, or any other irregular Passion."[36] The potential for tyranny in the third abuse, not to mention despotism, was stated by Jefferson when he wrote that the people's "Right of Representation in the Legislature" was "a Right inestimable to them and formidable to Tyrants only."[37]

The king's fourth abuse is virtually identical with another way of altering the legislative as stated in chapter 19 of the *Second Treatise:* namely, hindering the legislative. As Jefferson expressed that abuse,

"He has called together Legislative Bodies at Places unusual, uncomfortable, and distant from the Depository of their public Records, for the sole Purpose of fatiguing them into Compliance with his Measures."[38] Compare Locke's language to this effect: "When the Prince hinders the Legislative from assembling in its due time, or from acting freely, pursuant to those ends, for which it was Constituted, the *Legislative is altered.*"[39]

The fifth abuse is similar to the fourth except that it alleged that the king hindered (or altered) the colonial legislatives in the extreme by dissolving their "Representative Houses repeatedly." The more basic offense alleged here, however, was the king's "Invasions on the Rights of the People," and the reason the colonial legislatures were dissolved by the king, according to the Declaration, was that they were "opposing with manly Firmness his Invasions" on their rights.[40] The principal right claimed by the colonists was the freedom to govern themselves, a basic premise of Locke's *Treatise*.

The sixth abuse alleged by the Declaration, like the fourth and the fifth, involves hindering the legislative, which, as Locke stated, alters the legislative. In this allegation, however, Jefferson made explicit a Lockean principle: that the dissolution of legislative power is the effect of its having been altered by people other than those who established it—at which time that power devolves to the people. The king, wrote Jefferson of this allegation, "refused for a long Time, after such Dissolutions [of colonial representative houses], to cause others to be elected." As a consequence of this substantial alteration of government by the king, he then added, "the Legislative Powers . . . have returned to the People at large for their exercise."[41]

The thirteenth alleged abuse is the only one that does not name the king as the sole abuser: "He has combined with others to subject us to a Jurisdiction foreign to our Constitution, and unacknowledged by our Laws." Here "others" referred to the people of England, and "Jurisdiction" to their Parliament.[42] The allegation then condemned the king for "giving his Assent to their [Parliament's] Acts of pretended Legislation" over the colonists.[43] Both Parliament's claim of legislative authority and the king's assent to it were the Lockean legislative usurpation and alteration that dissolved the government, since Parliament had not been authorized by the colonial people to make laws for them. One such act of Parliament's "pretended Legislation" was "imposing Taxes on us without our Consent."[44] On this sensitive issue Locke specified in the *Second Treatise* that taxes "must be with his [each individual's] own *Consent,*—i.e., the Consent of the Majority, giving it either by themselves, or their Representatives chosen by them."[45]

Following the abuses alleged to have been committed jointly by king and Parliament, Jefferson again focused exclusively on the king, this time on his acts of war against the colonies: His Majesty had "plundered our Seas, ravaged our Coasts, burnt our Towns, and destroyed the Lives of our People."[46] In the next paragraph he made further allegations as to the king's acts of war, once again specifying abuses that, according to the *Second Treatise*, would dissolve government. As Locke put it, a prince "by actually putting himself into a State of War with his People," would thus "dissolve the Government, and leave them to that defence, which belongs to every one in the State of Nature." Since everyone was entitled, even obligated, to self-defense both in the state of nature and after a government was formed, according to Locke, even the actions of kings could be defended against: *"Self-defence is a part of the Law of Nature; nor can it be denied the Community, even against the King himself."*[47]

It is clear, then, that many of the specific abuses alleged in the Declaration are found in the *Second Treatise*. It seems equally clear that what Jefferson did when he drafted the Declaration was to analyze the offenses of king and Parliament against the colonies. He thereby noticed that many of them corresponded with abuses mentioned in the *Second Treatise*. He then arranged the allegations in the Declaration, as a lawyer would, to demonstrate that the colonies were justified in dissolving their government. Since any one of several specific abuses stated in the Declaration would, by itself, dissolve the government according to Locke, Jefferson used Lockean theory to support the Declaration's purpose, which was to make a formal statement that the authority of the British government over the colonies was dissolved. Hence, to a very great extent, the Declaration judged both the king and Parliament by criteria set forth in Locke's *Second Treatise*. Jefferson could not have used these criteria without knowledge of that work.

Emigration and Lockean Theory

One abuse mentioned near the end of the Declaration provides evidence that Jefferson had knowledge of Lockean political theory long before he wrote that document and shows that he used historical precedents much as they were used in the *Second Treatise*. Locke stated that governments of the world that began in peace were the result of the consent of free and independent men joining to form a commonwealth in the state of nature. History, Locke maintained, provided proof of this, which he made clear when he said there were "examples of History, shewing, that the *Governments* of the World, that were begun in Peace . . . were *made by the Consent of the People.*" He cited Rome and Venice as examples. Greece, he believed, provided another example when some of the Spartans left their native city "with *Palantas, mentioned by Justin.*" These Spartans were free men who, "*independent* one of another, . . . set up a Government over themselves, by their own consent." Locke was convinced that he had proved his theory of the origin of government by giving "several Examples out of History, of *People free and in the State of Nature,* that being met together incorporated and *began a Commonwealth.*"[48]

Jefferson, consistent with this Lockean approach, read history to find precedents for the American colonies' establishment of their own government. He was interested in the Greek colonies that broke away from or became disobedient to the cities that had colonized them and cited examples from the writings of Abraham Stanyan and Sir Walter Raleigh.[49] Chinard said of Jefferson that "even when writing the Declaration of Independence he was still preoccupied with precedents."[50] One precedent briefly mentioned in the Declaration concerned emigration. In the next to last paragraph of the printed copy is an innocuous and somewhat obscure statement: "We have reminded them [the British people] of the Circumstances of our Emigration and Settlement here."[51] Those circumstances are not elaborated. This statement and the preceding sentence, "We have warned them from Time to Time of Attempts by their Legislature to extend an unwarrantable Jurisdiction over us,"[52] give the impression that the historical circumstances of emigration to British colonial America must somehow have made null and void the attempts of Parliament to exert jurisdiction over the colonies. In fact, this was the case, according to Jefferson, since the emigration reference in the final approved Declaration was the vestige of a much longer statement he had made in the rough draft, most of which was eliminated by the Continental Congress. The original passage (with the deleted part in italics) read:

> We have reminded them of the Circumstances of our Emigration and Settlement here, *no one of which would warrant so strange a pretention: that these were effected at the expense of our own blood and treasure, unassisted by the wealth or the strength of Great Britain: that in constituting indeed our several forms of government, we had adopted one common king, thereby laying a foundation for perpetual league and amity with them: but that submission to their parliament was no part of our constitution, nor ever in idea if history may be credited.*[53]

Jefferson went on to say (and this part remained in the adopted version) that the colonists had urged the British people "to disavow these Usurpations" or parliamentary claims of jurisdiction.[54]

Thus, the historical precedent mentioned in the final approved copy of the Declaration was but a brief version of the way Jefferson drafted it originally. Even the original draft, however, was itself but a brief version of a cherished theory Jefferson had articulated more comprehensively two years earlier in *A Summary View of the Rights of British America*. That essay, written to instruct the Virginia delegates to a Continental Congress and ultimately to set before the king certain grievances of all the colonies, was not adopted by the Virginia assembly but was published in London about one year later. Like the Declaration, it denied the authority of Parliament over the colonies and condemned Parliament's "unwarrantable encroachments and usurpations" on the legislative power of the colonies.[55] Its denial and condemnation, as in the Declaration, were based on the circumstances of emigration—not only of the colonists who had emigrated to America but of the Saxons who had emigrated to England. The *Summary View* used the Saxons as a precedent to justify the American colonies' establishment of their own government and laws.

Jefferson had read a great deal about the Saxons, as his government commonplace book demonstrates. Chinard notes that he painstakingly reconstructed their history by reading such authors as "Pelloutier, Molesworth, Vertot, Sullivan, Kames and Blackstone." He also read the writings of John Dalrymple and Sir Henry Spelman, which provided him with the idea that feudalism had been imposed upon Saxon law as a result of the Norman Conquest.[56] Before that, the Saxons had established and governed themselves by their own laws since their arrival in England, according to Jefferson. These laws in their pure form were not imposed on them by either feudal kings or Judeo-Christian revelation and its priestcraft, since the Saxons arrived in England before they were converted to Christianity and long before the Norman Conquest. This Saxon law, according to Jefferson, was the origin of the English common law.[57] It was a system of law that arose from the people themselves and had as its basis the law of nature as mentioned in the last chapter. Jefferson argued that by exercising their natural right of freedom of emigration, the Saxons had placed themselves back in the state of nature.[58] At that time they had the freedom of that state to form their own government by their own consent in England and adopt laws of their own choosing without any interference from their mother country—which in fact did not interfere.

Having exercised their right of emigration, which put them in the state of nature, the Saxons were the perfect historical precedent for the colonists in America. Jefferson argued that the colonists, upon exercising their right of emigration from England, had the right like their Saxon predecessors to form their own governments and adopt their own laws. This precedent, analogous to Locke's historical examples, justified the colonists' claims of legislatures and laws independent of Great Britain. Thus Jefferson, aided by reading many authors during his historical research (some of whom had a different view of the Saxons and the origin of the common law than the ones he preferred), adapted the Saxon history and law to serve the interests of the colonists. In addition he did so in a way that was in accord with Lockean theory, which also served those interests. As Jefferson argued from historical precedent in the *Summary View*:

> Our ancestors, before their emigration to America, were the free inhabitants of the British dominions in Europe, and possessed a right, which nature has given to all men, of departing from the country in which chance, not choice, has placed them, of going in quest of new habitations, and of there establishing new societies, under such laws and regulations as, to them, shall seem most likely to promote public happiness. That their Saxon ancestors had, under this universal law, in like manner, left their native wilds and woods in the North of Europe, had possessed themselves of the Island of Britain, then less charged with inhabitants, and had established there that system of laws which has so long been the glory and protection of that country. Nor was ever any claim of superiority or dependence asserted over them, by that mother country from which they migrated.[59]

Jefferson went on to state that if a claim of governmental jurisdiction had been made by the mother country over England, the Saxons there had "too firm a feeling of the rights derived to them from their [Saxon] ancestors, to bow down the sovereignty of their state before such visionary pretensions."[60] The thrust of this argument was that what the Saxons did in England and were allowed to do by their mother country, the colonists had a right to do in America and should be allowed to do by *their* mother country.[61]

In specifying the "establishment of new societies, under such laws and regulations as to them shall seem most likely to promote public happiness" by emigrants in a land "less charged with inhabitants," Jefferson was applying the Lockean theory of government by consent of the people in a historical context as Locke did in the *Second Treatise*: "For there are no Examples so frequent in History, both Sacred and Prophane, as those of Men withdrawing themselves, and their

Obedience, from the Jurisdiction they were born under, and the Family or Community they were bred up in, and *setting up new Governments* in other places: from whence sprang all that number of petty Common-wealths in the beginning of Ages, and which always multiplied, as long as there was room enough."[62] This striking similarity between the *Second Treatise* and the *Summary View* leaves little doubt that Lockean political theory was entrenched in Jefferson's mind two years before he drafted the Declaration. This was when he wrote the *Summary View* and formulated his Lockean historical precedent, which was used in that document as well as the Declaration.

Subsequent to the *Summary View,* two other documents written by Jefferson gave him the opportunity to formulate grievances against Great Britain and the king that were consistent with Lockean political theory. The first was the "Declaration . . . setting forth the causes and necessity of taking up arms," which he drafted in 1775; the second was a proposed constitution for Virginia, drafted not long before the Declaration of Independence. Both documents, especially the latter, listed grievances similar to the ones stated in the Declaration. In fact, when Jefferson drafted the Declaration, he had with him a list of the grievances stated in his proposed constitution for Virginia, a list he had rearranged to suit the Declaration.[63]

Given all the similarities between the ideas of the *Second Treatise* and the Declaration, it is not surprising that Richard Henry Lee accused Jefferson of copying the latter from the former. Jefferson's later denial of this charge, made to James Madison, is revealing: "Richard Henry Lee has charged it [the Declaration] as copied from Locke's treatise on Government. . . . I only know that I turned to neither book nor pamphlet while writing it. I did not consider it as any part of my charge to invent new ideas altogether and to offer no sentiment which had ever been expressed before."[64] It is significant that he denied only copying Locke, not the use of his theory. In a similar denial to Henry Lee, Jefferson said the Declaration was "neither aiming at originality of principle or sentiment, nor yet copied from any particular and previous writing, it was intended to give expression of the American mind. . . . All its authority rests on the harmonizing sentiments of the day, whether expressed in conversation, in letters, printed essays, or in the elementary books of public right, as Aristotle, Cicero, Locke, Sidney, etc."[65] Again, there was no specific denial of using Lockean theory; Locke was mentioned with several other authors who may have contributed to the ideas contained in the Declaration. Yet it was Locke whom Jefferson singled out for praise in 1790, among all those authors mentioned to Lee when he said of the *Second Treatise,* "Locke's little book on Government is perfect as far as it goes. Descending from theory to practice, there is no better book than the Federalist [Papers]."[66] This high praise of Lockean theory is testimony to Jefferson's knowledge of it, a knowledge attained before 1776 and put to use during that year. Jefferson's statement to Lee that the Declaration "was intended to give expression of the American mind" has been interpreted by some to mean that the document is an expression of the collective mind of the American people or their representatives at the Second Continental Congress. The "American mind" expressed in the Declaration, however, was clearly Jefferson's. Apart from the fact that the language and ideas expressed in the first official printed text were, for the most part, Jefferson's, there were few if any members of the Congress, other than Benjamin Franklin, who shared the deist religious views Jefferson expressed in that document, even though most agreed with its political ideas.

As Julian Boyd has pointed out, some have seen parallels between the Declaration and James Wilson's pamphlet *Considerations on the Nature and Extent of the Legislative Authority of the British Parliament* (1775), or Jefferson's fellow Virginian George Mason's *Declaration of Rights* (1776), and regarded one or both as an influence on Jefferson when he drafted the Declaration.[67] Certainly these works, like the Declaration's ideological passages, do have a Lockean flavor.[68] One explanation is that Lockean ideology was so well known in the colonies before 1776, according to Carl Becker, Bernard Bailyn, and Steven Dworetz, that all expressions of it were bound to have similarities.[69] Jefferson's extensive pre-1776 knowledge of the *Second Treatise,* however, was such that he did not need Lockean intermediaries like Wilson or Mason to acquaint him with Lockean political theory.

Theology and Egalitarianism

Apart from political theory, Locke made a specific contribution to the theology of the Declaration. He seems also to have influenced Jefferson in a more general way in matters of theology prior to 1771. Jefferson firmly believed that each man's reason was his sole authority in theology and religion, but only for himself and no one else.[70] This idea arose partly from the influence of his extracts of Bolingbroke's writings, with their devastating attacks on revelation and the tradition of the church or ecclesiastical authority. These left man de facto with no authority in theology and religion but his own reason. The idea would also seem to have come from his reading of John Locke's *Of the Con-*

duct of the Understanding. This work too was on the list of books Jefferson recommended to Robert Skipwith in 1771.[71] In it Locke stated:

> There is indeed one science, as they are now distinguished, incomparably above all the rest, where it is not by corruption narrowed into a trade or faction for mean or ill ends and secular interests—I mean theology; which, containing the knowledge of God and his creatures, our duty to him and our fellow-creatures, and a view of our present and future state, is the comprehension of all other knowledge directed to its true end, i.e. the honour and veneration of the Creator and the happiness of mankind. This is that noble study which is every man's duty, and every one that can be called a rational creature is capable of. . . . This is that science which would truly enlarge men's minds, were it studied, or permitted to be studied everywhere with that freedom, love of truth, and charity which it teaches, and were not made, contrary to its nature, the occasion of strife, faction, malignity, and narrow impositions.[72]

Locke's ideas in *Conduct* on the study of theology, which included each individual's duty to God and to "our fellow-creatures" were succinctly echoed by Jefferson: "The relations which exist between man and his Maker, and the duties resulting from those relations, are most interesting and important to every human being, and the most incumbent on his study and investigation."[73] Although this statement was made in 1822, Chinard saw such statements as a reflection of the lasting impressions made on Jefferson's consciousness by his early reading.

In another statement from *Conduct* emphasizing individual reason in theology and religion, Locke pointed out that the vast majority of persons were inclined to accept popular opinion as truth, or, as he put it, "apt to conclude that what is common opinion cannot but be true." Yet he also maintained that this herd instinct of the masses could not lead to truth: "I do not remember wherever God delivered his oracles by the multitude, or Nature truths by the herd." He went on to state that anyone who wished to know "the truth of things must leave the common and beaten track, which none but weak and servile minds are satisfied to trudge along continually in" and exercise his own rational judgment.[74] Jefferson echoed these comments in a 1787 letter to his nephew Peter Carr: "Your own reason is the only oracle given you by heaven, and you are answerable, not for the rightness, but the uprightness of the decision." After cautioning against favoring novel or bizarre opinions on religious and theological matters, using phraseology similar to Locke's "servile minds," he went on to advise his nephew not to surrender his mind or reason to the views of others but to let it reach its own conclusions:

> Your reason is now mature enough to examine this object [religion and theology]. In the first place, divest yourself of all bias in favor of novelty and singularity of opinion. Indulge them in any other subject rather than that of religion. It is too important, and consequences of error may be too serious. On the other hand, shake off all the fears and servile prejudices, under which weak minds are servilely crouched. Fix reason firmly in her seat, and call to her tribunal every fact, every opinion. Question with boldness even the existence of a God; because, if there be one, he must more approve of the homage of reason, than that of blindfolded fear.[75]

Locke's specific contribution to the theology of the Declaration, however, was his affirmation of God-given equality. Yet probably even before Bolingbroke and Locke influenced him, Jefferson was imbued with the value of equality. Among the quotations he copied in his literary commonplace book, three indicate the emergent egalitarianism and theology of equality that would become the foundation of the Declaration's ideological passages. The first, an entry he made sometime before 1763 from book 8 of Milton's *Paradise Lost,* suggests that inequality disrupts any enjoyable and lasting "society" between human beings from the perspective of either the superior or the inferior of an unequal relationship:

> Among Unequals what Society
> Can sort, what Harmony or true Delight?
> Which must be mutual, in Proportion due
> Giv'n & received; but in Disparity.
> The one intense, the other still remiss
> Cannot well suit with either, but soon prove
> Tedius alike: . . . Id: l: 383.[76]

The second quotation, from Nicholas Rowe's play *Tamerlane* (1701), was also entered before 1763. It speaks of a universal God who treats all nations and faiths alike and who welcomes and accepts all forms of worship, in contrast to a partial God who accepts just one and rejects all others:

> Look round, how Providence bestows alike
> Sunshine & Rain, to bless the fruitful year,
> On different Nations, all of different Faiths;
> And (tho' by several Names & Titles worship'd)
> Heav'n takes the various Tribute of their Praise;

Since all agree to own, at least to mean,
One best, one greatest, only Lord of all.
    Rowe's Tamerl: Act. 3. Sc: 2.[77]

The third, copied in Greek from Euripides between 1762 and 1765, states that equality is based on natural law and that inequality disrupts human affection: "Better far, . . . prize equality that ever linketh friend to friend, city to city, and allies to each other; for equality is man's natural law; but the less is always in opposition to the greater, ushering in the days of dislike. Id. v. 538."[78]

It was in the *Second Treatise,* however, that Jefferson found the expression of egalitarianism and theology of equality that appears in the Declaration of Independence. Locke's statement *"All Men by Nature are equal"* is a major premise of that theology. God created all men "equal and independent," since they were "all the Workmanship of one Omnipotent, and infinitely wise Maker." Locke elaborated on what he meant by equality when he defined it in terms of what it is not: *"Age"* and *"Virtue," "Excellency of Parts and Merit,"* as well as *"Birth"* may cause men voluntarily "to pay an Observance to those whom Nature, Gratitude or other Respects may have made it due." Then, after this definition by negation, which acknowledges that men are not equal in all respects, he provided a positive definition of equality: "that *equal Right* that every Man hath, *to his Natural Freedom,* without being subjected to the Will or Authority of any other Man."[79]

This natural and equal right to freedom had certain limitations, however, for *"Liberty,"* Locke said, was *"not a State of Licence."* Those limitations were the moral rules of the law of nature, which "obliges every one: And Reason, which is that Law, teaches all Mankind, who will but consult it, that being all equal and independent, no one ought to harm another in his Life, Health, Liberty or Possessions." Locke took full account of the limitations that these rules placed on freedom in his definition of liberty, which he said was "a Liberty to follow my own Will in all things, where the Rule prescribes not. . . . *Freedom of Nature* is to be under no other restraint but the Law of Nature."[80]

According to Locke, it was precisely because of this equal freedom, the equal power that was natural to all men, and the ability to find the moral law of nature that each man in the state of nature had the capacity to judge whether or not other men had transgressed the law of nature and, if they had, to punish them.[81] To put it another way, in the state of nature each man was the source of moral knowledge as well as juridical and punitive authority in his relations with others. He was not dependent upon the authority of God's revelation, church, or priests, or that of kings to provide laws for good social behavior; rather, he was anterior and superior to these authorities and their rules. As a result, it was only by the authority of individuals that the legislative part of government could prescribe rules. It was because of the nature of men, particularly their equal freedom, that the consent of each was needed in order to form a legislature. Locke thus turned the traditional authority of government upside down. Instead of coming down from God via kings or priests who in the name of God imposed laws on humanity, that authority arose from the mutual consent of individuals, who then appointed a legislature and an executive as trustees to give and enforce laws consistent with the law of nature for the benefit of the people.[82] That legislature and executive and those laws were then under the ultimate authority of the people, who made the final judgment as to whether their trust was carried out.[83] The ability of the people to find the moral laws of nature with their reason was what enabled them to make that judgment.

The consequence of these Lockean ideas was that no one man or group of men could claim authority to rule others by the grace of God. God in Locke's political theory had in effect ordained all persons with equal authority in government at the time of creation and granted His grace for the purpose of governing to none. In this sense, God treated all men equally at creation. The Declaration of Independence echoed the thrust of this Lockean political theory and theology of equality. The second paragraph begins:

> We hold these Truths to be self-evident, that all Men are created equal, that they are endowed by their Creator with certain unalienable Rights, that among these are Life, Liberty and the Pursuit of Happiness. That to secure these Rights, Governments are instituted among Men, deriving their just powers from the Consent of the Governed, that whenever any Form of Government becomes destructive to these Ends, it is the Right of the People to alter or to abolish it, and to institute new Government, laying its Foundation on such Principles and organizing its Powers in such Form, as to Them shall seem most likely to effect their Safety and Happiness.[84]

The God of the Declaration, like Locke's God in the *Treatise,* created all men equal by treating them all equally at the time of their creation. He made this equal treatment manifest when He "endowed" each and every man with certain "unalienable Rights" and gave all men equal authority to form governments by their consent. The God of the Declaration, therefore, like the God of the *Treatise,* did not grant special favor or grace to anyone at the time of creation, as did the God of

Christian theology. Indeed, the Declaration's whole concept of equal creation and treatment by God at creation was contradictory to the concept of grace, particularly predestinating grace, which had become repugnant to Jefferson under Bolingbroke's influence. Grace was partiality on the part of God, and Jefferson followed Bolingbroke's lead in rejecting a partial God. Therefore, in the second paragraph of the Declaration Jefferson departed from the theology of the dominant versions of Christianity, both Catholic and Protestant, by rejecting their partial God who was a granter of grace.

It can be argued that God's equal treatment of men as spelled out in the *Second Treatise* and the Declaration—His giving them equal authority to form governments while simultaneously not granting His grace to any one man or group of men to govern—applied to God's grace only as respects matters of government; it had nothing to do with the saving grace that grants individuals salvation. This distinction may have been maintained by some, but Jefferson in the Declaration of Independence rejected all forms of divine grace, including that which provided salvation. Grace in any form was not in accord with "Nature's God" (see chapter 2).

By appealing to Bolingbroke's impartial "Nature's God" in the Declaration, Jefferson departed from the revealed theology of both the New and the Old Testament.[85] Bolingbroke's influence on the theology of the Declaration was thus considerable. Yet the specific influence on its theology of equality was Locke's idea that *"all Men by Nature are equal"* and that God, the "omnipotent and infinitely wise Maker" created them that way. This provided Jefferson with what he needed to construct his ideology: a God who was truly universal, whose love and benevolence included all mankind and excluded none. That universality began with God's first act toward men, for at the time of their creation He treated them all equally by endowing them all with equal rights while showing grace or partiality to none in matters of either government or salvation.

One part of Lockean political theory posed a problem to Jefferson, however. It had to do with the law of nature and the Lockean epistemology that provided access to that law. Jefferson's solution and those who helped him find it contributed to his concept of man as an independent moral agent.

4

Kames and the Moral Sense

According to the orthodox Christian concept of man, men and women, because of their depraved fallen condition, could not trust their own determinations of right and wrong. God was the only trustworthy source of moral knowledge, and individuals had only mediated access to that source through scripture, church, and clergy. This effect of the fall made humanity dependent upon one or more of these intermediaries for trustworthy moral knowledge. As a result these intermediaries, especially the clergy, became the authorities over others in moral considerations. Before writing the Declaration of Independence, Jefferson had rejected the orthodox Christian concept of human nature and adopted a heterodox view. As Adrienne Koch stated, he favored "systems of independent morality needing no sanction from church and state."[1] In Jefferson's heterodox concept of man, "Nature's God," or the God of natural theology, endowed individuals with the capacity to attain trustworthy moral knowledge independently. This capacity made the authority of the individual preeminent in moral determinations over that of church, scripture, and clergy.

This chapter will examine a major source of Jefferson's ideas on the moral nature of man and will explain—from the perspective of Lockean political theory and the problem posed by Locke's moral epistemology—why he adopted those ideas as part of the Declaration's theology. It will also explain how those ideas are linked to Jefferson's later revision of Christianity to a heterodox version, with a concept of man in accord with the one contained in the Declaration's theology.

The Problem of Moral Independence in Locke

Jefferson was familiar, before he wrote the Declaration, with the political implications of the individual's attaining moral knowledge independently. John Locke's *Second Treatise*, according to which individuals had rational access to moral knowledge, was no doubt one source of that familiarity. David Hume, whose essays were among the works that Jefferson recommended to Robert Skipwith in 1771, could also have contributed to that familiarity as well as to Jefferson's commitment to Lockean democratically derived political systems based on moral independence.[2] "Monarchies," said Hume, "receiving their chief stability from a superstitious reverence to priests and princes, have almost always abridg'd the liberty of reasoning with regard to politics and consequently to metaphysics and morals."[3] As a result of this "superstitious reverence to priests and princes," men voluntarily submitted to their moral and political authority, thus abridging the use of their own reason in morals and politics and leaving them dependent for moral knowledge on church or state. This dependency, by preventing them from making independent moral judgments about their government, effectively deprived them of the political control and power described by Locke in the *Second Treatise*. It also enabled unscrupulous princes and priests to exploit the people and morally justify their exploitations to their victims, who were dependent on them for moral knowledge.

This condition of a superstitious people, which was antithetical to Lockean political theory, was clearly repugnant to Jefferson at the time of the Declaration of Independence, when he rejected both the moral and political authority of the king because of His Majesty's exploitation of his colonial subjects. Jefferson was also anticlerical by that time and rejected the moral authority of the clergy. There is little doubt that his reading of Bolingbroke was a major source of his anticlericalism.[4] Even though he did not extract any of Bolingbroke's anticlerical statements in his commonplace book, Jefferson too believed that the priestcraft of any religion exploited the people.[5] Therefore, to him the medieval idea that the pope could pass moral judgment on monarchs and absolve the subjects of those judged unrighteous from any obligation to abide by their rule was akin to letting a wolf guard the sheep.[6] Although Jefferson early in life formulated his ideas on monarchical and institutional religious exploitation of people, perhaps his best expression of such exploitation may be found in a letter of 1815: "Government, as well as religion, has furnished . . . its devices for fattening idleness on the earning of the people. It has its hierarchy of emperors, kings, princes and nobles, as that has of popes, cardinals, archbishops, bishops and priests."[7]

In order to put an end to exploitation by kings and priests, the vast majority of individuals needed the capacity to attain trustworthy moral knowledge easily and independently. If human reason could provide that capacity, the moral dependency of the masses would be a thing of the past, and the people could morally judge their governments and their clergy as well. It was in this direction that John Locke moved in basing his political theory on the independently attained rational knowledge of the moral law of nature by each individual. The *Second Treatise* states that reason is the law of nature and "teaches all Mankind, who will but consult it, that . . . no one ought to harm another in his Life, Health, Liberty or Possessions."[8] This language suggests that knowledge of the moral law of nature is readily or easily accessible to each human being: to acquire that knowledge, all anyone has to do is consult his or her own reason. Once knowledge of the law of nature is thereby attained, individuals can judge the moral transgressions of other individuals in the state of nature, and a people can judge the transgressions of their government after one is formed.[9] This moral knowledge, which each individual could easily attain, places ultimate political judgment and thereby the ultimate political power that results from it in the hands of the people. As John Dunn put it, "divine will," which according to Locke is the moral law of nature, is to be found not in divine revelation accessible only to one or a few but in "a set of rationally intelligible prescriptions accessible to all men."[10]

Yet even though his political theory was based on individual possession of moral knowledge, Locke was not convinced that people would "consult" their reason and thereby possess such knowledge. Indeed the *Second Treatise* states in effect that most men would not make such consultations and therefore would remain ignorant of the moral law of nature: "For though the Law of Nature be plain and intelligible to all rational Creatures; yet Men, being biassed by their Interest, as well as ignorant for the want of study of it, are not apt to allow of it as a Law binding to them in the application of it to their particular Cases."[11] It is understandable that Locke would regard self-interest as preventing persons from applying moral law to their own actions, but to say that men were "ignorant" of the law of nature "for the want of study of it" was a plain statement that most people did not know that law. This sort of ignorance challenged the democratic aspect of Locke's political theory. It would seem likely that Jefferson was aware of this provision as a result of his detailed knowledge of the *Second Treatise* before he wrote the Declaration of Independence. Whether or not he knew of this specific provision, he was aware that Lockean epistemology had limitations as respects its ability to find the moral law of nature. He could have gained this knowledge by reading two other works of Locke: *An Essay concerning Human Understanding* and *The Reasonableness of Christianity.*

One purpose of *Human Understanding* was to state the law of nature, which Locke believed reason could deduce from self-evident propositions born of ideas in the mind obtained by sensory perceptions of the social material world. Locke compared natural law to *"the Sciences"* and stated that it was *"capable of Demonstration: wherein I doubt not, but from self-evident Propositions, by necessary Consequences, as incontestable as those in Mathematics."*[12] Yet he failed to actualize this purpose of *Human Understanding*. Asked by his friend James Tyrrel to provide a rational demonstration of the law of nature, he was, as John Dunn pointed out, "confronted by his inability to present morality as a system of universally intelligible obligatory truths" and, with that realization, broke off the *Essay concerning Human Understanding*.[13]

In *The Reasonableness of Christianity*, written later, Locke admitted—in a manner that indicted, tried, and convicted human reason—his failure to provide a rational formulation of the law of nature:

> 'Tis plain, in fact, that human reason unassisted failed men in its great and proper business of morality. It never from unquestionable principles by clear deductions, made out an entire body of the law of nature. . . . The greatest part of mankind cannot know [morality], and therefore they must believe. And I ask, whether one coming from Heaven in the Power of God, in full and clear evidence and demonstration of Miracles, giving plain and direct Rules of Morality and Obedience, be not likelier to enlighten the bulk of Mankind, and set them right in their Duties, and bring them to do them, than by reasoning with them from general Notions and Principles of human Reason? And were all the Duties of human Life clearly demonstrated; yet I conclude, when well considered, that Method of teaching Men their Duties, would be thought proper only for a few, who had much Leisure, improved Understandings, and were used to abstract Reasonings. But the instruction of the People were best still to be left to the Precepts and Principles of the Gospel.[14]

Locke here admitted that reason never deduced "an entire body of the law of nature" and that "the greatest part of mankind" are not able to attain moral knowledge with their own reason. These limitations did not preclude a small portion of mankind—those who had extraordinary rational capacity and who had consulted their reason and studied the law of nature—from having sufficient knowledge of a part of that law to make moral judgments. But the fact that such knowledge was accessible to only a few defeated the democratic aspect of Lockean political theory by making the major portion of mankind dependent for moral knowledge upon the few who *could* know it by rational means.[15] Such dependency would give these few persons moral authority over the masses similar to that of the clergy over their denominations or congregations, allowing opportunity for these few to exploit the many by distorting the moral knowledge they provided in a way that favored their own selfish interests.

Although there is evidence that Jefferson read *Human Understanding* before drafting the Declaration of Independence, none indicates that he had read *The Reasonableness of Christianity* by that time.[16] He had, however, read indirectly via Bolingbroke what Locke said in the foregoing quote from it.[17] Bolingbroke, in a passage immediately preceding one extracted by Jefferson, as Morton White pointed out, wrote of Locke's statement in *Reasonableness* on the insufficiency of "human reason, unassisted by revelation, in its great and proper business of morality." In that same passage, Bolingbroke also wrote of Locke's statement that reason "never made out an entire body of the law of nature from unquestionable principles, or by clear deductions."[18]

The Solution in Kames

Another source would also have given Jefferson knowledge of the limitations of Lockean epistemology and reason in determining the moral law of nature. That source was Henry Home, Lord Kames, the Scottish jurist and philosopher. Kames was one of Jefferson's favorite pre-Declaration authors; in his government commonplace book Kames's *Essays on the Principles of Morality and Natural Religion* is cited in a section of entries that precede the date of the Declaration of Independence, as are several articles from Kames's *Historical Law Tracts*.[19] According to Gilbert Chinard, the pre-Declaration influence of Kames on Jefferson was extraordinary. He asserted, without elaboration or explanation, that in Kames's writings Jefferson "found a complete exposition of the theory of natural rights; and from the evidence furnished by the *Commonplace Book* it cannot be doubted that the Scottish Lord was for him a master and a guide."[20]

There is little doubt that Kames's extensive writings on moral philosophy had a more profound impact on Jefferson than did those of Francis Hutcheson, whom Garry Wills considers a major early influence on Jefferson and the Declaration of Independence.[21] Ronald Hamowy, in his critique of Wills's *Inventing America*, noted that even though Jefferson owned three Hutcheson works at the time Congress bought his library in 1815, it is not known when these books were purchased or whether Jefferson had read them. *An Inquiry into the*

Original of Our Ideas of Beauty and Virtue, Synopsis Metaphysicae, and *A Short Introduction to Moral Philosophy* were the Hutcheson titles among the five thousand volumes owned by Jefferson at the time of the sale.[22] The last of these does appear in the list of books Jefferson recommended in the 1767 letter outlining a study plan for the education of a lawyer.[23] But not one work by Hutcheson was included on the 1771 Skipwith list, and Hutcheson does not appear in the commonplace books. Had he exerted so great an influence on Jefferson's early adult life as Wills maintains, these omissions seem inconceivable. In contrast to Hutcheson's absence from the Skipwith list, three works by Kames were included there: *The Elements of Criticism, Principles of Equity,* and the aforementioned *Essays on the Principles of Morality and Natural Religion.*

In the *Essays* Kames took the position—in response to the writings of Samuel Clarke—that complex or abstract reason was not effective in giving men knowledge of moral rules or the law of nature.[24] His rationale was similar to Locke's statement in *The Reasonableness of Christianity* that the majority of men have little capacity for moral reasonings, particularly complex or abstract moral reasonings.[25] Kames believed, as did Hutcheson, who influenced him, that man was endowed by his creator with inner feelings or emotions, called a moral sense, which gave him knowledge of his moral duties and enabled him to perform those duties. Using Locke's *Reasonableness* phrase "the bulk of mankind," Kames argued:

> Supposing our duty could be made plain to us, by an abstract chain of reasoning, yet we have good ground to conclude, from analogy, that the Author of nature has not left our actions to be directed by so weak a principle as reason: and a weak principle it must be to the bulk of mankind, who have little capacity to enter into abstract reasoning; whatever effect it may have upon the learned and contemplative. Nature has dealt more kindly to us. We are compelled by strong and evident feelings, to perform all the different duties of life.[26]

Kames took a similar position in his *Principles of Equity,* which Jefferson read while he was a student of law.[27] In that work Kames spoke specifically of the superiority of the internal moral sense in gaining access to the law of nature, compared with Lockean epistemology's reliance on demonstrations made by reason from ideas in the mind born of sensory perceptions of external objects:

> By perception alone, without reasoning, we acquire the knowledge of right and wrong, of what we may do, of what we ought to do, and of

what we ought to abstain from: and considering that we have thus a greater certainty of the moral laws than of any proposition discovered by reasoning, man may well be deemed the favourite of Heaven, when such wisdom is employ'd in qualifying him to act a right part in life: the moral sense or conscience may well be held the voice of God within us, constantly admonishing us of our duty; and requiring on our part no exercise of our faculties but attention merely. The celebrated Locke ventured what he thought a bold conjecture, that the moral duties may be capable of demonstration: how great his surprise to have been told, that they are capable of much higher evidence.[28]

Kames divided human nature into two aspects in his analysis of what caused moral behavior in man. The first he termed the "principles of action," which he defined in a general way as "appetites, passions and affections." These principles, as their name indicates, were what made men act. In his specific account of them Kames listed five main ones. The first was love of life, which gave rise to the desire to preserve it; he called this "the strongest of all instincts." The second was the desire for "our own happiness," which he termed "self-love." The third principle was fidelity, the "performance of promises, . . . and in general the execution of trusts." "Friendship" was categorized under this principle, since it involved a trust relationship, as did "love to children, who by nature are entrusted to our care." The fourth principle was "gratitude," and the fifth was "benevolence."[29] The inclusion of both selfishness and altruism among the principles of action reflects Kames's effort to synthesize the views of Hobbes and Shaftesbury, who saw human reality as motivated by these opposites.[30]

Kames maintained that these five principles, constituting the first aspect of human moral behavior, were governed by the second aspect: the moral sense itself. The purpose and province of the moral sense, he said, was "to instruct us which of our principles of action we may indulge and which of them we must restrain."[31] Kames stressed his contention that the moral sense, which he also termed conscience, did not need the help of rational reflection to inform the individual how he should behave:

The authority of conscience does not merely consist in an action of reflection. It proceeds from a direct feeling, which we have upon presenting the object [of moral actions], without the intervention of any sort of reflection. And the authority lies in this circumstance, that we feel and perceive the action to be our duty, and what we are indispensibly bound to perform. It is in this manner, that the moral sense, with regard to some actions, plainly bears upon it the works of authority over all our appetites and affections [principles of action].[32]

Although reason was not necessary in making moral determinations, reason could and often did play some role in finding the moral laws of nature, according to Kames, which he made clear when he stated: "In searching for these laws, it must be obvious that we *may* falsely indulge every principle of action, where the action is not disapproved of by the moral sense, and that we *ought* to perform every action which the moral sense informs us to be our duty. From this short proposition, may be readily deduced all the laws of nature which govern human actions."[33] Since "the laws of nature which govern human actions" were "readily" or easily "deduced" by reason when it was guided by the moral sense, the amount of reason required to make such deductions to qualify for the descriptive term "readily" was minimal. This quantity of reason would require none of the complex, abstract, or scientific deductions of which Kames, echoing Locke, said that "the bulk of mankind . . . have little capacity to enter into."[34] This much reason the majority of human beings would have, giving the "bulk of mankind" easy access to the laws of nature. This minimal reason could provide persons with moral knowledge when used in conjunction with the moral sense. Thus, the function of the moral sense in Kames's moral philosophy is similar to that of scripture in Locke's *Reasonableness of Christianity,* where scripture was deemed necessary to provide moral knowledge because "human reason unassisted failed" to provide that knowledge. Reason assisted by scripture, however, did play a role in determining morality in Locke's *Reasonableness,* in that it gave its suffrage to and provided confirmation of what was contained in God's revealed word.[35]

As to the enforcement of moral law by the moral sense, Kames made a distinction between justice and benevolence. Justice consisted in refraining from "actions directed against others, by which they are hurt"; benevolence, in performing acts that would benefit others. Kames called justice a "primary virtue" because it was necessary for society, which could not exist if men continually harmed each other, whereas benevolence, although helpful to others, was not necessary for society and was therefore a "secondary virtue." Further, benevolence was not a duty under most circumstances, though Kames believed that "where the object of benevolence is distress, there it becomes a duty, provided it is in our power to afford relief without hurting ourselves." There was a natural inducement in man to perform even those benevolent acts that were not duties, however, for such acts produced a feeling of "approbationary pleasure" in the moral sense that motivated their performance. Justice, on the other hand, was always a duty, and violation of this duty resulted in punishment, inflicted by one's moral sense or conscience, in the form of "remorse of conscience," which "proves the most severe of all tortures." Kames believed that acts of justice gave some pleasure but that it was small compared with the higher satisfaction given by benevolent acts, which he considered more meritorious because they were for the most part discretionary and not duties. It was the feeling of the moral sense that one ought to perform some acts and refrain from others, however, combined with its meting out reward and punishment, that gave that sense what Kames described as "the most complete character of a law." His definition of the law of nature took into consideration that the moral sense not only provided knowledge of the law but also punished or rewarded individuals as they breached or obeyed it.[36]

The human moral sense was capable of improvement. Kames believed the feelings of the mind that constituted this sense could be strengthened by exercise in the form of attending plays and reading good literature. While participating in such exercise, one experienced an attraction toward characters who performed moral acts and an aversion to those who committed moral transgressions. This experience magnified, refined, and intensified the moral sense, according to Kames, who stated: "Nothing conduces so much to improve the mind [moral feelings], and confirm it in virtue, as being continually employed in surveying the actions of others, entering into the concerns of the virtuous, approving of their conduct, condemning vice, and showing an abhorrence at it; for the mind acquires strength by exercise, as well as the body."[37] Jefferson's 1771 letter to Robert Skipwith sounded much like this Kamesean passage. He included several plays and other works of literature among the books he recommended and specified their impact on the moral sense:

> Every thing is useful which contributes to fix us in the principles and practice of virtue. When any signal act of charity or of gratitude, for instance, is presented either to our sight or imagination, we are deeply impressed with its beauty and feel a strong desire in ourselves of doing charitable and grateful acts also. On the contrary when we see or read of any atrocious deed, we are disgusted with it's deformity and conceive an abhorrence of vice. Now every emotion of this kind is an exercise of our virtuous dispositions; and dispositions of the mind, like limbs of the body, acquire strength by exercise. But exercise produces habit; and in the instance of which we speak, the exercise

being of the moral feelings, produces a habit of thinking and acting virtuously. We never reflect whether the story we read be truth or fiction.[38]

Jefferson's belief that God necessarily provided man with a moral sense because He intended men to be social paralleled Kames's statement that no society could exist "among creatures who prey upon one another"; therefore a moral sense "was necessary in the first place, to provide against mutual injuries."[39] Like Kames, Jefferson admired this moral aspect of the human system and criticized a God who would make moral knowledge available only to the few who were capable of complex or scientific reason. Such a God would be incompetent. If only those few individuals capable of scientific or abstract reason had knowledge of morality, then the majority in their moral ignorance would harm one another, and society could not exist. In a statement to this effect, Jefferson implied that the God of the Bible, who created mankind morally depraved or with a nature prone to fall into depravity, was incompetent in this way:

He who made us would have been a pitiful bungler, if he had made the rules of our moral conduct a matter of science. For one man of science, there are thousands who are not. What would have become of them? Man was destined for society. His morality, therefore, was to be formed to this object. He was endowed with a sense of right and wrong, merely relative to this. This sense is as much a part of his nature as the sense of hearing, seeing, feeling; it is the true foundation of morality. . . . The moral sense, or conscience, is as much a part of man as his leg or arm. It is given to all human beings in a stronger or weaker degree, as force of members is given them in a greater or less degree. It may be strengthened by exercise, as may any particular limb of the body. This sense is submitted, indeed, in some degree, to the guidance of reason; but it is small stock which is required for this: even a less one than what we call common sense. State a moral case to a ploughman and a professor. The former will decide it as well, and often better than the latter, because he has not been led astray by artificial rules. In this branch, therefore, read good books, because they will encourage, as well as direct your feelings.[40]

This statement, in a letter to Peter Carr dated 10 August 1787, corresponds with Jefferson's 1771 comment to Robert Skipwith but more elaborately expresses Kamesean moral-sense philosophy. It includes Kames's use of both the moral sense and minimal reason as instruments of obtaining moral knowledge, both of which Jefferson appealed to in the 1774 *Summary View of the Rights of British America* and the

1776 Declaration of Independence, as we shall see. We can conclude, then, that Jefferson held the views expressed in this passage before and during the drafting of the Declaration of Independence.

What attracted Jefferson to Kames's moral philosophy, it is important to point out, was that it put moral knowledge within the easy grasp of virtually everyone. As a result, the concept of man Kames promulgated was very different from that of orthodox Christianity. Kamesean man was not the depraved or semidepraved victim of the fall, dependent upon God's intermediaries in the form of revelation, church, and clergy and under their authority for trustworthy moral knowledge. He could find that knowledge independently. Moreover, Kames's moral-sense concept of man solved the problem caused by Lockean epistemology's failure to deliver moral knowledge to the "bulk of mankind," making most men dependent for moral knowledge on the few who had the capacity for complex, abstract, or scientific reason. Kamesean man's ability to acquire knowledge of the moral laws of nature easily and independently was exactly what Jefferson, as a proponent of Lockean political theory, was looking for: Kames's concept of man was one that would render Lockean political theory efficacious.[41]

To some scholars, however, moral-sense philosophies too restricted men's access to knowledge of morality, especially those that utilized reason as well as the moral sense as instruments to provide moral knowledge. Morton White interpreted Jefferson's statements in his letter to Peter Carr that the moral sense is "the true foundation of morality" and that this sense is guided by reason and that that degree of guidance is small, "less than what we call Common sense," to mean that the extraordinary rational capacity of only the most intelligent human beings—not the moral sense—was the principal means of attaining moral knowledge. He argued that in writing to Carr that there were few men of science and therefore God could not have made the moral behavior of man a matter of scientific reason, Jefferson may have meant that the moral sense gave men "the first glimmerings of moral precepts," and as a result the final determination of those precepts was not "a matter of science *alone*." In White's view, Jefferson was of the opinion that the few men of science or of extraordinary rational capacity established moral rules for all mankind through the use of Lockean reason based on intuitive perceptions born of the senses, since this type of reason was necessary to substantiate the faint "glimmerings of moral precepts" first given by the moral sense.[42] The rational capacity of ordinary men could not accomplish this substantiation even with the aid of the moral sense. Thus, according to White, moral-sense philosophies that had a rational element, such as the one adopted by Jefferson, still made human beings dependent for trustworthy moral knowledge upon the few who had extraordinary rational capacity.

White's interpretation, however, hardly seems fair to the text of Jefferson's letter to Carr, which deprecated the extraordinary reasoning ability of professors while simultaneously exalting the rational capacity of the average "ploughman" in making moral determinations. Jefferson clearly stated that a professor could be morally "led astray by artificial rules" born of their superior reason, whereas ploughmen with average reasoning ability would not. The main point of Jefferson's comments to Carr was that even though the moral sense was guided by reason to some extent, in making moral determinations, reason was guided by the moral sense to the same extent or perhaps more. Jefferson stressed that only a minimal amount of reason, "even a less one than what we call common sense," was required for attaining moral knowledge when used in conjunction with the moral sense. It did not require a philosopher or a man of science to exercise this minimal quantity of rational capacity; to do so was within the intellectual scope of the common man.

White is of the opinion it was Lockean intuitive reason that perceived the principles contained in the Declaration. He maintains that few men have the capacity for such Lockean rational perceptions, which are self-evident and based on mental impressions derived from the senses. He also maintains that Jefferson, at the time of writing the Declaration, was under the influence of "Burlamaqui's idea that [Lockean] intuitive reason can [and would be necessary to] verify the precepts which the Creator had impressed indelibly on our hearts" or the moral sense. This of course would give an undemocratic cast to the Declaration by limiting to the few access to the knowledge of its principles as well as to the precepts of morality. Consequently, White interpreted Jefferson's comments that seem to privilege the moral sense over reason as an instrument of gaining moral knowledge—most of which were made after the eighteenth century—to Jefferson's "fear" that democratic "social cohesiveness could not be entrusted to the very few, who might be able to arrive at the rational principles asserted in the Declaration." White even went so far as to state that Jefferson in his later years "began to sound like Locke in *The Reasonableness of Christianity,*" suggesting that Jefferson, like Locke, turned to revelation as the source of moral knowledge for all men.[43]

In fact, there is little evidence to support White's opinion that Jefferson was influenced by J.J. Burlamaqui when he wrote the Declaration. It is true that Jefferson obtained a copy of Burlamaqui's *Le Droit Natural* at the time he received a copy of Locke's *Second Treatise* in 1769.[44] He neither mentioned Burlamaqui's writings in his commonplace books, however, nor recommended them in his pre-Declaration letters or book lists—omissions inconsistent with the view that he wrote the Declaration under Burlamaqui's influence.

Further, in two ways I will show that White's interpretation of Jefferson and the Declaration is implausible: first, by demonstrating a thread of consistency that linked Jefferson's ideas on moral philosophy immediately before and during the drafting of the Declaration with those he held in the remaining years of his life, and the general consistency of those ideas with Kamesean moral thought; second, by demonstrating that this thread of consistency culminated in Jefferson's interpretation of Jesus and his teachings in the light of Kames's moral-sense philosophy, thereby bringing them into accord with the concept of man in the theology of the Declaration of Independence.

Kames, the Summary View, the Declaration, and After

In the 1774 *Summary View of the Rights of British America*, Jefferson acknowledged both the reason and the moral sense as an individual's means of knowing right and wrong. He accomplished this, as White pointed out, when he stated, "Not only the principles of common sense, but the common feelings of human nature, must be surrendered up, before his majesty's subjects here can be persuaded to believe that they hold their political existence at the will of a British parliament."[45] White believed that Jefferson's "common feelings of human nature" referred to the moral sense and "principles of common sense" to reason.[46] Both, according to the *Summary View*, perceived what was right and wrong. It seems clear, however, that "common sense" as used here was not the Lockean intuitive reason accessible to the very few, which, according to White, dominated Jefferson's thinking on the moral sense. Rather, it meant the minimal reason readily accessible to the vast majority of mankind. It also seems clear that the moral sense and common sense, as Jefferson used the terms in the *Summary View*, were on more or less equal terms as instruments of obtaining moral knowledge. In this way the *Summary View* was generally in accord with Kamesean thought, which provided for the use of minimal reason along with the moral sense in attaining moral knowledge.

White also stated that Jefferson did not refer to the moral sense in the Declaration.[47] But Jefferson did appeal to that sense in that document and did so in a way that followed the pattern of argument used in the *Summary View*. In the earlier work he had appealed to the moral sense of the king to judge the rational moral arguments it presented, yet he knew that the colonial interests of the king would very likely prevent His Majesty from making an objective moral judgment. Only if the king's interests were subordinate to his moral sense—a sense that flowed from the heart or breast, according to Kames,[48]—would the king fairly judge the rational moral arguments of the *Summary View*: hence, in an effort to induce such a subordination, Jefferson's exhortation "Open your breast, Sire, to liberal and expanded thought."[49] As I interpret this plea, "liberal and expanded thought" referred to what Jefferson deemed his rational moral arguments, and "breast" to the heart-based moral sense. Kames made a similar statement that could well have been the basis of this exhortation. Arguing for the existence of the moral sense in man, he said that he could offer no objective proof of that sense but that each person could find subjective proof of its existence by looking within himself. Men could not deny an inner moral sense if they paid heed to it by looking within. If they ignored their inner moral feelings, however, their "self affections" or selfish interests would dominate the moral sense and dispose them toward self-interest and prejudice against that sense, which would obscure its reality. Therefore, in order to prove the existence of their moral sense, Kames urged self-interested men to "Lay prejudice aside, and give fair play to the emotions of the heart."[50]

Having witnessed the failure of rational moral argument to impress the interested parties in England who had allegedly committed wrongs against the colonists, Jefferson adopted a different approach in the Declaration. In its preamble he appealed to "the Opinions of Mankind,"[51] or the moral sense of the people of the world—the first of two such appeals for judgment of that document's rational moral arguments. Jefferson wrote later that he regarded those appeals as "an appeal to the tribunal of the world."[52] Apart from political reasons, a principal one for addressing all "Mankind" was that ordinary people's moral sense could be relied upon for moral judgments because it was, for the most part, unobstructed and unobscured by interested or selfish designs on the colonies; hence there was no need for an exhortation—like that made to the interested king in the *Summary View*—to open their breasts or hearts. Jefferson's second appeal to the moral sense in the Declaration, immediately preceding the presentation of its rational moral arguments, merely stated, "let Facts be submitted to a candid World"[53]—referring of course to the people of the world whose lack of selfish interests made them candid or impartial and thus rendered their moral sense effective. The idea that candor was conducive to the efficacy of the moral sense could well have been the result of Jefferson's reading of Adam Smith's *Theory of Moral Sentiments* (1759), which he included on the Skipwith book list of 1771. I offer this work as a more plausible source of Jefferson's concept of candor than Thomas Reid as suggested by Garry Wills. Wills mentions Reid's *Inquiry into the Human Mind* (1764) as contributing to Jefferson's ideas in the Declaration yet quotes his *Essays* (1780s) on the meaning of candor.[54] Smith, when he wrote on candor, acknowledged its beneficent effect on the sentiments of an individual making moral judgments and the adverse impact of self-love, self-interest, and passion:

> When we are about to act, the eagerness of passion will seldom allow us to consider what we are doing with the candour of an indifferent person. The violent emotions which at that time, agitate us, discolour our views of things, even when we are endeavouring to place ourselves in the situation of another, and to regard the objects that interest us, in the light [in] which they will naturally appear to him. The fury of our own passions constantly calls us back to our own place, where every thing appears magnified and misinterpreted by self-love. . . . When the action is over indeed, and the passions which prompted it have subsided, we can enter more cooly into the sentiments of the indifferent spectator. What before interested us, is now become almost as indifferent to us as it always was to him, and we can now examine our own conduct with his candour and impartiality.[55]

In presenting rational moral arguments to the moral sense of the candid people of the world, Jefferson tried to be straightforward, even simplistic, in the Declaration. His statement "to place before mankind the common sense of the subject," in his letter to Henry Lee in 1825, describes his intent when he was drafting that document.[56] As in the *Summary View*, he was concerned with commonsense moral arguments understandable to virtually everyone, not complex Lockean rational demonstrations comprehensible to only a few.

Wills suggests that Jefferson used "common sense" in his letter to Lee as Thomas Reid did in his *Essays*. There Reid made a distinction between the ability of men to grasp self-evident truths when such truths were set before them in distinct terms, and the task of setting forth those terms distinctly. The latter, which only the philosopher could accomplish, was within the meaning of common sense as Reid defined it. Therefore, Jefferson was "closer to a boast than self-deprecation" in the letter to Lee (cited above), according to Wills.[57] It does not seem that Jefferson regarded himself as a philosopher when he drafted the

Declaration in 1776 or even later, as is indicated by his 1789 statement that he was not used to "abstract reasonings." A more plausible account of his disposition and intent when he drafted the Declaration's arguments is found in the letter to Lee, where he wrote that he had sought to express them "in terms so plain" that the people of the world to whom they were addressed could not help but "assent."[58] In this statement Jefferson sounded more like a lawyer, which he was, trying to accommodate his case to the jury of the world, to whom he was pleading it, rather than a philosopher, which he was not and never claimed to be. Therefore, the Lee letter's reference to plain terms and common sense with respect to the Declaration and Jefferson's appeal in that document to the moral sense show it to be based, like the *Summary View*, on a belief in both the moral sense and minimal reason as means to determine what is morally correct, and demonstrate that both documents were in accord with Kames's moral philosophy.

Implicit in Jefferson's appeal to the moral sense of mankind in the Declaration is a common standard of morality subscribed to by the vast majority of mankind. Such a standard was articulated by Kames in his *Essays on the Principles of Morality and Natural Religion* and later in his *Elements of Criticism*; Jefferson was familiar with both of these works before 1776, since both are on the Skipwith list. Kames seemed aware that a system in which each individual looked to his inner moral sense for judgment of right and wrong was too subjective: even if guided by a minimal amount of reason, it would result in different ideas as to what constitutes morality. This problem was compounded by Kames's contention that the moral sense is subject to improvement through the exercise of attending plays and reading good literature and through education and culture acquired by living in civilization.[59] Since different individuals would experience varying degrees of exercise, culture, and education, their moral sense would be in various stages of improvement, which would produce different and even conflicting ideas on morality.

In his *Elements of Criticism*, Kames acknowledged the variety of opinions on morality in the world, pointing to those who had no moral objections to selling their own children into slavery or murdering their enemies in cold blood as examples. Nevertheless, he was convinced that a common standard of morality did exist, one subscribed to by the vast majority of human beings. That standard was born of and included in a universal and unvarying ideal that Kames called "the common nature of man," which could be discerned despite individual and cultural differences: "With respect to the common nature of man, in particular, we have a conviction that it is invariable not less than universal; that it will be the same hereafter as at present, and as it was in time past; the same among all nations and in all corners of the earth. Nor are we deceived; because, giving allowance for the difference of culture, and gradual refinement of manners, the fact corresponds to our conviction."[60]

In explaining the common standard of morality in his *Essays*, Kames stated that each living thing was endowed not only with an external form unique to its species but also with an "internal constitution, which manifests itself in a certain uniformity of conduct peculiar to each species." In human beings, this internal constitution of the common nature of man was "the foundation of the laws of our nature," and before an act performed by a particular member of a particular species could be "considered regular and good," it had to be "conformable" to this aspect of the "common nature of the species." A man committing nonconforming actions, Kames maintained, was considered a "monster" by his fellowman and looked upon by them with feelings "of disgust" as if he had "two heads or four hands."[61]

In his letter of 13 June 1814 to Thomas Law, Jefferson sounded much like Kames:

> Some men are born without the organs of sight, or of hearing, or
> without hands. Yet it would be wrong to say that man is born
> without these faculties, and sight, hearing, and hands may with truth
> enter into the general definition of man. The want or imperfection of
> the moral sense in some men, like the want or imperfection of the
> senses of sight and hearing in others, is no proof that it is a general
> characteristic of the species. . . . I sincerely believe with you in the
> general existence of a moral instinct. I think it the brightest gem with
> which the human character is studded, and the want of it as more
> degrading than the most hideous of the bodily deformities.[62]

In fact, in this letter Jefferson made specific reference to Kames's *Essays*. Even though he said that "fifty years" had passed since he read that work, his memory of Kames's ideas included a common or general standard of morality: "A man owes no duty to which he is not urged by some impulsive feeling. This is correct, if referred to the standard of general feeling in the given case, and not the feeling of an individual."[63]

Kames believed that all persons paid homage to the common standard of morality, even those whose morals were of a lower standard. He also believed that the most perfect manifestations of the universal moral sense and morals born of that sense were found among people of old cultures, societies, and civilizations, who had been "long disciplined in society." With few exceptions individuals in such societies, as a result of an extended subjection to culture and education provided there, would have their moral sense and tastes honed to a refined state. Deviations or exceptions in such societies were few, according to Kames, and he regarded them as "aberrations" or remnants of "men, originally savage and brutal." To find "the rules of morality" of the common standard, all anyone needed to do was look to the moral sense "of men in their more perfect [civilized] state" and the rules or laws born of that sense. Then he narrowed the selection of such laws to the "most universal and the most lasting among polite nations." He concluded, "In this very manner, a standard for morals has been ascertained with a good deal of accuracy, and is daily apply'd by able judges with general satisfaction." By experience or by paying heed to "what is most universal and the most lasting among polite nations," in addition to considering the moral sense of men in such nations, one could determine the common standard of morality.[64]

Morton White has pointed out that Jefferson sometimes made statements about human determinations of morality that sounded pro-moral sense and antirational, both in the nineteenth century and before. A closer look at these statements, however, reveals that Jefferson was not antirational as respects Kamesean minimal reason used in conjunction with the moral sense. For example, in a 12 October 1786 letter to Maria Cosway, in which he conducted a dialogue between his head and his heart, Jefferson stated that the head or reason was often in the service of a man's selfish interests rather than his heart or moral sense; therefore, reason frequently worked against the moral sense when morality conflicted with selfish interests. To illustrate, Jefferson told of a "wearied soldier" who wanted a ride on "our [head and heart's] chariot." On this occasion, head's selfish calculations—such as "The road was full of soldiers and if all should be taken up, our horses would fail in their journey"—overruled heart's moral impulse to help the soldier by giving him a ride. After head's selfish calculations defeated heart's moral inclinations, heart said to head, "I do not know that I ever did a good thing on your suggestion, or a dirty one without it." Heart therefore concluded that "nature has not organized you [head] for our moral direction."[65] This repudiation of reason, at least selfish reason, was matched by a similiar repudiation of scientific reason in matters of moral determination: "Morals were too essential to the happiness of man, to be risked on the uncertain combinations of the head [reason]. She [nature] laid their foundation, therefore, in sentiment [heart], not in science [scientific reason]. That [sentiment or moral sense] she gave to all, as necessary to all: this [scientific reason] to a few only, as sufficing with a few."[66] Here Jefferson refers to the extraordinary rational capacity of the scientist, which he maintains is not commonly found among human beings and gives uncertainty when it attempts to determine what is moral.

Kames in his *Principles of Equity* made the same observation about the highly complex reasonings that only a few were capable of: "But reason employ'd in weighing an endless number and variety of circumstances, seldom affords any solid conviction; and upon the proposed system we would be often left in the dark about our duty, however upright our intentions might be." Kames went on to state that such complex reasonings, by obscuring "our duty" in matters of morality, caused the servitude of individual reason to self-interest or self-partiality. Once moral duty was obscured, this servitude manifested itself through the rationalization of moral transgressions that served self-interest. As Kames put it, "Our duty would vanish from our sight in [a] maze of subtilties; and self-partiality would always suggest plausible reasons, for slight [moral] transgressions at first, and afterward for the very boldest."[67] Jefferson's letter to Cosway, criticizing selfish and scientific reason, was in accord with these statements.

In a letter to James Fishbach of September 1809, Jefferson again echoed Kamesean statements, especially Kames's "maze of subtilties" that is the result of complex moral reasonings: "The practice of morality being necessary for the well-being of society, he [God] has taken care to impress its precepts so indelibly on our hearts that they shall not be effaced by the subtleties of the brain."[68] Jefferson here criticized as effacing moral knowledge the subtle reasoning that is beyond the scope of most human beings, as he had criticized reason in the service of self-interest, in the Cosway letter. In neither letter, however, did the criticism apply to minimal or commonsense reasoning—reason within the rational capacity of virtually anyone—working in conjunction with the moral sense in making moral determinations. Jefferson's statements in both letters are therefore in accord with the views of Kames and those of the *Summary View* and the Declaration, both of which invoked the moral sense and minimal reason to make moral determinations.

In a letter to Thomas Law, 13 June 1814, Jefferson once again seemed to privilege the moral sense to the exclusion of reason. After reflecting on the variety of moral philosophies born of complex reasonings, he said, "It shows how necessary was the care of the Creator in making the moral principle so much a part of our constitution as that no errors of reasoning or of speculation might lead us astray from its observance in practice." Conflicting moral philosophies would bring confusion about right and wrong, and confusion born of such moral intellectualization would give selfish human interests the opportunity to assert themselves and reason the opportunity to rationalize immoral actions that served those interests, as Kames had said. Jefferson's statement in the same letter, "Take from man his selfish propensities, and he can have nothing to seduce him from the practice of virtue," is consistent with these Kamesean ideas, since "selfish propensities" thrive in an atmosphere of moral confusion brought about by complex moral reasonings.[69] The seductive combination of selfish interests and the rationalization of immoral actions that serve those interests brought about by moral confusion was, according to Jefferson, an ever present potential in highly intellectual persons. The greater the intelligence, the greater the capacity for both intellectually induced moral confusion and rationalization of immoral selfish acts. Both Kames and Jefferson, however, argued that reason could be useful in moral determinations as long as it was minimal reason, like that of common sense, which was within the rational capacity of the vast majority of human beings, and as long as that minimal reason was used in the service of or in conjunction with the heart or moral sense.

The Influence of Kames on Jefferson's Interpretation of Jesus

Jefferson stressed the heart, or principle of love, in the moral sense in his letter to Thomas Law. Moral actions, he said, give pleasure to any individual who performs them "because nature hath implanted in our breast a love of others, a sense of moral duty to them, a moral instinct, in short, which prompts us irresistibly to feel and to succor their distresses."[70] To put it another way, an individual derives pleasure from moral actions because the love principle or moral sense in that individual is fulfilled by those actions. It was heart or the principle of love, the basis of the moral sense in Kamesean man, that Jefferson used as the basis of his interpretation of Jesus' teachings. As a result, Jesus emerged as a human, Kamesean-like moral-sense philosopher promulgating a religion in accordance with the theology of the Declaration of Independence, rather than the son of God who revealed God's truth to depraved sinners and died to atone for their sins.

Under Bolingbroke's influence (see chapter 2), Jefferson had rejected the idea that Jesus was the son of God before writing the Declaration of Independence, and he maintained this view in his later years. He wrote in 1820 that "Jesus did not mean to impose himself on mankind as the Son of God" and further that Jesus was not inspired by God, even though he might have suffered from this delusion.[71] Since Jesus was a man and not God incarnate as the second person of the Trinity, and since he was not even inspired by God, Jefferson considered his teachings devoid of divine authority. In other words they were not the word or revelation of God but the perceptions and conceptions of a man, a man named Jesus. Therefore, human beings could disagree with them, whereas they could not disagree with God or His revealed word.

Jefferson himself regarded Jesus' teachings critically with "a mixture of approbation and dissent," just as he would those of any other teacher or philosopher.[72] "This first of human sages," he said, taught not theology or metaphysics but morality exclusively.[73] The theology and metaphysics that orthodoxy claimed as part of the Christian religion were imposture—an idea instilled in Jefferson's mind by Bolingbroke and strengthened after 1793 by his reading of Joseph Priestley's *History of the Corruptions of Christianity,* plus his friendship with Priestley.[74] A letter to John Adams of October 1813 reveals his matured views on imposture:

> In extracting the pure [moral] principles which he [Jesus] taught, we should have to strip off the artificial vestments in which they have been muffled by priests, who have travestied them into various forms, as instruments of riches and power to themselves. We must dismiss the Platonists and Plotinists, the Stagyrites, and Gamalielites the Eclectics, the Gnostics and Scholastics, their essences and emanations, their Logos and Demiurgos, Aeons and Daemons, male and female, with a long train of etc., etc., etc., or, shall I say at once, of nonsense. We must reduce our volume to the simple evangelists, select, even from them, the very words only of Jesus, paring off the amphiboligisms into which they have been led, by forgetting often, or not understanding, what had fallen from him, by giving their own misconceptions as his dicta, and expressing unintelligibly for others what they had not understood themselves. There will be found remaining *the most sublime and benevolent code of morals which has ever been offered to man* [emphasis added]. I have performed this operation for my own use, by cutting verse by verse out of the printed book, and arranging the matter which is evidently his, and which is as easily distinguishable as diamonds in a dunghill.[75]

In this passage Jefferson described what he considered when he edited out what he deemed imposture from the four Gospels. He did this twice. The first effort, done hurriedly in 1804 while he was president, he called "The Philosophy of Jesus"; the second, done with more care in 1819–20, he titled "The Life and Morals of Jesus."[76] That Jefferson's interpretation of Jesus and his teachings had been in his mind for some time before he first edited the Gospels is evidenced by an 1800 letter to Benjamin Rush in which he stated that his perception of Jesus was in accord with rational Christianity and deism: "I have a view of the subject which ought to displease neither the rational Christian nor Deists, and would reconcile many to a character they have too hastily rejected."[77]

Jefferson maintained that the original moral teachings of Jesus were "within the comprehension of a child" and that their very simplicity posed a threat to the selfish interests of the priests and close followers of Jesus.[78] If virtually all men could understand Jesus' simple teachings, there would be no need for theologians and clergy to explain them. Only if they superimposed on Jesus' simple moral philosophy a complex set of theological doctrines that ordinary people found difficult or impossible to understand would the clergy be needed to explain those doctrines. According to Jefferson, this was why those who were allegedly the most devoted followers of Jesus became "dupes and impostors." The first of these was Paul, whom Jefferson described as "the great Coryphaeous, and the first corrupter of the doctrines of Jesus."[79] The close followers of Jesus and then the priests thereby made the people dependent upon them for the interpretation of the doctrines they imposed, and as a result of that dependency the priesthood could extract support and even wealth from the people. Jefferson described these causes of the corruption of Jesus' teachings when he said, "The mild and simple principles of Christian philosophy would produce too much calm, too much regularity of good, to extract from its disciples a support from a numerous priesthood, were they not to sophisticate it, ramify it, split it into hairs, and twist its texts till they cover the divine morality of its author with mysteries, and require a priesthood to explain them."[80]

The basis of Jesus' simple moral teachings was, according to Jefferson, the love principle in man—the same basis of the moral sense as in Kames's philosophy. Yet Jesus, as Jefferson interpreted him, exalted and stressed this love principle in an unprecedented manner. In Jesus' moral system the love principle purified human reason of any bias in favor of selfish interests, thereby preventing reason from rationalizing immoral actions that served selfish human interests. Pure love was devoid of any self-interest, and reason purified by love would serve the love-based moral sense in man rather than his selfish interests. The love principle was the divine spark in the heart of man, and Jesus' teachings as Jefferson perceived them probed the heart, thereby stimulating that spark so it would purify the head or reason. Jefferson expressed this view when he said, "He [Jesus] pushed his scrutinies into the heart of man erected his tribunal in the region of his thoughts, and purified the waters at the fountain head."[81]

Reason's function in determining morality in Jesus' moral philosophy was minimal and therefore within the scope of virtually every human being. From Jesus' principle "Love your neighbor as yourself" it was a simple matter to deduce a duty not to harm your neighbor and thence such basic precepts of justice as "Thou shalt do no murder, Thou shalt not commit adultery, Thou shalt not steal, Thou shalt not bear false witness."[82] Benevolence too could be easily deduced from the "Love your neighbor" principle. This process of moral determination, based on love and minimal reason in "The Philosophy of Jesus," as Jefferson called Jesus' moral teachings, is similar to the Kamesean approach to finding not only the laws of nature but criminal laws, which Kames believed were based on the laws of nature.[83] In his *Historical Law Tracts*, Kames referred to both rational reflection and the breast or love principle in man:

> Of the human system no part, external or internal, is more remarkable than a class of principles intended obviously to promote society, by restraining men from harming each other. These principles, as the Source of the criminal Law, must be attentively examined; and, to form a just notion of them, we need but reflect upon what we feel when we commit a Crime, or witness it. The first reflection will unfold Divine justice carried to execution with the most penetrating wisdom. Upon certain Actions, hurtful to others, the stamp of *impropriety* and *wrong* is impressed in legible characters, visible to all, not excepting even the Delinquent. Passing from the action to its Author, we feel that he is *guilty;* and we also feel that he ought to be punished for his guilt. He himself, having the same feeling, is filled with remorse; and, which is extremely remarkable, his remorse is accompanied with an anxious dread that punishment will be inflicted, unless it be prevented by his making reparation or atonement. Thus in the breast of man a tribunal is erected for Conscience; sentence passeth against him for every Delinquency.[84]

It is doubtful that Jefferson ever believed like Kames that *all* the laws of nature governing human actions were capable of being deduced by minimal reason from the feelings of the moral sense. He did seem to believe, however, that a sufficient number could be determined in this way to enable humans to govern their relationships in most circumstances.[85] Certainly, Jefferson never claimed that his edited version of the Gospels included a *complete* set of moral laws. He described Jesus' precepts as "more pure and perfect than those of the most correct philosophers, and greatly more so than those of the Jews," yet he simultaneously maintained that they were mere "fragments"— albeit "rich fragments"—of morality.[86]

It was Jefferson's opinion that his interpretation of Jesus' moral teachings made them consistent with the morality determined by the moral sense, a sense that included the use of minimal reason. In a letter to John Adams he equated Jesus' moral system, which he acknowledged as a common standard of morality, with morality determined by the moral sense, simultaneously maintaining that religion consisted of morality rather than theological dogma:

> If by *religion,* we are to understand *sectarian dogmas,* in which no
> two of them agree, then your exclamation on that hypothesis is just,
> "that this would be the best of all possible worlds, if there were no
> religion in it." But if the moral precepts, innate in man, and made
> part of his physical constitution, as necessary for a social being, if the
> sublime doctrines of philanthropism and deism taught by Jesus of
> Nazareth, in which all agree, constitute true religion, then, without it,
> this would be, as you say, "something not fit to be named even,
> indeed a hell."[87]

This statement has deistic overtones since, as John Marshall has pointed out, a number of deists saw "Christ's mission solely in terms of republishing natural law,"[88] and Jefferson saw the innate moral sense as providing knowledge of that law.

Contrary to what Morton White suggests, then, Jefferson in the nineteenth century was not concerned with using revelation to provide the masses of humanity with access to moral knowledge, as Locke was in the seventeenth century. Kames's moral-sense concept of man, which Jefferson adopted before writing the Declaration of Independence and continued to hold, provided that access. Further, Jefferson had rejected revelation from the time of his Bolingbroke extracts and maintained that position in his later years. What Jefferson did do in the nineteenth century was to adapt Christianity and Jesus to his early

Bolingbrokean natural theology and deism, as well as to Kamesean moral philosophy. When he edited the Gospels, he stripped them of the Virgin Birth, the resurrection, and all miracles contrary to the laws of nature that govern the material universe.[89] He thereby brought Christianity into accord with empiricism and the "Nature's God" of the Declaration. (In his rejection of miracles he adhered to Bolingbroke rather than Priestley, who acknowledged some Christian miracles that went against the laws of nature.)[90] In describing the effects of eliminating imposture (which he believed included miracles) from Christianity, Jefferson stated, "The Christian religion, when divested of the rags in which they [the clergy] have enveloped it, and brought to the original purity and simplicity of its benevolent institutor, is a religion of all others most friendly to liberty, science, and the freest expression of the human mind."[91] Among the passages Jefferson omitted as "rags" or imposture from the Gospels were the antisemitic statements of Jesus in John 8:42–47.[92]

When he referred to "liberty, science, and the freest expression of the human mind," Jefferson mentioned three themes that were dear to him from his student days on. All three were linked to his idea that human reason was a gift from God, a gift that God intended human beings to use to find truth in religion and science and, in conjunction with the moral sense, to make moral determinations and judgments of humanity's social and political well-being. This use of reason necessitated freedom of reason. Jefferson's valuation of such freedom put him on a collision course with what he deemed obstacles to that freedom.

5

Obstacles to Reason

Trust in man was a vital part of the heterodox theology of the American Declaration of Independence. That trust was antithetical to the Christian orthodox trust in God, not man. The basis of the Declaration's trust in man was due to the moral capacity given him by "Nature's God" and also the rational capacity or reason given him by this God of natural theology. Jefferson had great trust in human reason born of two factors. The first was his conviction that the human rational faculty was capable of providing knowledge of truth. The second was his conviction that reason was capable of putting that knowledge to use in a way that would generally improve the human condition, thus making reason the instrument of progress. Even reason itself was capable of improvement or progress, according to Jefferson, who was convinced that an ascending order of knowledge and progress awaited humanity when it improved its reason.[1]

Although there was no doubt in Jefferson's mind that reason and progress would eventually prevail, he was aware that inauspicious factors were working against reason and reason-based progress. Those factors were obstructions that repressed and oppressed the human rational faculty and thereby caused its suspension. Jefferson believed that the delay in progress caused by those obstacles to reason was especially manifest in the fields of science, government, and religion. Before the rational faculty could become an effective instrument of progress, therefore, it was necessary to remove those obstacles.

Francis Bacon was one thinker who had written of such obstacles. Many of Jefferson's early ideas on reason came from Bacon, who made a profound and lasting influence on his thinking and whom, along with John Locke and Isaac Newton, he exalted as an intellectual hero.[2] As a student Jefferson read Bacon's writings, and even though there is no record of which of Bacon's works he read, it would seem the *Novum Organon* was among them.[3] There Bacon presented a new method of arriving at truth in natural philosophy or science while he criticized the existing methods, especially those of speculative philosophy. He believed that because philosophers jumped to conclusions not based on a comprehensive gathering of facts observed by the senses, their conclusions were often erroneous. According to Bacon, numerous facts had to be gathered on a specific subject and then analyzed with reason in order to find the truth of that subject. The test of truth discovered in this way was correspondence to the facts observed. This approach to truth was not easy because of the severe limitations of the senses and reason that Bacon acknowledged: "Neither the bare hand nor the intellect left to itself have much power." He then concluded that "results are produced by instruments and helps."[4]

The purpose of Bacon's new method was to lead mankind via these "instruments and helps" to "a better and more perfect use of Reason in discovery of things" and thereby enable human reason "to scale the steep and dark ascents of Nature." "Helps" were especially needed as respects gathered facts since they could not be analyzed by reason unless they were organized. Therefore his method prescribed that the facts of a particular subject be presented in organized tables, or "Tables of Discovery." These "tables," as "instruments and helps" to the senses and reason, would enable thinkers to analyze facts obtained with the senses and thereby gain access to the truth of the material world. Bacon expressed these ideas when he wrote: "When there is so great a number and host of particulars, and these too so scattered and diffused as to disconnect and confuse the Intellect; no good Hopes can be entertained from the skirmishings, light movements, and transitions of the Intellect; unless there be an arrangement and marshalling of those things which pertain to the subject on which we are making inquiry, by means of fit, well arranged, and, as it were, living Tables of Discovery; and unless the mind be applied to the prepared and digested assistance afforded by these Tables." Bacon believed that the knowledge thus attained should be used to benefit and bring progress to mankind: "The true and legitimate goal of the Sciences is none but this: that human life be enriched with new discoveries and wealth."[5]

Examples of Baconian influence on Jefferson can be found in the data-recording methods of his *Garden Book* (beginning in 1766) and his *Farm Book* (from 1774). Jefferson was persistent in keeping these records; the last entries in the *Garden Book* were made in 1824, just two years before his death. Among other facts, he recorded what was planted and when and the period of blooming and fruiting. As Edwin Betts pointed out, these data provided "the time the different articles came to the table, and their disappearance," facts that would be useful to any gardener or farmer.[6] Another example of the *Novum Organon*'s influence is found in Jefferson's *Notes on the State of Virginia*. Bacon's impact on *Notes* is such that Robert Ferguson described it as "the primal vision of order" within that work.[7] Many of the materials and facts contained in *Notes* were collected by Jefferson before the time of the Declaration of Independence, although he did not actually write the book until 1780–81.[8] The subject matter was, for the most part, the geography of North America, especially the state of Virginia. One Baconian feature of this work is its criticism of the Count de Buffon's hypothesis that the environment of the Old World was more conducive to animal life than that of the New World. According to Jefferson, Buffon jumped to an erroneous conclusion not based on facts with this hypothesis in the fashion of the philosophers criticized by Bacon. *Notes* condemned this approach by stating that truth is "inscrutable to us by reasonings a priori." It then promulgated Bacon's method of finding knowledge by maintaining, "Nature has hidden from us her modus agendi. Our only appeal on such questions is to experience. . . . But when we appeal to experience, we are not to rest satisfied with a single fact."[9] Numerous charts and tables in *Notes* affirm the Baconian idea that knowledge is attained by continuous gathering and careful organization and analysis of facts. Among these were a comparison of animals found in Europe and America; birds of Virginia; monthly rainfall, temperature, and wind variations; population growth; aboriginal tribes in each county of Virginia; aboriginal tribes located within the United States and northward and westward of the United States; crimes punishable by death, by dismemberment, and by labor; and exports.[10]

Philosophical Skepticism as an Obstacle

In the *Novum Organon*, Bacon described obstacles to scientific reason as "Phantoms which lay siege to human minds." Of particular concern to Jefferson among these "Phantoms" was philosophical skepticism, a subject on which he did considerable reading. His concern stemmed from the fact that skepticism undermined the very foundation of the human rational faculty. In discussing this obstacle, Bacon said he was against the extremes of, on the one hand, granting assent to truth based on too few facts, which was the practice of the dogmatic philosophers such as Aristotle, and, on the other hand, unduly withholding assent to factually based truth, which was the practice of the skeptical philosophers: "The excess is of two kinds; the one that of those who dogmatise readily, and render the Sciences positive and dictatorial; the other, that of those who have introduced *Acatalepsy* ("Incomprehensibility") and vague inquiry without limit. The former of these depresses the Intellect, the latter enfeebles it." The enfeebling of the intellect by "vague inquiry without limit" was Bacon's reference to philosophical skepticism, which maintained that man could not perceive or rationally determine the truth. The *Novum Organon* elaborated on skepticism's origin and effects:

> Plato's school introduced *Acatalepsy*: first as in jest and irony, through hatred of the ancient Sophists, Protagoras, Hippias, and the rest, who feared nothing so much as appearing to doubt upon any subject. But the new Academy made a dogmatism of its *Acatalepsy*, and held it as their tenet. And although this is more honest than the license of dogmatising, since they say for themselves that they do not at all confound inquiry, like Pyrrho and the Sceptics, but have something which they can follow as Probability, though not what they can hold as Truth; nevertheless after the human mind has once despaired of the discovery of truth, all things in all ways become more languid, and therefore men prefer to turn aside to pleasant disputations and discourses, and sundry wanderings through the fields of knowledge, rather than sustain any severity of inquiry.[11]

The philosophers of the Academic school of skepticism used reason to make it known that man could not rely on the perceptions of the senses and that even reason itself was unreliable. The result was a long shadow of doubt cast on the veracity of any judgment based either on the senses or on reason. The Pyrrhonian school of skepticism, founded by Pyrrho of Elis, which came into being shortly after the Academic school, rejected what it deemed the extreme claims of both the Dogmatist philosophers and the Academic skeptics, who respectively stated that "Something can be known" and "Nothing can be known." The Pyrrhonists did not want to commit themselves either way and therefore avoided making any judgment on anything that was not evident. In addition, they opposed all evidence, either pro or con, on any question in order to maintain a suspension of judgment. These efforts led to mental ataraxia, an indifferent, serene, or detached state wherein an individual lived by customs and appearances within his sphere of experience without making any judgments concerning them. Sextus Empiricus was one of the principal Pyrrhonists during the time this movement was at its zenith in about 200 A.D.[12]

Among the authors Jefferson read on skepticism was Kames, who touched on the subject in his *Essays on the Principles of Morality and Natural Religion*.[13] Two other works on the 1771 Skipwith book list indicate Jefferson's concern with skepticism as an obstacle to the use of the human senses and reason in finding truth: one was Pierre Bayle's

Dictionary, and the other was Thomas Reid's *Inquiry into the Human Mind.*[14] Bayle's *Dictionary* would have given Jefferson a general knowledge of skepticism, since, according to Richard Popkin, Bayle's "critical technique" in that work when "pursued long enough exhibits the sad fact that rational effort is always its own undoing." That "high road to scepticism" would soon cause reason to appear "perplexing" even though it "at first looks like a way to explain something."[15] Evidence of Jefferson's familiarity with the contents of the *Dictionary* may be seen in his noting the cost of each item on the list of books he recommended to Skipwith: by far the most expensive was the five-volume English translation of the *Dictionary,* listed at £7.1 (by way of comparison, the five-volume set of Bolingbroke's works was listed at £1.5). Jefferson's recommendation that his friend make such a sizable expenditure indicates the importance he attributed to the *Dictionary,* an importance he could scarcely have determined without being familiar with its content.

Of Pyrrho of Elis, one of the subjects of the *Dictionary,* Bayle stated that this great skeptic was "a disciple of Anaxarchus, and accompanied him as far as India" in his travels and "then followed Alexander the Great." During his journeys Pyrrho "went to see the Magi of Persia, and the Gymnosophists of India." Bayle recounted how Pyrrho and the Pyrrhonians questioned the capacity of the senses to deliver accurate impressions of objects to man by stating, "Every one of us may say, *I feel heat before a fire,* but not *I know that fire is such in itself as it appears to me.* Such was the style of the ancient Pyrrhonists." When it came to Pyrrho's use of reason to find truth, Bayle wrote that Pyrrho "suspended his assent after he had well examined the arguments *pro* and *con*" on any subject and that this suspension was permanent, born of Pyrrho's having "reduced all his conclusions to a *non liquet, let the matter be further enquired into.*" As a result of this commitment to endless inquiry on a given subject, Bayle added, Pyrrho "sought truth as long as he lived, but he so contrived the matter, as never to grant that he had found it."[16]

Bayle went on the describe the perplexing effect of this Pyrronian suspension of judgment, as elaborated on by Sextus Empericus:

> When a man is able to apprehend all the ways of suspending his judgement, which have been laid open by Sextus Empericus, he may then perceive that that Logic is the greatest effort of subtilty that the mind of man is capable of; but he will see at the very same time, that such a subtilty will afford him no satisfaction: it confounds itself; for if it were solid, it would prove that it is certain that we must

doubt. . . . But you need not fear that things would come to that: the reasons for doubting are doubtful themselves: one must therefore doubt whether he ought to doubt. What chaos! what torment for the mind! it seems therefore, that this unhappy state is the fittest of all to convince us, that our reason is the way to wander, since when it displays itself with the greatest subtilty, it throws us into such an abyss.[17]

Since reason had such an abysmal effect, Bayle stated that men should renounce it as a guide to truth and "beseech the cause of all things to give us a better." God did indeed provide a better guide in faith or revelation, according to Bayle, who put reason under the authority of faith when he said, "We should captivate our understanding to the obedience of faith." He maintained, however, that skepticism could be valuable in leading to faith. The man who saw that the senses and reason could not find truth and would therefore lead him nowhere would be more inclined to turn to God or faith for "the persuasion of the truths which he ought to believe, than if he should flatter himself with a good success in reasoning and disputing."[18]

These arguments posed a fundamental threat to the importance Jefferson placed on the human sensory and intellectual faculties as instruments of finding truth. If the senses and reason could not lead to truth, then empiricism and science, which were based on the senses and reason, were exercises in futility. As Kames summed up the impact of skepticism in his *Essays:* "If the testimony they [the senses] give to the real existence of a material world, be a mere illusion, as some have held, all belief founded on our own feelings is at an end. . . . [For] no reasoning, no experience, can discover the power or energy of what we term a cause, when we attempt to trace its source."[19] In addition to their adverse impact on science, if the claims of the skeptics were not defeated, Bayle's offering of faith would be a favorable alternative to reason as the guide to truth. Placing faith over reason, however, would have been anathema to Jefferson as a disciple of reason. Therefore he looked for champions to defend the honor of the human senses and intellect against skepticism. He found them in Kames (see chapter 6) and especially in Thomas Reid, the Scottish philosopher of common sense.[20]

The Defeat of Philosophical Skepticism

Reid was a graduate of Marichal College in Aberdeen, which was also the college of William Small, Jefferson's teacher at William and Mary. Small, Reid's younger contemporary, was probably the one who introduced Jefferson to Reid's writings.[21] He was also very likely the one who gave Jefferson an interest in the theory of knowledge, which Reid wrote on extensively, since epistemology was a standard subject in Scottish higher education in the eighteenth century.[22] Reid's work, *An Inquiry into the Human Mind,* as has been stated, was on the 1771 list of books Jefferson sent to Skipwith. In that work Reid called Pyrrho the father of skeptical philosophy, which arose out of discrediting the senses. Pyrrho was so dedicated to the concept that the senses gave illusory perceptions, Reid explained, that he would "not stir a foot to avoid the danger" of confrontation with a vicious dog or a precipice.[23]

It was not the senses themselves, however, so much as ideas—mental images or representations of objects perceived by the senses—that Reid deemed the foundation of modern skepticism. "Ideas," he said, "seem to have something in their nature unfriendly to other existences" or objects.[24] Once ideas mediated in one's mind between one's self and the worldly objects they represented, one was effectively cut off from the world: that is, unable to know whether or not one's perceptions of worldly objects were accurate. To put it another way, if ideas mediated between one's self and the world, one had no way of knowing whether those mediators were true representations of the world. Skepticism, therefore, was the logical result of the concept that ideas, as representations of the worldly objects perceived by the senses, mediated between one's self and the world.

John Locke's *Essay concerning Human Understanding,* according to Reid, gave a huge impetus to the view of sense-derived mediating ideas as a basis of skepticism. Locke defined an idea as "the Object of the Understanding when a Man thinks." He also stated that "the Mind knows not Things immediately, but only by the intervention of the *Ideas* it has of them."[25] Added to these views was Locke's insistence that the secondary qualities of matter such as color, sound, and taste were not part of the objects that appeared to have those qualities. Something in the primary qualities of the object, such as bulk, figure, and texture, merely stimulated the mind via the senses to perceive those secondary qualities as if they were part of the object.[26] To Locke, for example, a red ball was not itself red; redness was an appearance born of the senses and the mind. Redness was posited on the ball by the senses and the mind. If Locke was right, according to Reid, this effectively prevented man from perceiving the world as it actually is.[27] In short, it was impossible to have an accurate view of the objective world, since one could perceive it not directly but only through the medium of ideas, ideas that were distortions of reality, distortions that were caused by the human sensory apparatus and mind.

Reid attributed to Locke's concept of ideas what he deemed the absurd philosophy of George Berkeley and the skeptical one of Hume.[28] S.A. Grave presents a simple diagram that "crudely" illustrates Reid's perception of how Hume's ideas derived from Locke's via Berkeley's. Locke's views are represented in this diagram by three concentric circles, the outermost symbolizing the material objects of the world; the innermost, one's self; and the one between, ideas.[29] Berkeley's philosophical system nullified the reality represented by the outer circle; Hume's nullified those represented by both the inner and outer circles. It was Berkeley's view that reality consists of perceiving entities or spirits (such as men) and ideas that are perceived. Ideas, however, had no need to be based on any material objects separate from those ideas; hence, the material world was superfluous and even nonexistent.[30] Spirits, ideas, and God were all that was necessary to account for reality, according to Berkeley.

Hume took Locke's ideas one step further than Berkeley, which resulted in complete skepticism, according to Reid: "The triumph of ideas was completed in Hume's *Treatise of Human Nature*," since it "discards spirits also, and leaves ideas and impressions as the sole existences in the universe." Reid believed Hume discarded "spirits" or men as perceivers by denying any substratum to the mind or self of man. As Reid put it, Hume believed that the "mind is only a succession of ideas and impressions, without any subject" and that ideas in the mind "came together, and arranged themselves by certain associations and attractions."[31] This rendered man incapable of perceiving or making any cause-based scientific conclusions about the world founded on sense perceptions and rational determinations. The conclusion, for example, that the sun will rise in the morning is born of human psychology and custom, not the causal determinations of reason, according to Hume.[32]

Reid railed against these ideas of Berkeley and especially those of Hume:

> The little I know of the planetary system; of the earth which we
> inhabit; of minerals, vegetables, and animals; of my own body, and of
> the laws which [we] obtain in these parts of nature, opens to my mind
> grand and beautiful scenes, and contributes equally to my happiness
> and power. But when I look within, and consider the mind itself,
> which makes me capable of all these prospects and enjoyments; if it is
> indeed what the *Treatise of Human Nature* makes it, I find I have

been only in an inchanted castle, imposed upon by spectres and apparitions. I blush inwardly to think how I have been deluded; I am ashamed of my frame, and can hardly forbear expostulating with my destiney: Is this thy pastime, O Nature, to put such tricks upon a silly creature, and then to take off the mask, and shew him how he hath been befooled? If this is the philosophy of human nature, my soul enter thou not into her secrets. It is surely the forbidden tree of knowledge; I no sooner taste of it, than I perceive my self naked, and stript of all things, yea even of my very self. I see myself, and the whole frame of nature, shrink into fleeting ideas, which, like Epicurus's atoms dance about in emptiness.[33]

Reid's approach to defeating skepticism born of ideas was three-fold. First, he attacked the validity of the Lockean concept of ideas as representations and mediators of objects in the world and the belief that these mediators were necessary to a knowledge of objects. Second, he explained sensory perception as a direct encounter with objects of the world without the mediation of ideas, an encounter sufficient to give knowledge of worldly objects. Third, he relied on what he called first principles of human nature, an inherent and inexplicable part of man that accounted for the phenomenon of human perception and conceptual understanding of the objective material world.

Reid used Bacon's new method of science in the first approach. He praised Bacon as the one who "first delineated the strict and severe method of induction," which had been applied "with very happy success" but was limited in its application to only "some parts of natural philosophy . . . and hardly in any thing else." Baconian induction was not the source of knowledge of the mind of man and ideas, according to Reid. He believed that the concept of the mind as the seat of ideas conveyed to it by the senses, with those ideas being mediators necessary to conceptions, thoughts, and conclusions about the world, was unproven "hypothesis" and even "invention" on the part of philosophers such as Locke. Such "invention" went beyond a "just induction from facts," and facts were for Reid the measure of truth. He was critical in a Baconian way of any philosophers or philosopher, no matter "how great soever his genius and abilities may be," who gave us "a system of human nature" when many parts of that nature "never came under their observation." Systems invented or hypothesized by such philosophers, under such circumstances, often caused them to stretch and distort their ensuing observations of the world in order "to fill up blanks and complete the system" they had invented. Reid expressed his disgust for this inventive approach of philosophers when he said,

"Christopher Columbus or Sebastian Cabot, might almost as reasonably have undertaken to give us a complete map of America."[34]

Reid's second approach to the defeat of skepticism centered on countering John Locke's definition of knowledge as the result of recognizing the connection between the ideas of things and comparing those connected ideas. Stated Locke: "*Knowledge* then seems to me to be nothing but *the perception of the connexion and agreement, or disagreement and repugnancy of any of our Ideas*. In this alone it consists. Where this perception is, there is knowledge, and where it is not, there, though we may fancy, guess, or believe, yet we always come short of knowledge."[35]

Reid, by contrast, attempted to account for knowledge from the perception of things by the senses and conclusions drawn from those perceptions without any mediation by and comparison of ideas: "Every operation of the senses, in its very nature implies judgement or belief, as well as simple apprehension. Thus, when I feel the pain of the gout in my toe, I have not only a notion of pain, but a belief of its existence, and a belief of some disorder in my toe which occasions it; and this belief is not produced by comparing ideas, and perceiving their agreements or disagreements; it is included in the very nature of the sensation." Reid did not confine this observation to sensations of bodily pleasure and pain but extended it to sensations which gave the perception of objects external to the individual: "When I perceive a tree before me, my faculty of seeing gives me not only a notion or simple apprehension of the tree, but a belief of its existence and of its figure, distance, and magnitude; and this judgement or belief is not got by comparing ideas, it is included in the very nature of the perception."[36]

In his third approach to the defeat of skepticism, Reid stated that the "original and natural judgements" that accompany sensations born of the senses were "a part of our constitution." They were, he said, part of that constitution "no less than the power of thinking." These sensations and the original judgments arising from them made up what Reid called "the common sense of mankind." Another name Reid applied to these constituents of human nature was "first principles," on which "all the discoveries of our reason are grounded." He believed that mankind could not rationally understand or explain these "first principles"; they were truths that reason could "neither make nor destroy." Moreover, man could not help but abide by the first principles of common sense: "By the constitution of our nature, we are under a necessity of assenting to them." It was God who provided man with these first principles of common sense, according to Reid. Therefore, belief in them and what they delivered to man in the form of knowledge was something man should not throw off because if human beings were deceived by these first principles of the human constitution, then "we are deceived by him that made us and there is no remedy."[37] Reid, however, did not believe that God deceived man. It was the view of commonsense philosophy that the first principles of common sense "are principles by which our cognition is conformed to its objects, to things as they really are in themselves."[38]

The principles of common sense are often the strongest "in those who are not acute in reasoning," according to Reid. Those who deviated from such principles suffered from what he politely described as "a disorder in the constitution" and not so politely as "lunacy." Therefore, Reid believed philosophers who deviated from the principles of common sense by presenting arguments in favor of skepticism were either fools (as a result of their lunacy) or, if not fools, sophists, and one should not listen to fools or sophists. As he put it, "He must be either a fool, or want to make a fool of me, that would reason me out of my reason and senses. I confess I know not what a sceptic can answer to this, nor by what good argument he can plead even for a hearing; for either his reasoning or his sophistry, and so deserves contempt."[39]

Jefferson's interest in arguments against philosophical skepticism did not wane when he ceased to be a student, and that interest was linked to Reid. In Paris as minister plenipotentiary to France—between the American Revolutionary War and George Washington's presidency—Jefferson developed a friendship with Dougald Stewart, who had studied under Reid, became a teacher of mathematics at Edinburgh, and later succeeded Adam Ferguson as a professor of moral philosophy. According to S.A. Grave, Stewart "always saw his work as an extension of Reid's."[40] Jefferson found Stewart an able successor to the antiskepticism philosophy of Reid. He also placed the Frenchman Destutt de Tracy beside Stewart as a scourge of skepticism. Writing to Robert Walsh in 1818, Jefferson said of Tracy's *Principes logiques:* "It is an examination into the *certainty* of our knowledge, and the most complete demolition of the Skeptical doctrines which I have ever met with. You know his character and peculiar strength in Ideological enquiries. I place him and Dugald Stewart so much in a line, that I can decide no more than that they are the two greatest men in that line at present known to the world."[41]

Although written in 1818, this reference to Tracy and Stewart as the two best critics of skepticism "at present known to the world" is significant. It left room to include Thomas Reid, who influenced

Jefferson early in his life, in the exalted category of Tracy and Stewart since Reid's presence was no longer known to the world. He had died in 1796. The continuing impact on Jefferson of Reid's antiskepticism and that of his followers is clear in a statement he made to John Adams in 1820: "Rejecting all organs of information, therefore, but my senses, I rid myself of the pyrrhonisms with which an indulgence in speculations hyperphysical and antiphysical, so uselessly occupy and disquiet the mind. A single sense may indeed be sometimes deceived, but rarely; and never all our senses together, with their faculty of reasoning. They evidence realities."[42] This commonsense approach that established the efficacy of the senses and reason removed skepticism as an obstacle to reason—especially scientific reason—in Jefferson's mind.

Faith as an Obstacle

Another obstacle to science and scientific reason discussed in the *Novum Organon* was faith or religion. Religion, according to Bacon, fostered blind unquestioning faith or belief in superstition. Such belief was antithetical to natural philosophy or science based on Bacon's method of observed sensory facts analyzed by reason. As Bacon put it, "Natural Philosophy has in all ages had a troublesome and stubborn adversary in Superstition, and a blind and immoderate zeal for religion." Bacon was particularly critical of what he called the "Deification of Error" by faith and religion in the sciences, which he regarded as "the worst of all things" and "the plague of the Intellect." He cited the accounts of the origin and development of the world in Genesis and Job as examples of this "Deification" and excoriated those who attempted to reconcile scripture with natural philosophy or science: "Some of the moderns have indulged in this vanity with the greatest carelessness: and have endeavoured to found a natural Philosophy on . . . Scriptures, so 'seeking the dead among the living.'"[43]

Jefferson, like Bacon, expressed his distaste for the deification of error in science by faith, especially when it was backed by government: "Galileo was sent to the inquisition for affirming that the earth was a sphere: the government had declared it to be as flat as a trencher, and Galileo was obliged to abjure his error. This error however at length prevailed, the earth became a globe." Here Jefferson was pointing out the absurdity of making erroneous science "an article of faith" enforced by church or government. He also specifically ridiculed the enforcers of scientific errors in the name of faith by pointing out that such errors were corrected despite their enforcement as soon as free reason based on induction took place. As he put it, errors "fled" as soon as "Reason and experiment have been indulged."[44]

Bacon implicitly offered a method of removing faith or religion as an obstacle to science and scientific reason when he said, "Those things only be rendered to Faith, which are Faith's." What he implied was the converse of this statement: "Those things only be rendered to natural philosophy that are natural philosophy's." This statement, along with its explicit counterpart, suggests that two kinds of truth—truth resulting from faith or blind unquestioning belief in scripture or religious tradition, and truth resulting from determinations made by sensory observations combined with rational analysis—should be confined to their own separate jurisdictions: salvation and the material world, respectively. Jefferson followed this pattern by separating religion or church from education when he founded the University of Virginia, thus marking, as Gilbert Chinard stated, "to a large extent . . . the beginning of the secularisation of scientific research in America."[45]

Jefferson saw faith in the sense of blind, unquestioning acceptance of, belief in, and obedience to the doctrine and authority of institutionalized religions as an obstacle to the use of reason not only in science but also in government. He believed that institutionalized religions based on faith, via the priestcraft of those religions, had such a hold over the reason of the people that they could and often did make political judgments for them. Because of faith the people often followed the political dictates or suggestions of their clergy without question. This nullified the exercise of even that minimal amount of reason which, along with the aid of the moral sense, enabled individuals to make moral determinations and judgments applicable to their government. Jefferson lamented this impact of faith and described people in religions of faith who did not exercise their individual reason as the "willing dupes and druges" of institutionalized religions and their clergy.[46] The suspension of individual reason among the members of the populace, allowing their clergy to think for them in political matters, rendered a democracy a de facto aristocracy, an aristocracy of the priests or clergy. Jefferson stated this view when he spoke of the people as the victims of "slumber under the pupilage of an interested aristocracy of priests and lawyers, persuading them to distrust themselves, and to let them think for them."[47] As his reference to lawyers as well as priests here indicates, Jefferson was opposed to any group that usurped or attempted to usurp the rational judgment-making capacity of the individuals who constituted the masses. He was especially opposed to the clergy's usurpations in this respect in politics, since the Lockean political theory reflected in the Declaration of Independence was based on the free reason of the individual or the judgment-making capacity of that reason. Institutionalized religious and priestly authority born of faith vitiated the *Second Treatise*'s theory because it obstructed that free reason without which individuals in the state of nature, if institutionalized religions were to exist there, would not be able to make the judgments of consent necessary to form a government.

The idea that the authority of faith and the religions of faith were antithetical to Lockean political systems based on the free reason of the individual would seem to have been infused in Jefferson's mind by the writings of Bolingbroke that he read before drafting the Declaration of Independence. Consider this Bolingbroke comment:

> The principles and duties of natural religion arise from the nature of things, and are discovered by the reason of man, according to that order which the author of all nature, and the giver of all reason, has established in the human system. From hence too would arise the institutions of civil government, in a natural state; if the minds of legislators were not corrupted previously by superstition. In these cases, religion and civil government, arising from the same spring, their waters would be intermixed, they would run in one stream, and they might be easily confined to the same channel; if revelation did not introduce mysterious doctrines and rites, which it becomes soon a trade to teach and celebrate.[48]

From reason would arise "the institutions of civil government, in a natural state" only if "the minds of legislators were not corrupted by superstition." Since superstition is faith or belief in the unproved or unverified claims of religion, Bolingbroke was referring to the religions of faith in his reference to superstition. His message in the foregoing statement made it clear that faith religions founded on revelation and tradition were not in accord with—and indeed were opposed to—political systems founded on the free reason of man. This view gave Jefferson a political motivation to reject and oppose faith-based religions, since he was an advocate of the reason-based Lockean political theory. Bolingbroke also pointed out that natural religion and political systems that arose in a state of nature, such as those Locke described, were both based on reason and were therefore complementary. This idea gave Jefferson political grounds for preferring and subscribing to natural religion and natural theology.

He also adhered to Bolingbroke's idea put forth in the foregoing statement that one cannot reconcile politics based on free reason and religion based on faith. To put it another way, the people could not be half slave and half free: that is, accept the authority of the religions of faith with their scriptures, their institutions, and their clergy and yet claim to be politically free under the authority of their own free reason. As Jefferson commented to this effect: "History, I believe, furnishes no example of a priest-ridden people maintaining a free civil government," and "In every country and in every age, the priest has been hostile to liberty."[49] That he used "priests" in the broadest sense of the term, meaning the clergy of all denominations and religions, is evidenced by the phrase "in every country and in every age." Clearly, Jefferson viewed the priesthood as striving for or possessing control over the reason of individuals, a control that he deemed an obstruction to the use of individual reason in politics.

Just as faith obstructed the exercise of free individual reason in politics, so it obstructed the search for religious truth, according to Jefferson. He maintained that the priesthood's preaching of the efficacy of faith as the vehicle of salvation and the people's acceptance of such preaching destroyed the mind and critical reason of individuals in religion. He made this clear when he said: "Man, once surrendering his reason, has no remaining guard against absurdities the most monstrous, and like a ship without a rudder, is the sport of every wind. With such persons, gullibility, which they call faith, takes the helm from the hand of reason, and the mind becomes a wreck."[50] This statement, although made in 1820, is similar to a passage on faith promulgated by priests from act 5 of Thomas Otway's *Venice Preserved,* which Jefferson copied during his student years:

> You want to lead
> My Reason blindfold, like a Hamper'd Lion,
> Check'd of its nobler Vigour; then when bated
> Down to obedient Tameness, make it couch,
> And shew strange tricks, which you call signs of Faith
> So silly souls are gull'd, & you get Money.
> Away; no more.[51]

Jefferson was of the opinion that faith or blind unquestioning belief in doctrinal, scriptural, and priestly authority perpetuated error and imposture in religion, and the corruption that resulted from error and imposture. This was because the faithful believer was gullible, as he made clear in the aforementioned statement, and therefore would not think of critically questioning his faith with his reason. Further, to think critically of one's faith would bring that faith, which was contingent upon blind unquestioning belief, to an abrupt conclusion, and no person of faith would want to do this. Even if one was inclined to criticize faith, if one lived in a society dominated by a particular faith and persisted in critically questioning it with reason and concluded that it was not true, one would be branded a heretic. Thus, faith and religions based on faith were opposed to the use of critical reason in matters of religion. Only scholastic reason or reason that, under the authority of scripture and church, confirmed the conclusions of those authorities was permitted by religions based on faith. Jefferson, contrary to religions based on faith, believed the exercise of the critical reason of each individual without any restraints was the great friend of religion, since it could redeem religion of the errors, impostures, and corruptions perpetrated by scriptural and ecclesiastical authority. He stated this in *Notes on the State of Virginia,* written in 1781, and the basis of his comments was no doubt his earlier advocacy of Bolingbroke's strict empirical tests to determine the veracity of the truth claims of religion (see chapter 2):

> Reason and free enquiry are the only effectual agents against error.
> Give a loose to them, they will support the true religion, by bringing
> every false one to their tribunal, to the test of their investigation. They
> are the natural enemies of error, and of error only. Had not the
> Roman government permitted free inquiry, Christianity could never
> have been introduced. Had not free inquiry been indulged, at the aera
> of the Reformation, the corruptions of Christianity could not have
> been purged away. If it be restrained now, the present corruptions will
> be protected, and new ones encouraged.[52]

One of the effects, when each individual regarded and used his own reason as the authority for himself in determining religious and theological truth, was religious pluralism. This was due to the very nature of the human mind or rational faculty, according to Jefferson. He believed that the mind, as well as the body, of each individual was structured differently from others and that differences in mental structure would cause each mind to function differently. These differences in function would then lead individuals to different conclusions about God, who as a result of His nonobjective nature was not subject to objective verification. Jefferson believed that the differences in human mental structure and the resultant differences in thinking on God were caused by God, who had created humans with different mental structures. Therefore, the different opinions of individuals on God should be respected; they were of divine origin, as Jefferson wrote to James Fishbach in 1809: "The varieties in the structure and action of the human mind as in those of the body, are the work of our Creator, against which it cannot be a religious duty to erect a standard of uniformity."[53] This line of thought dated back to Jefferson's student days, when he had copied a passage from act 3 of Nicholas Rowe's play *Tamerlane* that stated that it was the nature of the thinking faculty—

often referred to as the soul in the seventeenth and eighteenth centuries—to think differently because of individual variations:

> . . . to subdue th'unconquerable Mind,
> To make one Reason have the same Effect
> Upon all Apprehensions; to force this,
> Or this Man, just to think, as thou & I do;
> Impossible! unless Souls were alike
> in all, which differ now like human Faces.[54]

Clearly, Jefferson saw faith, the institutionalized religions that were based on faith, and especially the clergy of those religions as obstacles to the free use of reason in science, politics, and religion. It is therefore understandable why he reacted with indignation to a comment made by Benjamin Rush shortly before he was elected president. Rush, unlike Jefferson, believed that Christianity was conducive to republicanism and, concerned about Jefferson's lack of commitment to Christianity, made an effort to alter the views of the man who would soon hold the young country's highest office. On 22 August 1800 he wrote to Jefferson, "It is only necessary for Republicanism to ally itself to the Christian Religion, to overturn all the corrupted political and religious institutions in the world."[55] Jefferson took Rush's comment to be advocacy of an established national church supported by the government. Given his long-standing opinions on that subject—including his opposition to the established church in Virginia in the 1770s,[56]—his response to Rush was what one might expect:

> The clergy [had] a very favorite hope of obtaining an establishment of
> a particular form of Christianity through the United States; and as
> every sect believes its own form the true one, every one perhaps
> hoped for his own, but especially the Episcopalians and Congrega-
> tionalists. The returning good sense of our country threatens abortion
> to their hopes, and they believe that any portion of power confided to
> me, will be erected in opposition to their schemes. And they believe
> rightly: for I have sworn upon the altar of God, eternal hostility
> against every form of tyranny over the mind of man.[57]

Jefferson made it clear in this statement that he regarded the faiths of institutionalized Christianity as obstacles to reason in that they tyrannized "the mind of man," and that he had taken an oath to oppose such tyranny. It would seem he took that oath when he was a student as a result of his extensive reading and study of those who opposed any authority—including scriptural or ecclesiastical authority—over the reason of each individual. Jefferson suggested as much to Thomas

Cooper in describing his student days as those when he never feared "to follow truth and reason to whatever results they led, and bearding every authority which stood in their way."[58]

The Removal of Faith as an Obstacle

Jefferson prescribed education, "the diffusion of instruction" among the people, as the long-term or "remote remedy" for the removal of faith, which he described as the "fever of fanaticism" that constituted a tyrannizing obstacle to human reason.[59] The education he recommended was public or government-funded secular education, not in any way controlled by the clergy of religious institutions. Jefferson was of the opinion that when the clergy, who preached the doctrines of faith, determined what was to be taught in educational institutions, free reason and truth were compromised to accommodate those doctrines. This compromise would result in obscurantism and regressive, not progressive, education, like the pattern of education in the Middle Ages, a pattern that some clergy preferred, according to Jefferson. He expressed these ideas in a letter to Joseph Priestley: "What an effort, my dear Sir, of bigotry in politics and religion have we gone through! The barbarians really flattered themselves they should be able to bring back the times of Vandalism, when ignorance put everything into the hands of power and priestcraft. All advances in science were proscribed as innovations. They pretended to praise and encourage education, but it was to be the education of our ancestors."[60]

In 1779 Jefferson drafted a bill to establish public education in Virginia. The bill spelled out his basic ideas for education and prescribed three levels: elementary, grammar, and university.[61] The clergy would have no authority whatsoever at any level. Indeed, Jefferson wrote in 1820 in connection with his original plan, that he preferred election methods that would tend to "keep elementary education out of the hands of fanaticising preachers" if his plan was ever actualized on that level.[62] Although that bill did not pass, part of his plan was actualized subsequent to his presidency, after the Virginia legislature finally approved the establishment of the University of Virginia (1819). It was Jefferson who aroused interest in that project, Jefferson who became the architect not only of that institution's buildings but also of its curriculum and format.[63] Gilbert Chinard wrote that the University of Virginia "was his in every sense of the word."[64] Jefferson summed up the new university's policy on academic freedom, which reflected his own views on reason, when he wrote, "This institution will be based on the illimitable freedom of the human mind. For here we are not afraid to follow truth wherever it may lead, nor to tolerate any error so long as reason is left free to combat it."[65]

Jefferson paid tribute to the people of Virginia when he wrote of his new university, "The liberality of this State will support this institution, and give fair play to the cultivation of reason." He believed that "the priests of the different religious sects" were "serious enemies" of such cultivation, that they put "spells on the human mind" that would cast an "ominous" cloud over the efforts to improve it.[66] The clergy of various sects confirmed his belief by complaining about the allegedly unorthodox religious views of Dr. Thomas Cooper. Cooper had been chosen to be a member of the faculty of the new university, but the clergy's complaints forced his resignation before classes ever began. Jefferson, smoldering at this priestly interference, sarcastically criticized his fellow Visitors of the university for yielding to the clergy's pressure by accepting Cooper's resignation. "For myself," he stated, "I was not disposed to regard the denunciations of these satellites of religious inquisition."[67]

That the mind and reason could be improved and cultivated by education in the context of freedom, especially freedom from religious restraints, was an idea Jefferson found in Locke's *Of the Conduct of the Understanding,* which he would have been familiar with since he had recommended it to Skipwith in 1771:

> He that will inquire out the best books in every science, and inform himself of the most material authors of the several sects of philosophy and religion, will not find it an infinite work to acquaint himself with the sentiments of mankind concerning the most weighty and comprehensive subjects. Let him exercise the freedom of his reason and understanding in such a latitude as this, and his mind will be strengthened, his capacity enlarged, his faculties improved; and the light which the remote and scattered parts of truth will give to one another will so assist his judgement, that he will seldom be widely out, or miss giving proof of a clear head and a comprehensive knowledge. At least, this is the only way I know to give the understanding its due improvement to the full extent of its capacity, and to distinguish the two most different things I know in the world, a logical chicaner from a man of reason.[68]

Locke's "man of reason," although a reader of the ideas of others, was not a mere follower but an independent thinker who made his own determinations of truth. This rational independence was actualized by Locke's method of education, as he made clear in *Some Thoughts concerning Education.* Jefferson would also have been familiar with this work, since it, along with *Conduct,* was on the list of books he sent to Skipwith in 1771. Quoting and recommending the ideas of a "judicious author," Locke stated in *Thoughts:*

> The study of the original text can never be sufficiently recommended. 'Tis the shortest, surest, and most agreeable way to all sorts of learning. Draw from the spring-head, and take not things at second hand. Let the writings of the great masters be never laid aside, dwell upon them, settle them in your mind, and cite them upon occasion; make it your business thoroughly to understand them in their full extent and all their circumstances; acquaint yourself fully with the principles of original authors; bring them to a consistency, and then do you yourself make your deductions. . . . [Yet] content not yourself with those borrowed lights, nor guide yourself by their views but where your own fails you and leaves you in the dark. Their explications are not yours, and will give you the slip. On the contrary, your own observations are the product of your own mind, where they will abide and be ready at hand upon all occasions in converse, consultation, and dispute.[69]

This Lockean approach—developing reason through reading the "original" texts of "great masters" while maintaining the freedom and independence of the rational faculty—seems to have shaped Jefferson's own early education and reading, which liberated him from faith.[70] Therefore, he believed that once individuals became imbued with the idea of pursuing truth with reason in the context of freedom—as a result of improving their own reason through reading at the lower levels of his system of education—they too would emerge as independent thinkers. Consistent with this independence, they would no longer uncritically follow religious doctrines or blindly accept the authority of the clergy. People followed doctrines and priests with blind, uncritical faith as a result of ignorance, which, Jefferson said, "would seem impossible" in "an intelligent people, with the faculty of reading and the right of thinking" actualized by education.[71] Significantly, Jefferson proscribed Bible reading at the lowest level of his system, claiming that the "judgements" of children at that level "are not sufficiently matured for religious enquiries."[72]

It was science in particular that Jefferson believed would ultimately tame the tyranny of faith and superstition over the human mind. People who became accustomed to Baconian questioning and testing of knowledge in order to confirm its correspondence to observed facts, which was the method of science, would eventually subject their own faith to such tests, tests similar to the empirical religious tests of Bolingbroke.

This is not to say that Jefferson thought one needed to become a scientist to adopt this approach; he did not believe that everyone had the rational capacity to do so.[73] Familiarity with and appreciation of scientific method would suffice for individuals to apply the method to their own faith and reject aspects of it that could not be objectively verified. Jefferson believed that the clergy, who made their living from what he deemed the superstitions of faith, anticipated this impact of science with a great deal of apprehension: "The priests of the different religious sects . . . dread the advance of science as witches do the approach of day-light; and scowl on the fatal harbinger announcing the subdivision of the duperies on which they live."[74]

Jefferson made perhaps his most complete statement of what he deemed the progressive method of science and regressive method of faith in a letter to Elbridge Gerry in 1799. There he said Christianity's use of the crucifixion, which conjures up images of the agonizing death Jesus suffered on the cross to atone for the effects of original sin, is responsible for "awing" men to distrust their reason and rely on that of others:

> And I am for encouraging the progress of science in all its branches; and not for raising a hue and cry against the sacred name of philosophy; for awing the human mind by stories of raw-head and bloody bones to a distrust of its own vision, and to repose implicitly on that of others; to go backwards instead of forwards to look for improvement; to believe that government, religion, morality, and every other science were in the highest perfection in ages of the darkest ignorance, and that nothing can ever be devised more perfect than what was established by our forefathers.[75]

Jefferson believed that general progress could be made in the human condition, especially in government and religion, and that reason would be the instrument of progress once the general education of the people removed the obstructions to reason:

> Enlighten the people generally, the tyranny and oppressions of body and mind will vanish like evil spirits at the dawn of day. Although I do not, with some enthusiasts, believe that the human condition will ever advance to such a state of perfection as that there shall no longer be pain or vice in the world, yet I believe it susceptible of much improvement, and most of all, in matters of government and religion; and that the diffusion of knowledge among the people is to be the instrument by which it is to be effected.[76]

Without general public education of a kind that would produce men of independent reason, as described by Locke in *Some Thoughts concerning Education,* Jefferson feared that the minds of the people would be defenseless against eventual domination by authoritarians in religion and government. This domination would result in the collapse of democracy, which he believed was born of and nurtured by the free and independent reason of the individuals who made up the populace. He stated this to George Wythe, a friend and former teacher who had supported his bill for public education in Virginia: "Preach, my dear Sir, a crusade against ignorance; establish and improve the law for educating the common people. Let our countrymen know, that the people alone can protect us against these evils, and that the tax which will be paid for this purpose, is not more than the thousandth part of what will be paid to kings, priests and nobles, who will rise up among us if we leave the people in ignorance."[77]

"Educating the common people," the principal objective of Jefferson's bill for public education in Virginia, despite the fact that it was actualized only on its highest or university level, would enable the people to read and think for themselves and not fall prey to "kings, priests and nobles." Jefferson believed that reading history on the first level of education prescribed by his bill was the foundation that would enable the people to think for themselves.[78] Therefore his educational program was not elitist as respects its application to the "common people" in politics, who he believed were the foundation of democratic government, even though his educational ideas were elitist in other respects, as were those of Locke.[79] The statement to Wythe indicates his trust in the rational capacity of the populace in politics, as well as their moral capacity. As a result of this trust, Jefferson exalted human nature, especially that of the common man. His greatest and most universal exaltation of human nature, however, is found in his ideas on natural rights, which, according to his concept of man contained in the theology of the Declaration of Independence, he believed to be an inherent and sacred part of each individual.

6

Self-Evident Truths

The Lockean idea that "all Men by Nature are equal"[1] and that God created them that way was echoed by Jefferson in the ideological passages of the Declaration of Independence where he wrote, "We hold these Truths to be self-evident, that all Men are created equal."[2] He went on to state how men were created equal by "Nature's God," or the God of natural theology, when he said, "They are endowed by their Creator with certain unalienable Rights, that among these are Life, Liberty and the Pursuit of Happiness."[3] This ideology of God-given equal rights was used in the Declaration as a leveler: by exalting the status of each man to one equal to that of any other, it tamed those who, as a result of deeming themselves superior beings, claimed authority over the common man. This gave the common man a basis to reject and resist anyone who claimed authority over him without his consent, since equals have no authority over equals. Such an ideology of equality, especially equal natural freedom, was of course fundamental to Locke's consent theory of government,[4] which Jefferson used in the Declaration when he stated, "Governments are instituted among Men, deriving their just Powers from the Consent of the Governed."[5]

The idea that individuals have God-given equal rights is a vital element of Jefferson's concept of man as contained in the theology of the Declaration of Independence. To him, the "unalienable Rights" specified there were no mere postulates but realities, described as "Truths." What led him to believe that those rights were "Truths"? The answer to this question lies in Jefferson's ideas on the epistemology of rights, or how he believed that people come to know the "Truths" of their natural "unalienable Rights." Significantly, Jefferson stated the means by which men gain access to knowledge of the truths about themselves and their rights in the Declaration's ideological passages when he wrote, "We hold these Truths to be self-evident."[6] The question then is what Jefferson meant by "self-evident," since this term is key to understanding his epistemology of rights.

I want to emphasize that "self-evident" was Jefferson's own terminology, inserted in place of "sacred and undeniable" when he amended his original rough draft. Carl Becker believed that the handwriting of "self-evident" in the amendment to the rough draft was more like Franklin's than Jefferson's.[7] Julian Boyd disagreed, pointing out that the s's and t's resemble the unusual way Jefferson wrote these letters.[8] I agree with Boyd, especially since the t in words ending with that letter has a very distinctive A-like structure. The t in "self-evident" and those in the words "respect" and "government," which are found in the third line preceding and the fifth line succeeding the line in which "self-evident" appears in the rough draft, have this unusual feature in common.[9] In addition to this evidence, John Adams claimed that neither he nor Franklin nor the other two members of the Declaration's drafting committee altered Jefferson's rough draft before it went to the Continental Congress for final approval, at which time it contained the word "self-evident."[10] Proceeding on the basis that "self-evident" was indeed Jefferson's language, then, let us come back to the consideration of what he meant by this term.

Morton White believed that Jefferson used "self-evident" in the Declaration as Locke did in *An Essay concerning Human Understanding,* where the philosopher specified exactly what he meant by this term. White pointed out that, according to Locke, a "self-evident principle must be certified by a man's intuitive reason," which consisted in seeing "the truth of the principle immediately upon understanding its terms."[11] As Locke put it:

> If we will reflect on our own ways of Thinking, we shall find, that sometimes the Mind perceives the Agreement or Disagreement of two *Ideas* immediately by themselves, without the intervention of any other: And this, I think, we may call *intuitive Knowledge.* For in this, the Mind is at no pains of proving or examining, but perceives the Truth, as the Eye doth light, only by being directed toward it. Thus the Mind perceives, that *White* is not *Black,* That a *Circle* is not a *Triangle,* That *Three* are more than *Two,* and equal to *One* and *Two.* Such kind of Truths, the Mind perceives at the first sight of the *Ideas* together, by bare *Intuition,* without the intervention of any other *Idea;* and this kind of Knowledge is the clearest, and most certain, that humane Frailty is capable of. This part of Knowledge is irresistible, and like the bright Sun-shine, forces it self immediately to be perceived, as soon as ever the Mind turns its view that way; and leaves no room for Hesitation, Doubt, or Examination, but the Mind is presently filled with the clear Light of it. 'Tis on this *Intuition,* that depends all the Certainty and Evidence of all our Knowledge, which

Certainty every one finds to be so great, that he cannot imagine, and therefore not require a greater.[12]

This intuitive reason is related to Locke's demonstrative reason, which is used to find the truth of something beyond the scope of intuition such as "the Agreement or Disagreement in bigness, between the three Angles of a Triangle, and two right ones," to use Locke's own example. The mind, as Locke stated, "cannot by an immediate view and comparing them" determine which of these combinations of angles is larger; there must be intervening steps or "Proofs" whereby "the Mind does at last perceive the Agreement or Disagreement of the *Ideas* it considers." But in each of the intermediate steps or "Connections" leading to a final conclusion or "truth," self-evident intuition born of intuitive reason is necessary to perceive the agreement or disagreement of the ideas considered at each intermediate step.[13] Both Locke and Jefferson, however, considered that gaining moral knowledge by Lockean demonstrative reason was beyond the capacity of most persons (see chapter 4).

Despite Locke's assertion that all men can have intuitive or self-evident perceptions, there is a potentially undemocratic element in this intuitive reason (anticipated by Thomas Aquinas) as White pointed out. What is self-evident to a highly educated and intelligent individual, seen clearly like "bright Sun-shine," would often appear as darkness to an uneducated and unintelligent person. The latter, if he "did not have certain ideas" or "know the meanings of certain words," simply "*could not* see that certain propositions were self-evident." Therefore, Jefferson's Lockean use of "self-evident" in the Declaration, according to White, rendered the "truths" or principles or rights of man specified there knowable to only a few highly intelligent and educated men. As a result, White argued, "the doctrine of self-evident truth . . . *could have been* easily turned into . . . a tool of haughty dictators of Principles." An advocate of the doctrine of self-evident truth who claimed to see the self-evident principles of the Declaration "could claim that those who did not agree with him on the self-evidence of some proposition were biased" and "incapable of using their reason."[14] To put it another way, Lockean "self-evident" epistemology established possibilities for an intellectual elite to exercise normative control over a democracy just as demonstrative reason did (see chapter 4). This elite would then give a democracy its normative direction, even though that democracy was established by the people with the intent that they themselves would supply its moral direction.

I agree with White's analysis of Locke's epistemology and its implications for the Declaration, but I disagree that it was the Lockean meaning of "self-evident" that Jefferson used in that document. I argue that Jefferson's meaning entailed a different epistemology, one that he believed gave virtually all persons easy access to knowledge of their natural "unalienable Rights." I also argue that that epistemology, like the one he believed provided knowledge of morals, came from Lord Kames. Indeed, they were similar epistemologies. The one in connection with rights, however, was linked to Kamesean ideas promulgated to defeat David Hume's skepticism as respects the self of man.

In his *Treatise of Human Nature*, Hume argued that man has no personal identity or self in the sense of an idea of himself that has "identity and simplicity." By "identity," Hume meant an "idea of self" that would "continue invariably the same, thro' the whole course of our lives; since the self is suppos'd to exist after that manner." By "simplicity," he meant an idea of self born of "one impression," which, he said, was what "gives rise to every real idea." The impressions that gave rise to the real ideas Hume referrred to were, like the ideas of Locke, born of contact by the senses with objects external to the self. The problem with such impressions and the ideas they produced in the mind, however, was that they were not "constant and invariable," according to Hume. On the contrary they were successive and short-lived and could therefore not give a single continuous idea of one's self that would endure throughout one's entire life. Hume expressed this view when he said: "Pain and pleasure, grief and joy, passions and sensations succeed each other, and never all exist at the same time. It cannot, therefore, be from any of these impressions, or from any other, that the idea of self is deriv'd; and consequently there is no such idea." Hume went on to emphasize that ideas based on sense impressions were scattered. He then challenged the concept that they could be in any way related to or connected with the self: "All these are different, and distinguishable, and separable from each other, and may be separately consider'd, and may exist separately, and have no need of any thing to support their existence. After what manner, therefore, do they belong to the self; and how are they connected with it?"[15]

Hume was responding to "some philosophers" (including Locke) who argued, according to Hume, that the experience of "pain or pleasure" or the "strongest sensation" or "most violent passion," even though fleeting, was enough evidence of the self to enable men to "feel its existence and its continuance in existence."[16] Locke had maintained in *Human Understanding* that an individual's personal identity or continuous unchanging self was his thinking faculty or consciousness. He did not claim to have an idea of that self or consciousness but maintained that one could intuit knowledge of one's self. He stated that it was "impossible for any one to perceive, without perceiving, that he does perceive. When we see, hear, smell, taste, feel, meditate, or will any thing, we know that we do so [with our consciousness]." Memory was crucial in gaining knowledge of the self as a continuous entity, according to Locke: "As far as this consciousness can be extended backwards to any past Action or Thought, so far reaches the Identity of that *Person*; it is the same *self* now it was then; and 'tis by the same *self* with this present one that now reflects on it, that that Action was done."[17]

This knowledge of one's continuous self, which Locke described as intuitive, was not the same, however, as what he described as intuitive or self-evident knowledge, where two ideas were, without the "pains of proving or examining," immediately perceived to agree or disagree ("*White* is not *Black*, . . . *Three* are more than *Two*," and so on). Hence, Locke's proof of the self did not leave David Hume without "Hesitation, Doubt, or Examination," as Locke had said intuitive or self-evident knowledge would. There was no idea of self in the sense of consciousness or mind, Hume pointed out, as there was of white, black, one, two, and three. In what is perhaps the most quoted statement from his *Treatise*, Hume described what happened when he tried to gain knowledge of his own self or mind: "For my part, when I enter most intimately into what I call *myself*, I always stumble on some particular perception or other, of heat or cold, light or shade, love or hatred, pain or pleasure, I never can catch *myself* at any time without a perception, and never can observe any thing but the perception." Hume went on to compare the mind or self to an unknowable theater where the performers are impressions, perceptions, or ideas born of the senses:

> The mind is a kind of theatre, where several perceptions successively make their appearance; pass, re-pass, glide away, and mingle in an infinite variety of postures and situations. There is properly no *simplicity* in it at one time, nor *identity* in different; whatever natural propension we may have to imagine that simplicity and identity. The comparison of the theatre must not mislead us. They are the successive perceptions only, that constitute the mind; nor have we the most distant notion of the place, where these scenes are represented, or of the materials, of which it is compos'd.[18]

Like Thomas Reid, Kames was appalled by Hume's skepticism, especially as respects the self.[19] In his *Essays on the Principles of Morality and Natural Religion,* he wrote:

Had we no original impressions but those of the external senses, according to the author of the treatise of human nature, we never could have any consciousness of *self;* because such consciousness cannot arise from any external sense. Mankind would be in a perpetual reverie; ideas would be constantly floating in the mind; and no man would be able to connect his ideas with *himself.* Neither could there be an idea of *personal identity.* For a man, cannot consider himself to be the same person, in different circumstances, when he has no idea or consciousness of *himself* at all.[20]

What Kames offered as counterpoint to Hume's points about ideas born of the external senses was the internal sense that provided each individual with an idea of the self or, as Kames put it, with "an undoubted truth, that he has an original feeling, or consciousness of himself, and of his existence." This feeling or consciousness was of a continuous self that "for the most part, accompanies every one of his impressions and ideas, and every action of his mind and body." Kames's qualifying phrase "for the most part" allowed for the occasions when persons were without this feeling and consciousness of self: in deep sleep they had no ideas at all; in some dreams and even some waking hours there were moments of "reverie," which Kames defined as a "wandering of the mind through its ideas without carrying along the perception of self." What Kames perceived via the internal sense was an idea "of the liveliest kind" that, even though sometimes interrupted, was dominant and persistent in an individual's life. That idea was "self preservation," an idea that an individual "carried through all the different stages of life, and all the variety of action, which is the foundation of personal identity." The idea of self-preservation, therefore, substantially met Hume's criterion of continuity through time, or "identity." Being one idea, it also met Hume's criterion of "simplicity." The idea of self-preservation, which had both identity and simplicity, was thus used by Kames as proof of the self in response to Hume's skepticism. It was an idea he observed in himself via "the internal sense, which is the cause of this particular perception." Kames wrote of this proof: "It is not by any argument or reasoning, I conclude myself to be the same person, I was ten years ago. This conclusion rests entirely upon the feeling of identity, which accompanies me through all my changes, and which is the only connecting principle, that binds together, all the various thoughts and actions of my life. Far less is it by any argument, or chain of reasoning, that I discover my own existence."[21]

Moreover, Kames not only relied on feelings born of the inner sense to give self-knowledge but simultaneously denied reason as a means to attain such knowledge. In the foregoing statement he renounced any "chain of reasoning" of a Lockean demonstrative type as a method of gaining self-knowledge. In addition, Kames criticized Descartes's rational argument *cogito ergo sum* ("I think, therefore I am") to defeat doubt or skepticism as respects the self. "For surely," he said, "I am not more conscious of thinking, than of existing."[22] Kames preferred a sometimes interrupted but ever persistent inner feeling or consciousness of self-preservation, perceived by the inner sense, to thinking or reason as proof of the truth of his existence.

According to Arthur McGuinness, one characteristic of several Enlightenment thinkers was that they made observations of their own consciousness and then drew conclusions that they applied to all mankind; Kames was in this category.[23] So was Descartes with his "I think therefore I am." Even David Hume fit this pattern: his arguments in support of the lack of simplicity and identity of ideas of the self came from examining his own consciousness.[24] Thomas Hobbes, whom both Kames and Jefferson read (see chapter 4), gave perhaps the best description of this method of gaining knowledge of human nature: "*Wisdome* is acquired, not by reading of *Books*, but of *Men*." Hobbes went on to offer "*Nosce teipsum, Read thy self,*" as a specific way in which men "might learn truly to read one another."[25] This approach of these authors fits generally into what Arthur E. Lovejoy described as "Uniformitarianism" practiced by Enlightenment thinkers.[26]

Jefferson was familiar with writings from all of the foregoing authors when he wrote the Declaration (with the possible exception of Descartes, although he was aware of the famous *cogito ergo sum* via Kames). He was especially familiar, of course, with the ideas of Kames; therefore, it was quite natural for him to look to his own inner sense for the truth of his own existence or self, as Kames did. The fact that he did so can be seen in his letters to John Adams and John Manners. To comments on skepticism in an Adams letter, Jefferson responded, "Its crowd of scepticisms kept me from sleep. I read it, and laid it down; read it, and laid it down, again and again; and to give rest to my mind, I was obliged to recur ultimately to my habitual anodyne, 'I feel, therefore I exist.'"[27] This letter was written in 1820. But given the similarity of Jefferson's "anodyne" phrase "I feel, therefore I exist" to Kames's proof of the self from "an undoubted truth" in the form of "an original feeling" of his "existence" from his internal sense,[28] plus the fact that Jefferson read Kames in his student days, it would not seem unreasonable to conclude that Jefferson's "anodyne" had been "habitual" since those days and that he could well have adopted it as a result of reading Kames.

It can be argued that Jefferson did not specify whether the feeling that confirmed his existence or self was derived from his external or internal sense. When explaining to John Manners the source of his ideas on rights, however, he specified they were born of sense in a way that meant the internal sense and in a way related to his proof of his self "I feel, therefore I exist." The right of expatriation, emphasized in his 1774 *Summary View*, was what Jefferson discussed in his 1817 letter to Manners by explaining the method by which individuals gained knowledge of their right to move as well as all the "unalienable Rights" stated in the approved copy of the Declaration:

> My opinion on the right of Expatriation has been, so long ago as the year 1776, consigned to record in the act of the Virginia code, drawn by myself, recognizing the right expressly, and prescribing the mode of exercising it. The evidence of this natural right, like that of our right to life, liberty, the use of our faculties, the pursuit of happiness, is not left to the feeble and sophistical investigations of reason, but is impressed on the sense of every man. We do not claim these under the charters of kings or legislators, but under the King of kings. If he has made it a law *in* [emphasis added] the nature of man to pursue his own happiness, he has left him free in the choice of place as well as mode.[29]

Here Jefferson not only stated that the evidence of natural rights was "impressed on the sense of every man" by God but that rights were "law *in* the nature of man" as a result. Much like Kames, when he wrote of the knowledge of self and self-preservation, Jefferson emphasized that because God made impressions *in* individuals, there was no need for them to look to the "feeble and sophistical investigations of reason" for knowledge of their rights. This was especially true of Lockean reason, born of conclusions drawn from ideas derived from impressions made by objects external to the self via the external senses, or senses that put man in contact with external objects. External perceptions had nothing to do with the knowledge of rights that were "impressed on the sense of every man" or placed "*in*" every man by God.

In effect Jefferson was saying to Manners that an individual's consciousness or knowledge of his rights welled up or emoted from within as an impulsion or inner feeling born of the impressions God made on his inner sense. In the Declaration Jefferson in effect said the same thing when he wrote of "the causes which impel" or inwardly direct the people of the colonies to "Separation"[30] just before the descriptive

phraseology on rights. "Impel" in this context connotes a manifestation of the feeling or consciousness of natural rights that emerges within
an individual via the inner sense, whereby individuals gain knowledge
of their rights, especially when those rights are violated or transgressed
in the ways alleged by the Declaration. This emergent manifestation is
a central point made in the Declaration. Jefferson's original draft description of the rights stated there as within or "inherent and inalienable" in individuals supports this interpretation of "impel." Significantly, it was the Continental Congress, not Jefferson, that deleted
"inherent" in the final approved copy.[31] This interpretation of the
Manners letter and the Declaration is consistent with Jefferson's comment that the colonists "felt their rights before they had thought of
their explanation" which he made in a letter written in 1812 discussing how the colonists knew their rights prior to and at the time of the
Declaration.[32]

In 1824 Jefferson's views on the source of the knowledge of natural
rights had not changed. As he said at that time, "Nothing then is unchangeable but the inherent and unalienable rights of man."[33] Here he
not only called rights "inherent and unalienable," as in the draft language of the Declaration, but also described them as persistent or "unchangeable." According to this description, which echoed Kames's
views on the persistence of the idea of self-preservation in an individual's
life, rights were stable "truths" or ideas in the constantly changing
human mind. Other ideas in the mind might come and go, but during
all periods of life one had persistent or "unchangeable" feelings and
consciousness of the right to "Life," the right to "Liberty," and the
right to "the Pursuit of Happiness."

It is significant that in the original draft of the Declaration's list of
rights, "Life" appeared as "the preservation of life."[34] I maintain that
Jefferson used these terms interchangeably. He probably finally settled
on "Life" because it was the more succinct expression of "the preservation of life." A precedent for this interchangeable use is found in Sir
William Blackstone's *Commentaries on the Laws of England,* which
Jefferson read as a law student and recommended to Skipwith. Blackstone referred to the absolute right of "personal security" (or preservation of life) and then immediately stated that "LIFE is the immediate gift of God, a *right* [emphasis added] inherent by nature in every
individual."[35] Jefferson's view that "Life" or "the preservation of life"
was an "unchangeable" reality in man, made known by an inner feeling or inner sense, when combined with his habitual anodyne "I feel,
therefore I exist," was the equivalent of Kames's view that the inner

feelings and consciousness of self-preservation in man were the stable connecting links, in the ever changing kaleidoscope of his mind, that gave him evidence of self.

It seems, then, that when Jefferson said in the Declaration, "We hold these Truths to be self-evident, that all Men are created equal, that they are endowed by their Creator with certain unalienable Rights, that among these are Life, Liberty, and the Pursuit of Happiness,"[36] he used "self-evident" in the sense of evidence born of feelings or consciousness within the individual self, provided by the individual's inner sense for the truth of the rights mentioned and not evidence born of ideas derived from sense impressions made by things external to the self, as Locke used the term. Therefore, all that individual persons had to do to find evidence for their unalienable natural rights, according to Jefferson, was to look to their inner sense. The effect of this epistemology was that none were dependent on a philosopher or on someone highly intelligent or highly educated for knowledge of their rights.

Jefferson's letter to John Manners in effect stated that he subscribed to this individual method of gaining knowledge of unalienable rights. For despite his statement in that letter that rights were impressed by God on the inner being or sense of "every man," he had no way of knowing the inner reality or sense of another human being. He could only have known that he found rights impressed on his own inner being and sense, and then concluded that other men were similarly impressed. Kames's expression of this meaning of "self-evident," which I believe Jefferson borrowed from the Scottish jurist, is found in his *Essays on the Principles of Morality and Natural Religion:* "If natural feelings, whether from internal or external senses, are not admitted as evidence of truth, I can not see, that we can be certain of any fact whatever." Those "natural feelings" derived from the "internal or external senses" provided individuals with "self-evident" truths, both of one's self and the world external to one's self, respectively, according to Kames. Consistent with this line of thought, Kames went on to state, in a way applicable to the truths of ourselves obtained with our internal sense that we then attribute to others, "We know little about the nature of things, but what we learn from a strict attention to our own nature."[37]

Given the foregoing interpretation of "self-evident," when Jefferson substituted this term for "sacred and undeniable" in his rough draft, he apparently believed that he benefited the text in two ways. First, he clarified the Declaration's epistemology of "unalienable Rights"—not realizing, in my opinion, that "self-evident" would be mistaken for a term from Lockean epistemology. Second, he avoided repetitious language in a document meant to be a succinct expression of the colonies' position. The term "sacred" would have been a redundancy if used to mean that rights were God-given; the statement that all men are equally "endowed by their Creator" with "unalienable Rights" carries this meaning of the word. Or, if it meant that God-given rights were "sacred" in the sense of being inviolable, the word could have been construed as contradictory to one of the main purposes of the Declaration, which was to call attention to the king's violations of rights. Consistent with this line of thought, the removal of "undeniable" was necessary to avoid contradicting the Declaration's allegations that the king through certain actions *had* denied the colonists' rights.

It would seem that what Jefferson had meant by "undeniable" as respects rights was that no man could deny his inner feelings and consciousness of his rights if he paid heed to his inner sense or being. Jefferson had a Kamesean precedent for this meaning of "undeniable," since the Scottish jurist used it as proof of the moral sense (see chapter 4). But again, given this meaning, "undeniable" would have created a redundancy in the Declaration if it had not been deleted and replaced by "self-evident," since "unalienable" carries a similar connotation. The 1774 *Summary View* implies the similar meaning of the two words: "The god who gave us life, gave us liberty at the same time: the hand of force may destroy, but cannot disjoin them."[38] Here Jefferson acknowledged that force might in fact take away or destroy outward manifestations of an individual's freedom, but it could not inwardly alienate or make him inwardly deny the feeling derived from the core of his being of his right to freedom as long as he was alive. It was in this sense that rights were "unalienable" and "undeniable."

Apart from equal unalienable rights, three other self-evident "Truths" are spelled out in the Declaration, as Michael Zuckert has pointed out.[39] First, to secure those rights, "Governments are instituted among men, deriving their just Powers from the consent of the Governed." Second, "whenever any Form of Government becomes destructive of these Ends, it is the Right of the People to alter or to abolish it." Third, the people may then institute "new Government, laying its Foundation on such Principles and and organizing its Powers in such Form, as to Them shall seem most likely to effect their Safety and Happiness."[40] (For the original version of this passage and the subsequent changes made, see chapter 3, note 84.) Unlike "unalienable rights," however, these self-evident "Truths" were not impressed by the Creator on the internal sense; they have nothing to do with the perception by individuals of their inherent rights. Rather they have to do with government, which is external to and separate from the individual. Thus Jefferson shifted in the Declaration from the "Truths" of internal reality perceived by the internal sense to those of external reality perceived by the external senses. Yet he applied "self-evident" to both kinds of "Truths." This seems puzzling until one looks at these internal and external "Truths" in the light of Kames's philosophy. Kamesean thought foreshadowed the commonsense philosophy of Thomas Reid and contains a great deal of commonsense philosophy of its own.[41] In the context of Kames's commonsense meaning of "self-evident," which could be born of both the internal sense and the external senses, since Kames specified that both gave self-evident perceptions of truth, Jefferson's leap from internal to external truths becomes understandable. Indeed, it supports the view that Jefferson used Kames's idea of "self-evident."

Property Rights

In the context of its Lockean content, one peculiarity of the Declaration is its omission of property rights, which Locke includes in his *Second Treatise* along with the right to the preservation of life and the right to liberty as fundamental rights of man.[42] He especially emphasized property rights, and yet the Declaration, with its specified rights of "Life, Liberty, and the Pursuit of Happiness," accords with only two of Locke's trinity of rights. The questions then arise, what was Jefferson's disposition toward Lockean property rights, and why did he substitute the "Pursuit of Happiness" for them in the Declaration?[43]

Answering the first of these questions necessitates briefly describing what Locke meant by property rights in movable things and land. The right of self-preservation, he maintained, was the source of these property rights. He stated this in the *Second Treatise,* chapter 5, "Of Property," when he said, "Men . . . have a right to their Preservation, and consequently to Meat and Drink, and such other things, as Nature affords for their Subsistence." Locke developed his ideas on the origin of property rights from this right to the things in nature required for sustenance. He argued that although in the state of nature the "things" of nature belonged to mankind in common, each man had a right to take what he needed and could therefore separate a portion of those things from the common ownership. Such things became the private property of an individual. This separation was accomplished by means of each individual's labor. Locke believed that each man had a right to the fruits of his labor, a right born of a basic property right each person had in himself. If a man's self was his property, that property extended to his labor, which was part of himself, and thence to things external to himself upon which he exerted his labor. These ideas were expressed by Locke when he said:

> Though the Earth, and all inferior Creatures be common to all Men, yet every Man has a *Property* in his own *Person*. This no Body has any Right to but himself. The *Labour* of his Body, and the *Work* of his Hands, we may say, are properly his. Whatsoever then he removes out of the State that Nature hath provided, and left it in, he hath mixed his *Labour* with, and joyned to it something that is his own, and thereby makes it his *Property*. It being by him removed from the common state Nature placed it in, it hath by this *labour* something annexed to it, that excludes the common right of other Men.[44]

Jefferson subscribed to Locke's ideas on the labor theory of property, which is seen in his 1801 inaugural address, where he spoke of "a due sense of our equal right to the use of our own faculties" and "to the acquisitions of our industry."[45] In addition, Jefferson subscribed to Locke's idea that "the great and *chief end* . . . of Mens uniting into Commonwealths, and putting themselves under Government, *is the Preservation of their Property,*" which included the "Lives, Liberties and Estates" of individuals.[46] Once a government was formed, laws passed by the legislative and enforced by the executive became the instruments of protecting property in Locke's system of government.[47] Evidence that Jefferson accepted Locke's "chief end" and methods of accomplishing it may be seen in his proposed revisions to the laws of the state of Virginia, begun in 1776. In the preamble of his Bill for Proportioning Crimes and Punishments (which was never passed by the legislature), he wrote:

> Whereas it frequently happens that wicked and dissolute men, resigning themselves to the dominion of inordinate passions, commit violations on the lives, liberties and property, of others, and, the secure enjoyment of these having principally induced men to enter into society, government would be defective in its principal purpose were it not to restrain such criminal acts, by inflicting due punishments on those who perpetrate them . . . it becomes a duty of the legislature to arrange in a proper scale the crimes which it may be necessary for them to repress, and to adjust thereto a corresponding gradation of punishments.[48]

Given Jefferson's acceptance of many of Locke's ideas on property, why did he not list the right to property in the Declaration? His concept of unalienable rights provides the answer to this question. Jefferson believed that each man had a right to the preservation of his person or life and a right to his liberty and that these rights were an inherent part of his own nature or being. Such rights could not be inwardly alienated or renounced even though external coercion or duress could cause an individual to renounce these rights externally or to lose the physical manifestations of them. The right to one's life and liberty were in this sense unalienable. To put it another way, one could not inwardly alienate or separate one's self from something that was part of one's self. Property in the form of movable goods and land, however, was not part of one's self; hence, one could alienate such property and the right to it from one's self. Therefore, Jefferson could not list the right to property as an unalienable right. Kames was again the likely source of this element in Jefferson's thinking. In his *Historical Law Tracts* (passages from which Jefferson commonplaced as a law student),[49] Kames wrote that it was not only possible for men to alienate property in the form of movable goods and land but that they had the right to do so in law:

> Cattle are killed every day for the sustenance of the proprietor and his family. From this power, the transition is easy to that of alienation; for what doubt can there be of my power to alien what I can destroy? The right or power of alienation must therefore have been early recognized as a quality of moveable property. . . . We have reason, before-hand, to conjecture, that a power of alienating land . . . was not early introduced; because land admits not, like moveables, a ready delivery from hand to hand. And this conjecture will be verified in the following part of our history. Land, at the same time, is a desirable object; and a power to alien, after it came to be established in moveable property, could not long be separated from the property of land.[50]

God and Property Rights

Although Locke maintained that men had property and rights in their lives and liberties in relation to one another, his theology put men and God in a very different relationship. God, according to Locke, owned men; they were "all the Servants of one Sovereign Master, sent into the World by his order and about his business, they are his Property."[51] Although in the theology of the Declaration Jefferson adopted Locke's idea of a God who treated all men equally at the time they were created, he rejected the view of God as a "Sovereign Master" who owned men, which reduced men to the status of God's slaves. Evidence of this rejection is manifest in his statement to the Republicans of Georgetown in 1809 about the Declaration and the behavior of the colonists when it was made: "The principles on which we engaged, of which the charter of our independence is the record, were sanctioned by the laws of our being, and we but obeyed them in pursuing undeviatingly the course they called for. It issued finally in that inestimable state of freedom which alone can ensure to man the enjoyment of his equal rights."[52] Here Jefferson mentioned that the "principles" on which the colonists acted in 1776 were in accord with the "laws" of the "being" of man, and as the Declaration stated, it was "Nature's God" who placed these laws in human nature. They were "law in the nature of man," as Jefferson wrote to John Manners. Yet "laws" was a descriptive term, as Jefferson used it in this statement to the Georgetown Republicans, one that described human nature, which included the "unalienable Rights" in each individual's being, not precepts or rules to be obeyed. Therefore, in saying that "we but obeyed" the "laws of our being in pursuing undeviatingly the course they called for," Jefferson was saying that men were acting in accordance with their human nature in 1776 when they asserted their rights. They were acting in accordance with the "unalienable Rights" that were part of their God-given human nature. Since it was "Nature's God" who created man with his nature and rights, including the right of "Liberty" or freedom, He would not, as Locke had stated about his God, regard Himself as Master and man as His servant and property.

"Nature's God," in contrast to Locke's God, was Bolingbroke's deistic God of natural theology (see chapter 2). Therefore, He would not interfere with or go against His creation by going against the laws He established in nature or the universe at the time of creation; to do so would be to go against Himself. Since man was part of God's created nature, God would not go against the laws he placed in man. Once "Nature's God" made man with a certain nature or being of which laws or rights were an inherent part, He would not go against Himself and man by going against the laws or rights He had established in man. "Nature's God," therefore, made man his own man, who went about his own business, not God's. "Nature's God" made man a free being not only in relation to other men but also in relation to Himself.

To put it another way, God made each individual sovereign as respects his natural rights, no matter how much more intelligence or power another being—divine or human—might have. Jefferson expressed this view to Henri Gregoire: "Because Sir Isaac Newton was superior to others in understanding, he was not therefore lord of the person or property of others."[53] Despite Jefferson's concept of God-given equal rights, he acknowledged that there were unequal capacities in intelligence and power among men. In *Notes of the State of Virginia,* for example, he wondered whether blacks might have less intelligence than whites.[54] But he did not believe that these unequal capacities justified the usurpation of or infringement upon an individual's sacred natural rights, as he stated to Gregoire. Jefferson also acknowledged that men had unequal moral capacity, and he praised that capacity in blacks.[55] Because of this praise and because he believed that morality was more important to being a good citizen than intelligence, blacks as citizens would be in the same category as Jefferson's "ploughman," whose morality made him a good citizen even though only moderately intelligent.[56] (Noteworthy too is Jefferson's admission in the Gregoire letter that his doubts about the intelligence of blacks could well be erroneous and that he would be pleased to have them refuted.)[57]

In the Declaration itself, Jefferson stated clearly that "Nature's God" put the "laws of nature" or "unalienable Rights" in "all men," including black men. He stated this in the rough draft's allegation (deleted by the Continental Congress in the approved copy) that the king was responsible for the initiation and continuance of slavery in the colonies. That allegation referred to the king's violation of human nature's "sacred rights of life & liberty" by carrying "a distant people" into slavery and by his "crimes committed against the liberties" of those who were enslaved in the colonies.[58] In *Notes on the State of Virginia* (1781), where Jefferson stated many of his early views, he wrote of God's objection to any violation of the God-given right of liberty through the practice of slavery by citizens of the United States: "Can the liberties of a nation be thought secure when we have removed their only firm basis, a conviction in the minds of the people that these liberties are of the gift of God? That they are not to be violated but with his wrath?"[59] In short, the God of the Declaration did not own men or believe that other men should own men.

Women too were equally endowed with rights by the God of the Declaration. Jefferson wrote in his rough draft passage deleted by the Continental Congress that in violating the "*sacred rights* of life and liberty" of blacks, the king "waged cruel war against *human nature* itself" (emphasis added). He referred to blacks as "*a distant people*" because they came from Africa (emphasis added). "Human nature" and "a people," general terms inclusive of both men and women, suggest that when Jefferson wrote "All Men are created equal," he used "Men" in reference to the entire human species. This is exactly the way he used "Men" in the passage deleted by the Continental Congress, where he accused the king of being "determined to keep open a market where *MEN* are bought and sold" (emphasis added). It seems clear that Jefferson used "*MEN*" here to mean the entire human species, since both sexes were traded as slaves in the "market." It seems equally clear that Jefferson included women as well as men when he wrote that "all Men are created equal, that they are endowed by their Creator with certain unalienable Rights" in the light of a specific reference to his belief in women's natural equality and rights in *Notes on the State of Virginia,* a work, as has been mentioned, that expresses many of his views formulated before 1776: "It is civilization alone which replaces women in the enjoyment of their natural equality. That [civilization] first teaches us to subdue the selfish passions and to respect those rights in others, which we value in ourselves."[60]

The view of Jefferson and the Declaration that "Nature's God" endowed women with "natural equality" and "rights" differs sharply from the concept of male superiority and legitimate subjection of wives to the rule of their husbands contained in Christian theology, as stated in the writings of Paul and the words of Genesis. Their husbands' "rule" and "sorrow" in childbirth were punishments to which women were sentenced by the God of the Bible because of Eve's role in the fall of man (Genesis 3:16). The rule of her husband made a wife's right of "Liberty" nonexistent, as well as her right to the "Pursuit of Happiness," which necessitates "Liberty" or freedom, as Jefferson stated in his letter to John Manners. Though he was not immune to the cultural disposition of his time against women serving in government,[61] Jefferson went far beyond Locke, who in the *First Treatise on Government* maintained that God had cursed women in Genesis 3:16 and foretold "what should be the Womans Lot, how by his Providence he would order it so, that she should be subject to her husband, as we see that generally the Laws of Mankind and customs of Nations have ordered it so; and there is, I grant, a foundation in Nature for it."[62] Not only scripture but "a foundation in Nature" made women subject to their husbands, according to Locke.

Paul made matters even worse for women in Christianity by asserting their inferiority to men. Following the implications of the Adam's rib view of the creation of women (Genesis 2:21–22), he explained why women should and men should not cover their heads during worship: "But I would have you know, that the head of every man is Christ; and the head of the woman is the man; and the head of Christ is God. . . . For a man indeed ought not to cover his head, forasmuch as he is [created in] the image and glory of God: but the woman is the glory of the man. For the man is not of the woman; but the woman of the man. Neither was the man created for the woman; but the woman for the man" (1 Corinthians 11:3, 7–9). Paul's view that men are superior, Godlike beings relative to women, who were created "for the man," combined with the injunction of God in Genesis that a husband was to be lord and master over his wife, made women virtual slaves to men. The antithesis of this view is found in the concept of equal rights given at creation to all human beings, regardless of race or gender, by the "Nature's God" of the Declaration of Independence.

Rights, Duties, Resistance, and Jesus

Jefferson believed that the specific right of "Liberty" was restricted by a duty to respect the rights of others. A letter to Isaac Tiffany in which he quoted or paraphrased an unknown author in defining "Liberty" reveals much about his ideas on the nature of unalienable rights: "Liberty is 'unobstructed action according to our will; but rightful Liberty is the unobstructed action according to our will, within the limits drawn around us by the equal rights of others.'"[63] This definition is reminiscent of Locke's reference in the *Second Treatise* to "a Liberty to follow my own will in all things where the rule [law of nature] prescribes not."[64]

The fact that Jefferson subscribed to the Kamesean moral philosophy that men had the moral duty of justice, not to harm others, sheds light on the definition of liberty in the letter to Tiffany. Kames maintained that the duty of justice was born of the moral sense within each human being. Since violating the rights of others harmed those whose rights were violated, the restriction imposed on liberty by respect for the rights of others in the letter to Tiffany was moral in nature. What men were left with after fulfilling their moral duty of justice, according to this concept of the right of "Liberty" or "rightful Liberty," was an "active right," which, as Richard Tuck states, is one that could be exercised by its possessor even if not recognized by others. The idea that such recognition was not needed enabled the possessor of an active right to control that right.[65] The Declaration of Independence was an exercise of active rights since the colonies actively asserted their rights, despite the absence of recognition. In this respect, Jefferson's ideas on rights paralleled those in Locke's *Second Treatise* that men should actively assert their rights to one another in the state of nature and to their government, after one was formed, if those rights were not recognized.[66]

Unlike Locke, however, Jefferson adopted a deistic approach to rights, and this approach precludes any possibility that Burlamaqui's ideas on rights (as Morton White believes) influenced him in writing the Declaration. Burlamaqui, according to White, saw rights as duties rationally derived from considering the nature of man and God. If an individual had a certain God-given nature with certain observable attributes, then God—since He was wise, good, and powerful—would will that man to attain ends consistent with the nature God gave him. Burlamaqui believed that God did nothing in vain and wanted the best for us because of His wise and good nature. Therefore, since God gave us life, it could be inferred that God "proposed" or willed "the preservation of our life" for us, and because God gave us a desire for happiness, he proposed or willed "the pursuit of that happiness" for us as ends of life. It then became each individual's duty to try to attain the ends that God proposed or willed for him.[67] Since duties and rights could not be separated, from each other, according to Burlamaqui, duties entailed rights and vice versa: "Right therefore and obligation are two correlative terms: one of these ideas necessarily supposes the other."[68] But according to Jefferson, rights that were part of man's inner nature or being, even though God created that nature or being, did not need to be rationally derived from considering the nature of man and God and God's will; they emerged as feelings from man's inner nature or being once God put them there.

Men endowed by God with active rights behaved and valued behavior diametrically opposed to certain teachings of Jesus. Nonviolent, passive endurance of the moral transgressions of others was a part of Jesus' instruction to the victims of such transgressions. Indeed, Jesus went beyond teaching mere passiveness. He instructed a victim of moral transgressions to do three things: to perform actions that would encourage a transgressor who had inflicted pain to inflict more physical pain; to perform actions that would encourage a transgressor who had attained part of a victim's property to seek more of his property; and to perform actions that would encourage a transgressor who forced a victim to perform labor to seek more of his labor. Jesus' specific instruction to this effect is in Matthew 5:39–41: "Resist not evil: but whosoever shall smite thee on thy right cheek, turn to him the other also. And if any man will sue thee at the law, and take away thy coat, let him have thy cloak also. And whosoever shall compel thee to go a mile, go with him twain."

This Christian ideal was not conducive to preventing or overthrowing would-be or actual despots or tyrants, however, and possessors of active rights would not behave this way. If anyone transgressed against their "Life," "Liberty," or "Pursuit of Happiness," they would resist these moral transgressions in defense of their rights and with violence if necessary. Such resistance was encouraged in the Declaration: "But when a Long Train of Abuses and Usurpations . . . evinces a Design to reduce them [the people] under absolute Despotism, it is their Right, it is their Duty, to throw off such a Government, and to provide new Guards for their future Security."[69]

The idea that the people had a "Right" and "Duty" to resist and oppose those who transgressed against them was very Lockean. In the *Second Treatise* Locke said of the state of nature that "all Men may be restrained from invading other's Rights, and from doing hurt to one another" if individuals themselves would punish those who transgressed the "Law of Nature." The term "may" implies a right to do this and, Locke added, punishment was a necessity to "restrain offenders," thereby making individual resistance to and punishment of violators of rights not only a right but a duty. After a government was formed, this idea of punishment extended to any magistrate who exceeded his authority under the law or transgressed it to "another's harm." In such instances, according to Locke, "a Magistrate" was "acting without Authority" and therefore could be "opposed, as any other Man," since he "by force invade[d] the Right of another."[70] Jefferson believed that those who opposed or resisted violators of rights manifested their humanity. In the Declaration he spoke of "opposing with manly Firmness" the king's "Invasions on the Rights of the People."[71] This aspect of human nature, as found in Jeffersonian thought, gave rise to resistance against those who violated rights, which Daniel Boorstin described as the "largely unreflective answer of healthy men to the threat of tyranny."[72] There is no doubt, however, that both Locke and Jefferson were diametrically opposed to Jesus' teaching of "resist not evil." Both encouraged resistance to evil, which became an ideal of how man should behave, according to the concept of man contained in the theology of the Declaration of Independence.

The Pursuit of Happiness

Having explained why Jefferson eliminated property from the *Second Treatise*'s trinity of rights when he drafted the Declaration, I turn to the question of where he got the ideas on the "Pursuit of Happiness" that he specified there as an unalienable right. Among the authors he read before 1776 who dealt with this subject were John Locke, Lord Bolingbroke, Francis Hutcheson, David Hume, Lord Kames, William Blackstone, Jean-Jacques Burlamaqui, Thomas Hobbes, and Cesare

Beccaria.[73] Of these, the one who seems to have had the greatest impact on Jefferson's ideas was Locke, who not only used the exact phrase "pursuit of happiness" but also discussed at length what he meant by it. It was not in the *Second Treatise,* however, that Locke discussed "the pursuit of happiness." It was in *An Essay concerning Human Understanding.*

In book 2, chapter 20, "Of Modes of Pleasure and Pain," Locke used "Good and Evil" not merely to describe moral relationships or actions but, rather, in a hedonistic way to describe anything that causes "Pleasure or Pain": "That we call *Good*" is that "which *is apt to cause or increase Pleasure, or diminish Pain in us.* And on the contrary, we name that *Evil,* which *is apt to produce or increase any Pain, or diminish any Pleasure in us.*" Whatever causes pleasure and pain gives rise to passions, with love and hate being principal among them. We love what gives us pleasure and hate what gives us pain. A man "*loves* Grapes," wrote Locke, because "the taste of Grapes delights him." On the other hand, "the Thought of the Pain, which any thing present or absent is apt to produce in us, is what we call *Hatred.*" Yet an object that once caused pleasure and was therefore an object of love, could, with a change of circumstance, cause pain and become an object of hatred. For example, a man would "*love* grapes no longer" and even come to hate them if "an alteration of Health or Constitution destroy the delight of their Taste."[74] Locke showed in this way that human pleasure and pain are phenomenal or short-lived feelings, since the conditions that determine which objects give pleasure or pain, and are therefore loved or hated, are subject to change.

In book 2, chapter 21, "Of Power," Locke defined happiness and misery in terms of pleasure and pain enjoyed or suffered by body and mind. His definition included maximal and minimal happiness along with the good and evil causes of happiness and misery:

> *Happiness* then in its full extent is the utmost Pleasure we are capable of, and *Misery* the utmost Pain: And the lowest degree of what can be called *Happiness,* is so much ease from all Pain, and so much present Pleasure, as without which any one cannot be content. Now because Pleasure and Pain are produced in us, by the operation of certain Objects, either on our Minds or our Bodies; and in different degrees: therefore what has an aptness to produce Pleasure in us, is what we call *Good,* and what is apt to produce Pain in us, we call *Evil,* for no other reason, but for its aptness to produce Pleasure and Pain in us, wherein consists our *Happiness* and *Misery.*[75]

Locke believed that "all Men desire Happiness"; it was the "great end" of every human being. Therefore, men were devoted to the "pursuit of happiness."[76]

Locke saw an element of determinism in this pursuit, however, deriving from his concept of will. He defined will as the *"Power* which the mind has . . . to prefer the motion of any part of the body to its rest, and *vice versa* in any particular instance." This preference or will was a motivating force: it motivated action that was in accord with the will or actualized the will's preferences. Locke went on to distinguish between the will and *"Volition or Willing,"* which he defined as "the actual exercise of that power [will], by directing any particular action, or its forbearance." The will's preference of an act or its forbearance implies Locke's conclusion that the will was not free, not an indifferent faculty that could make its own determinations or choose its preferences. Rather, those preferences were determined by something separate from the will, something Locke called "uneasiness." The nature of uneasiness, which was a variety of pain, and its impact on the will he described by stating: "This is that which successively determines the *Will,* and sets us upon those Actions, we perform. This *Uneasiness* we may call, as it is, *Desire;* which is an *uneasiness* of the Mind for want of some absent good. All pain of the body of what sort soever, and disquiet of the mind, is *uneasiness:* And with this is always join'd Desire, equal to the pain or *uneasiness* felt." Uneasiness caused the will to prefer acts that would lead to happiness by ridding an individual of a particular uneasiness, whether they be acts for the alleviation of physical pain or for the acquisition of "some absent good." Locke expressed this idea when he pointed out that "the present *uneasiness* . . . does naturally determine the will, in order to that happiness which all aim at in our actions."[77]

This concept of the will as an unfree, determined faculty would seemingly leave man with no freedom or liberty. But Locke believed that liberty was a faculty separate from will or volition. It was *"not an* Idea *belonging to Volition,* or preferring"; rather, liberty belonged "to the Person having the Power of doing, or forbearing to do, according as the Mind shall chuse or direct." With respect to the movement of an individual's hand, Locke believed, for example, that a man had liberty as long as he had the power to move or not move his hand. If no external impediment or bodily incapacity prevented this power over the hand, liberty, as respects its movement, was a reality.[78] It was the will or volition, however, that directed the power of liberty; the preferences of the will and volition determined whether that power to move the hand or keep it still would be exercised. In stating the relationship of the will and volition to liberty, Locke said that volition, 'tis plain, is an Act of the Mind knowingly exerting that Dominion it takes it self to have over any part of the Man, by employing it in, or withholding it from any particular Action. And what is the *Will*, but the Faculty to do this? And is that Faculty any thing more in effect, than a Power, the power of the Mind to determine its thought, to the producing, continuing, or stopping any Action, as far as it depends on us? . . . *Will* then is nothing but such a power. *Liberty*, on the other side, is the power a Man has to do or forbear doing any particular Action, according as its doing or forbearance has the actual preference in the Mind, which is the same thing as to say, according as he himself *wills* it.[79]

Now it can be seen that when Jefferson wrote to Isaac Tiffany, "Liberty is 'unobstructed action according to our will,'" he was using the terms *liberty, will,* and *obstruction* the way Locke used them in discussing the "pursuit of happiness." Since Jefferson read *Human Understanding* before he wrote the Declaration, he probably formulated his own views on the third unalienable right stated there at that time. Jefferson's use of "Pursuit of Happiness" was basically Lockean because "Happiness," or that "which we all aim at" in actions determined by the will, was elusive in Locke's analysis. This elusiveness was largely due to what Locke described as multiple uneasinesses in man. The determination of the will in regard to a present action in the context of these manifold uneasinesses was, according to Locke, made by one uneasiness. The degree of intensity placed present uneasinesses in hierarchical order, the one with the greatest intensity having the greatest and most immediate impact on the will and the action it preferred. Thus, the most intense uneasiness was what determined the present action of an individual, an action intended to satisfy the most intense uneasiness among those "which are present to us." Once satisfaction of that intense uneasiness was attained through action, another uneasiness would "be ready at hand to give the *will* its next determination." A succession of determinations of the will was thereby made by multiple uneasinesses.[80]

Locke did not believe anyone would ever be free from multiple uneasinesses in this world, given "the multitude of wants, and desires, we are beset with in this imperfect State." Thus, it was impossible to rid one's self completely of the pain caused by uneasiness, even though one acted to attain this end. This impossibility no doubt had much to do with Locke's choice of the word "pursuit": an individual could pursue happiness but never quite attain as much of it as he would like because some uneasiness would always be gnawing at him and prevent him from attaining complete happiness. In addition it was not only multiple uneasinesses that contributed to the elusive nature of happiness but also the changing circumstances that altered objects of pleasure and love to those of pain and hate. Because of changing circumstances, what gave people happiness and what they wanted to make them happy were in a state of flux, causing them to be in a constant outreach for different objects or goods in their "pursuit of Happiness."[81]

The elusive aspect of Lockean happiness was not taken into consideration in George Mason's Virginia Declaration of Rights, a document Jefferson was no doubt familiar with in 1776; some think it influenced him when he wrote the Declaration (see chapter 3). Mason listed "pursuing and obtaining happiness" among his "inherent natural rights."[82] The right of "obtaining happiness," however, was inconsistent with Locke's idea of the elusive nature of happiness. There were so many contingencies involved in obtaining happiness, according to Locke, that no man could realistically claim a right to obtain it; he could only claim a right to pursue it. Therefore when Jefferson specified the "Pursuit of Happiness"—not obtaining it—as a right in the Declaration, he was more Lockean than Mason had been. Indeed, the fact that he did not include "obtaining happiness" as a right indicates that he was not influenced by Mason's Virginia Declaration of Rights when drafting the Declaration of Independence.

Arthur M. Schlesinger argues that Jefferson must have meant obtaining happiness, not its mere pursuit. To support his view, he cites the language following "the Pursuit of Happiness" in the Declaration, which states that governments by consent of the people are "to effect their Safety and Happiness."[83] What he fails to mention is the preceding qualification that such government is chosen by the people "as to them shall seem most likely to effect their Safety and Happiness."[84] The tentativeness of the words "most likely" in relation to effecting happiness is not consistent with the right of obtaining happiness but *is* consistent with the elusive nature of happiness put forth by Locke and Jefferson via the word "pursuit."

Jefferson also shared Locke's belief that the efforts of individuals to satisfy an immediate "uneasiness" prevented them from attaining maximal happiness. "Pursuing trifles" or frivolous immediate pleasures, Locke said, often dominated the will and caused persons to neglect some greater "remote Good" or happiness that might be enjoyed in the future. One remote good often neglected was the "State of Bliss" or salvation after death, which could be attained by observing moral norms. According to Locke, however, men could overcome the domination of immediate "trifles," and he prescribed a method for doing so. An individual could alter his will by first suspending it and then, while it was suspended, discover and cultivate a desire for a remote good that would lead to greater happiness than the pursuit of trifles. The absence of that greater or remote good would give rise to a new uneasiness in the mind, which would determine the will to prefer new actions conducive to attaining the greater remote good. Every individual, Locke said of this method, "may suspend the act of his choice from being determined for or against the thing proposed." During such a suspension, "since the *will* supposes knowledge to guide its choice," an individual would have time to scrutinize "each successive desire" with reason in order to determine where each desire might lead, relative to his greatest long-term happiness if he acted on it. Then he could judge with reason in favor of a greater remote good over some immediate good or trifle.[85] As Locke summarized this view:

> The forbearance of a too hasty compliance with our desires, the moderation and restraint of our Passions, so that our Understandings may be free to examine, and reason unbiased give its judgement, being that, whereon a right direction of our conduct to true Happiness depends; 'tis in this we should employ our chief care and endeavours. In this we should take pains to suit the relish of our Minds to the true intrinsick good or ill, that is in things; and not permit an allow'd or supposed possible great and weighty good to slip out of thoughts, without leaving any relish, any desire of it self there, till, by a due consideration of its true worth, we have formed appetites in our Minds suitable to it, and made our selves uneasie in the want of it, or in the fear of losing it.[86]

Although the will was a determined faculty, Locke made clear here that human reason and knowledge born of education could shape the will. With education and contemplative reason an individual could perceive a good not perceived previously as a source of greater long-term happiness; in addition, education with reason could motivate his will to act upon such a good that it might not have been previously motivated to act upon.

Evidence that Jefferson was aware of and subscribed to Locke's rationally determined hedonistic approach to maximizing happiness before writing the Declaration is seen in a 1770 letter to John Page. Describing a friend who was "the happiest man in the universe," Jefferson mentioned that he lived "in a very small house, with a table" and "half a dozen chairs," manifesting "an utter neglect of the costly apparatus of Life." Yet the man was not an ascetic; he was committed to pleasure and had the ability to attain it because "every incident in life he so takes as to render it a source of pleasure." The principal object of the friend's pleasure, however, was his child; he "speaks, thinks, and dreams of nothing but his young son."[87] The thrust of Jefferson's comments was that although his friend could have lived in better material surroundings, he had made a rational decision to forgo some immediate materialistic or frivolous pleasures in favor of lavishing attention on a greater long-term good or pleasure: the well-being and future of his child. Clearly, Jefferson admired a man who had rationally determined what would give him the greatest happiness in life and lived according that determination.

A similar expression of Jefferson's commitment to the Lockean pursuit of maximal happiness is found in *Notes on the State of Virginia,* where he commented on the curriculum for children in the public education system he proposed in 1779:

> The first stage of this education . . . wherein the great mass of the people will receive their instruction, the principal foundations of future order will be laid here. . . . Their memories may here be stored with the most useful facts from Grecian, Roman, European and American history. The first elements of morality too may be instilled into their minds; such as, when further developed as their judgements advance in strength, may teach them how to work out their own greatest happiness, by shewing that it does not depend on the condition of life in which chance has placed them, but is always the result of a good conscience, good health, occupation, and freedom in all just pursuits.[88]

Now, in saying that the "first elements of morality" acquired in the early stage of education would assist individuals later when they were "further developed" by the "advance in strength" of their judgments, Jefferson seemed to be saying that morality was derived from reason—a view contradictory to his ideas on the moral sense in man. But in fact the thoughts Jefferson expressed here were Kamesean and not at all opposed to the moral-sense basis of morality.

The Scottish jurist was of the opinion that if an individual had the capacity for rational judgment and used it in connection with his self-interest born of "self love," which seeks happiness independent of moral considerations or motivation, that capacity would help an individual to be moral. This rational capacity would not in any way increase the capacity of the moral sense, but it would help persons regulate their selfish desires and passions in a way that would best help them attain happiness. Rational capacity could provide restraint and direction for the selfish interests born of self-love in the pursuit of happiness. According to Kames's ideas on morality, this capacity gave the moral sense a context in which it could function effectively.[89] If a man had rational control over himself and his passions in his selfish pursuit of happiness, he would have more capacity to abide by the dictates and restraints of the moral sense. Hence, when Jefferson stated that morality becomes "further developed" as rational "judgements advance in strength," he was promulgating the Kamesean idea that morality, born of the moral sense, becomes more effective with increasing rational capacity. Kames's application of rational judgment to the attainment of happiness born of self-love was strikingly similar to the way Locke used it in "Of Power" as respects men pursuing their own pleasure or happiness. Therefore, "judgement," as Jefferson used the word in the foregoing statement, could be either a Kamesean or a Lockean term.

Manifest in this passage from *Notes* is what Charles Maurice Wiltse described as Jefferson's belief that a hedonistic "pursuit of happiness" was not inconsistent with an "innate moral sense."[90] This belief would seem to be due to Kames's reconciliation of hedonism and the moral sense in his system of morality (see chapter 4). Despite its Kamesean flavor, however, the passage also has an element of the Lockean view of long-term or remote good. It demonstrates a conviction on Jefferson's part that individuals, by using their matured and strengthened rational judgment along with the moral sense or "conscience," would be able "to work out their own *greatest* happiness" (emphasis added), by which he meant happiness born of attaining long-term goods. This is evidenced by his allusion to the "remote goods" that would be chosen as a result of rational "judgements" made by an individual in pursuit of his long-term or "greatest happiness." The specific "remote goods" mentioned by Jefferson—"good conscience, good health, occupation, and freedom in all just pursuits"—implied that through the use of reason individuals would restrain their desires and passions for "trifles" or frivolous immediate goods and, as Locke said, would make reasoned "judgements" that the aforementioned "remote goods" were more conducive to their greatest happiness than "trifles." They would then sacrifice or restrain the latter in favor of the former.

I would point out that by defining freedom as "freedom in all just pursuits" in *Notes*, Jefferson was emphasizing that freedom was license to do not anything at all in order to attain one's "greatest happiness" but only what was consistent with the moral sense of justice. This approach to freedom was identical to his idea that "Liberty" had to be bound by moral constraints, which made it "rightful Liberty," as he wrote to Isaac Tiffany. This emphasis on freedom in the context of morality in the pursuit of greatest happiness demonstrates that morality was an essential ingredient in Jefferson's idea of happiness. Morality or moral behavior fulfilled the moral nature of man, and Jefferson maintained that a man could be happy only if he lived according to that nature. Therefore, it was prudent to be moral. Jefferson expressed this idea when he said, "And if the Wise be the happy man, as these sages say, he must be virtuous too; for, without virtue, happiness cannot be."[91] Further, Jefferson maintained that right vocation or "occupation," mentioned in the passage from *Notes* as a long-term good, enabled men to be both virtuous and happy, and this also demonstrates his concern for morality as a vital element in attaining happiness. Hence his advocacy of husbandry as an "occupation": he believed that Americans would "be more virtuous, more free, and more happy, employed in agriculture, than as carriers or manufacturers."[92] Jefferson also maintained that morality was conducive to general happiness in that if most persons were moral in their behavior toward others, few would suffer the miseries of having their natural rights transgressed, and most would thereby be able to enjoy happiness derived from exercising those rights unimpeded by the moral transgressions of others. "All the tranquillity, the happiness and security of mankind," stated Jefferson on this subject, "rest on justice or the obligation to respect the rights of others."[93]

Jefferson's confidence in the capacity of each individual's reason or rational judgments, which he stated in *Notes* would "teach" people "how to work out *their own* greatest happiness" (emphasis added), stressed an individualistic approach to happiness. Implicit here is the idea that each person must use reason to find his or her own unique path to happiness. This idea is consistent with Locke's belief that individuals must travel different paths to find happiness because they have different tastes. As Locke stated:

> For as pleasant Tastes depend not on the things themselves, but their agreeableness to this or that particular Palate, wherein there is great variety: So the greatest Happiness consists, in the having those things, which produce the greatest Pleasure; and in the absence of those, which cause any disturbance, any pain. Now these, to different Men, are very different things . . . this, I think, may serve to shew us the Reason, why, though all Man's desires tend to Happiness, they are not moved by the same Object. Men may chuse different things, and yet all chuse right, supposing them only like a company of poor Insects, whereof some are Bees, delighted with Flowers, and their sweetness; others, Beetles, delighted with other kind of viands.[94]

Confidence in the individual's rational capacity to find his own unique way to happiness was a facet of Jefferson's optimistic view of human nature. This confidence, combined with his overall concept of man as a being to whom his heterodox "Nature's God" of natural theology had given a moral sense, a rational faculty, and unalienable rights, gave Jefferson an extraordinarily optimistic, even exalted, view of human nature that became part of the theology of the Declaration of Independence. It was this exalted concept of man, Jefferson maintained, that resulted in and justified a political system of minimal government with limited powers over the people and the right of the people, not kings or aristocrats or priests, to supply rational and moral guidance to that government. Indeed he asserted that this exalted view of human nature justified and resulted in a Lockean political structure in which the people would control and judge their government.

That these were in fact the ideas of man in relation to government held by Jefferson and the many others in the Continental Congress who approved the Declaration is specified in a letter he wrote to Judge William Johnson in 1823 about that Congress: "We believed . . . that man was a rational animal, endowed by nature with rights, and with an innate sense of justice; and that he could be restrained from wrong and protected in right, by moderate powers, confided to persons of his own choice, and held to their duties by dependence on his own will."[95] This view was in stark contrast to the European concept of human nature, which, as Jefferson perceived it, included an implicit depravity due to belief in the fall. According to that view, the people were incapable of supplying rational and moral direction to government; they were instead dependent upon powers temporal and spiritual apart from themselves to direct society. Jefferson found this concept of man antithetical to democracy and conducive to authoritarian political and religious structures, as he stated in his letter to Judge Johnson: "The doctrines of Europe were, that men in numerous associations cannot be restrained within the limits of order and justice, but by forces physical and moral, wielded over them by authorities independent of their will. Hence their organization of kings, hereditary nobles and priests."[96]

Such an organization was odious to Jefferson. Theoretically, the priests would supply the moral force necessary for civilization, and the kings and hereditary nobles the physical force, but in practice, according to Jefferson, this alliance of church and state was responsible for transgressions against the rights of man. It manifested itself in an unchecked caste system of priests and rulers who assisted each other in their transgressions of rights. As Jefferson put it, "The priest . . . is always in alliance with the despot, abetting his abuses in return for protection to his own."[97] The priests benefited in this alliance by enlisting the temporal power of government in support of their particular doctrines. With that power they could exert varying degrees of compulsion on the people to accept those doctrines. This or any sort of compulsion in religion, Jefferson believed, violated a fundamental human right, the right of "freedom of religion," which he regarded as "the most inalienable and sacred of all human rights."[98] Protection of this right, he believed, would uphold not only religious but political freedom.

7

Religious Freedom

The right of religious freedom was given to each individual by the deistic God of natural theology, in Jefferson's view. "Nature's God," who created the universe with law to govern it and then left it alone, did not intervene in the affairs of a people or a nation or the lives of individual human beings by choosing them or granting them grace over others. He left all peoples, nations, and individuals free to work out their own destiny, including their spiritual destiny or salvation. When it came to salvation, individuals did not need divine intervention or grace to attain that state because "Nature's God" gave them the capacity to earn it through moral actions. That capacity was born of the ability to know and abide by the moral laws of nature, which was itself born of the moral sense and reason given to each individual by "Nature's God." It was because individuals had God-given moral capacity that "Nature's God" gave them the freedom, as well as responsibility, to attain their own salvation without His intervention or grace. Further, having endowed each individual with the faculty of reason, "Nature's God," the God of reason, left individuals alone to find religious truth and God with that faculty.

Very often, however, men and their religions did not respect the right of religious freedom. They did not leave one another alone to attain their own salvation and find religious truth; in fact, they often persecuted one another. As a result, religious tyranny was often practiced by individuals, their religions, and their political institutions.

The root cause of religious tyranny and persecution, according to Jefferson, was theological exclusivism, manifested in the authoritarian truth claims of orthodox institutionalized religions and sects. These claims resulted in sectarian bigotry or intolerance, which gave rise to repression, oppression, and persecution. Each religion and sect claimed that its prophet or incarnation or scripture was the principal if not the only source of religious truth. Each maintained further that only its interpretation of its prophet or incarnation or scripture was true, thereby claiming a monopoly on religious truth and in effect, if not explicitly, denying the truth claims of all others. John Locke, in a statement from his *Letter concerning Toleration* that Jefferson paraphrased in 1776, summed up the effect of theological exclusivism on each church: "For every church is orthodox to itself; to others, erroneous or heretical. Whatsoever any church believes, it believes to be true; and the contrary thereunto it pronounces to be error."[1]

Since each sect or sectarian religion denied all truth claims but its own, its claims were an offense, even an insult, to all others. This bred bitterness, hatred, and enmity that all too often led to war. Moreover, convinced of their own truth and equally convinced that other religions and sects were erroneous, many felt justified in using force to compel those with other religious views to accept theirs. Those who had this sectarian perspective did not consider the use of force in religion evil. On the contrary they considered it charitable; since the doctrines of other sects and religions were false, those who followed them would never enjoy the bliss of heaven after death unless they were converted. The use of force in religion demonstrated love for those with erroneous beliefs and an earnest desire to put them on the one true religious path leading to salvation so that they would not roast in hell—even if this meant, as it sometimes did, that they were roasted or tortured here on earth.

The third Earl of Shaftesbury mentioned this sectarian disposition of religion in his *Characteristics of Men, Manners, Opinions, Times.* Jefferson read this work in late 1776 and paraphrased Shaftesbury by stating that contemporary religion, instead of practicing toleration toward different and conflicting religious ideas, as the Greeks had, adopted "a new sort of policy, which considers the future lives & happiness of men rather than the present," a policy that "has taught [us] to distress one another."[2] John Locke attacked this policy of Christianity in *A Letter concerning Toleration,* which Jefferson read carefully, as is evidenced by his 1776 notes on that work. Jefferson's paraphrase of Locke's attack queried, "Why persecute for diffce. in religs. opinion?" and answered sarcastically, "for love to the person."[3] Locke, however, did not believe that such persecution was born of love. He maintained that it was caused by a desire to increase the followers of a particular religion or sect, because those who persecuted were not concerned with the moral behavior of their victims. Locke argued that if one tries "to convert those that are erroneous unto the faith, by forcing them to profess things that they do not believe" and yet allows them to commit moral transgressions that "the Gospel does not permit," then that person "is desirous to have a numerous assembly joined in the same profession with himself."[4] Jefferson paraphrased a similar Lockean passage:

> When I see them persecute their nearest connection & acquaintance for gross vices, I shall believe it may proceed from love. till they do this, I appeal to their own consciences if they will examine, why they do nt. . . . why not then level persecution at the crimes you fear will be introduced? burn or hang the adulterer, cheat &c. or exclude them from offices. strange should be so zealous against things which tend to produce immorality & yet so indulgent to the immorality when produced. these moral vices all men acknolege to be diametrically against Xty. [Christianity] & obstructive of salvation of souls, but the fantastical points for which we generally persecute are often very questionable as we may be assured by the very different conclusions of people.[5]

Jefferson abhorred the monopolistic truth claims of sectarian Christianity and their resultant intolerance and tyrannical persecution. His early reading of thinkers such as Bolingbroke and Locke had much to do with this abhorrence, as did his general reading of history. His knowledge of historical events—the Crusades, the Inquisition, the French wars of religion, and the Thirty Years' War—during which millions were slaughtered in the name of Christianity and God no doubt prompted his response when asked what he thought of a particular sectarian creed: "You ask my opinion on the items of doctrine in your catechism. I have never permitted myself to meditate a specified creed. These formulas have been the bane and ruin of the Christian church, its own fatal invention, which, through so many ages, made of Christendom a slaughter-house, and at this day divides it into castes of inextinguishable hatred to one another."[6] Even though Jefferson made this statement in 1822, the words "I have never" in reference to accepting or contemplating accepting any specific creed, indicate his rejection of the sectarian approach to religion early in life.

It was to combat that approach and to protect the right of religious freedom that Jefferson wrote the Virginia Statute for Religious Freedom soon after the signing of the Declaration of Independence. Protection provided by that statute extended to all persons regardless of their religious, irreligious, or nonreligious opinions, and to all religions regardless of the content of their beliefs. Many of Jefferson's ideas on religious freedom are contained in the statute and in papers that document his research for and participation in the legislative process that led to its passage.

Legal Persecution and Law Reform

Jefferson objected to all forms of religious persecution. Governmental power taking sides in the conflicting truth claims of different religions and sects by aiding one through the persecution of others via the instrumentation of its laws was especially offensive to him, as it was to Locke. In 1776, just after the signing of the Declaration of Independence, the governmental power of the state of Virginia was a great offense to Jefferson as a result of its persecutory laws. At that time Virginia was replete with law that enforced the doctrine of the Anglican Church, which was the established or government-supported church in that state. There were three sources of that law: the common law of England, statutes made by Parliament, and statutes made by the Virginia legislature. Laws pertaining to religion from all three sources were extraordinarily repressive and formed a legal basis for intolerance and persecution of all dissenters from the Anglican Church, even though most of them were not strictly enforced.

One exception was a law that forced dissenters to contribute to the financial support of the Anglican clergy. Dissenters perceived this law, wrote Jefferson, as "unrighteous compulsion to maintain teachers of what they deemed religious errors."[7] By mid-1776, however, dissenters who had migrated to Virginia in the preceding decades had replaced Anglicans as the majority there.[8] Immediately after the signing of the Declaration, this dissenting majority clamored for relief from their legal obligation to support Anglicanism financially. As a result, Jefferson drafted resolutions not only to repeal that law but to disestablish the Anglican Church and nullify all law pertaining to its doctrinal support—thereby providing a foundation for religious freedom in Virginia. Although he did this to accommodate the majority, Jefferson had a personal interest in this legislation. If the religious laws of Virginia were ever enforced, he would suffer as a result of his own dissenting religious views, which were heterodox and heretical, according to those laws.

His arguments to the Virginia assembly in favor of his resolutions indicate his personal concern over the legal implications of his "heresy." He mentioned in his 1776 outline of those arguments that "Mos[t] men imag[i]ne [that] persec[utio]n [is] unkn[ow]n t[o] our l[and]s," where the "leg[e]l sta[tus of] Relig[io]n [is] little und[er]st[oo]d." In order to enlighten the assembly on the persecution prescribed by law in Virginia, he described some of the parliamentary religious statutes that were applicable there. Among them was one that called for punishment of recusancy, or failure to worship in the Anglican Church and submit to its authority. Others called for prison terms for individuals who did not subscribe to the Thirty-Nine Articles, the Athanasian Creed, and commination. A specific statute against heresy made heretics of Arians, since the church and state had adopted the trinitarian Athanasian creed, whereas Arians believed in the unity of God.[9] Jefferson mentioned that Arians had been "burnt" under that statute, which must have given him cause for personal concern, since he too believed in the unity of God and rejected the Trinity.[10]

That he was in fact concerned is evidenced by his research on heresy in relation to the Trinity and the unity of God. His notes refer to and quote Daniel Waterland's theological tracts; William Chillingsworth's *Religion of the Protestants, a Safe Way to Salvation;* the *Vita Constantini* and *Historia Ecclesiastica* of Eusebius, Bishop of Caesarea in Palestine; Conyers Middleton's *Miscellaneous Works;* the historical works of Joannes Zonaras, whom he cited from a French translation by Louis Cousin; and Thomas Broughton's *Dictionary of All Religions.*[11] He used the materials gathered in his research as arguments to defend his belief in the unity of God against the charge of heresy. Those materials and arguments had little or nothing to do with the irrationality of the concept that three are one and one is three, as he argued on other occasions.[12] Rather, they challenged the authority used by law to determine heresy. Jefferson described that authority as statements made by "the canonical scriptures, or by one of the four first general councils, or by other council having for the grounds of their declaration the express and plain words of the scriptures."[13]

He began his arguments in his 1776 research notes on heresy by defining a heretic as "an impugner of fundamentals."[14] He then dismissively left to others the task of determining whether or not the Trinity was clearly mentioned in the scriptures and thereby a "fundamental." His dismissiveness seemed an invitation on the part of a trial lawyer who, knowledgeable of scripture, knew that such a determination would be difficult to make and relished the opportunity to ridicule any attempts to make it during a trial with his own witnesses and cross examination. Next, he argued that the earliest Christians did not profess or teach the Trinity. The absence of trinitarian theology among them implied that the unity of God rather than the Trinity was fundamental to Christianity. He then focused on the authority of councils as a principal legal criterion for determining heresy, especially the Council of Nicea, held in the first half of the fourth century during Constantine's regime. There the dispute between trinitarian and Arian unitarian theologians was settled by vote in favor of the Trinity, which thereby became doctrine in orthodox Christianity.[15] Jefferson concluded that the determinations of councils were not to be relied upon as sources of religious fundamentals, since the Council of Antioch, for example, affirmed that the Son was *not* of one substance with the Father, in diametric opposition to the conclusions of the Council of Nicea.[16] In short, since there was little or no agreement among legally recognized authorities on the fundamentals of doctrine, it was impossible to identify a heretic. Jefferson's research arguments in effect put on trial the authorities who judged heresy and the Trinity as a fundamental doctrine in orthodox Christianity. As he stated those arguments:

> A heretic is an impugner of fundamentals. what are fundamentals? the protestants will say those doctrines which are clearly & precisely delivered in the holy scriptures. Dr. Waterland would say the Trinity. but how far this character [of being clearly delivered?] will suit the doctrine of the Trinity I leave others to determine. it is no where expressly declared by any of the earliest fathers, & was never affirmed or taught by the church before the council of Nice [Chillingw. Pref. 18.33.] Irenaeus says "who are the clean? those who go on firmly, believing in the father & in the son." the fundamental doctrine or the firmness of the Xn. faith in this early age then was to believe in the *father* & *son*.—Constantine wrote to Arius & Alexr. treating the question "as vain foolish & impertinent as a dispute of words without sense which none could explane nor any comprehend &c." this Ire is commended by Eusebius [Vit. Constant. 1b.2.c. 64 &c.] and Socrates [Hist. Eccles. 1.1.c.7.] as excellent admirable & full of wisdom. 2.Middleton.115. remarks on the story of St. John & [. . . .] . . . the second council meant by Zonaras was that of Constantinople ann 381. D hist. Prim. Xty. pref. XXXVIII. 2d. app. to pref. 49. the Council of Antioch [ann] expressly affirmed of our saviour . . . that he was not Consubstantial to the father. the Council of Nice affirmed the direct contrary. D hist. Prim. Xty. Pref. CXXV.[17]

That Jefferson did not present these research arguments to the Virginia assembly is evidenced by his notes on the arguments he did make to that legislative body. Perhaps he thought they would cause the assembly to suspect him of heretical beliefs. He did, however, include a general argument against the legal punishment of heresy in a way calculated to appeal to the orthodox of Virginia. After pointing out that the "Spir[i]t of [the] times [was] in fav[o]r. of [the] r[igh]ts of Consc[ien]ce" or freedom of belief, he continued: "Let gentlemen who happen [to be] of [the] Religion of [the] state make [a] case of other [religion] than their own [i. e., assume that some other religion than theirs is the established one]. What would be their Sensations [in such a case] if [there were] no Security [for] civil rights but [the] Moderation of [the spirit of the] times. [They] would be uneasy till [such were] fixed on [a] legal basis. Rights of Conscience [are] much more tender [even than our civil rights]."[18] In effect, what Jefferson suggested here was that Anglicans should put themselves in his uneasy position as a heretic under the law.

His arguments were of no avail, for his resolutions were not passed. The assembly did pass a measure that rectified the injustice of forcing those in dissenting sects to contribute financially to the Anglican Church; instead, it made the financial support of every religion or sect compulsory. It also repealed parliamentary laws that supported Anglican doctrine, but it left intact the establishment of the Anglican church as well as the Virginia statutes and common law that supported its doctrines.[19] It was in an effort to disestablish Anglicanism, repeal *all* law that supported it, and to make financial support of religion voluntary that Jefferson drafted the Virginia Statute for Religious Freedom in 1777.[20]

In his *Notes on the State of Virginia,* Jefferson described the condition of Virginia's religious law between the passage of the foregoing partial measure and the passage of the Statute for Religious Freedom. As his 1776 arguments to the assembly indicated a personal interest in his legislative efforts, so did the *Notes* account of the legal penalties of the religious laws.[21] For example, under Virginia common law, heresy was a capital offense. Further, an assembly statute "made it penal in parents to refuse to have their children baptised" and provided harsh penalties, including death, for Quakers who persisted in coming to Virginia. According to another statute, a person raised as a Christian who denied the existence of God or the Trinity or believed in multiple gods, or denied "the Christian religion to be true, or the scriptures to be of divine authority" was subject to an "incapacity to hold any office" on the first offense and a "disability to sue, to take any gift or legacy, to be guardian, executor, or administrator" as well as "three years' imprisonment, without bail" on the second offense. Jefferson pointed out that a father's right "to the custody of his own children" was "founded in law on his right of guardianship," and with this right removed as a result of violating the law he cited, a father's children could "be severed from him, and put by the authority of a court into more orthodox hands." Certainly the enforcement of this law in Jefferson's case would have deprived him of his children, and this must have made him uneasy. Finally, he pointed to the irony that men who condoned such laws had pledged their "Lives" and "Fortunes" for political freedom in the Declaration of Independence when he said, "This is a summary view of that religious slavery, under which a people have been willing to remain, who have lavished their lives and fortunes for the establishment of their civil freedom."[22]

Considering the status of religious law in Virginia, Jefferson's belief that alliances between church and state resulted in tyrannical rights violations (see chapter 6) is not surprising. Locke, it would seem, contributed to this belief. His *Letter concerning Toleration* stated that the church often sought government support for its aspirations to establish tyranny and reciprocated by supporting the tyrannical aspirations of those who had political power. Locke emphasized the clergy's role in this arrangement: "For who does not see that these good men are indeed more ministers of the government than ministers of the Gospel, and that by flattering the ambition and favouring the dominion of princes and men in authority, they endeavour with all their might to promote that tyranny in commonwealth which otherwise they should not be able to establish in the church? This is the unhappy agreement that we see between the church and state."[23]

The establishment of tyranny or help in its establishment was, of course, a great offense, according to Locke in his *Second Treatise*. Since an alliance between church and state augmented tyranny, he suggested in *A Letter concerning Toleration* that these institutions be separated. Locke saw this separation as logical because church and state had separate interests and functions. The church's interest was sacred, involving "the salvation of souls."[24] Its function was to provide a system of beliefs or faith and a form of worship conducive to salvation. Locke's definition of church, which Jefferson paraphrased in 1776, depicts this function and reveals Locke's latitudinarian disposition[25] toward religion:

> No man by nature is bound unto any particular church or sect, but every one joins himself voluntarily to that society in which he believes he has found that profession and worship which is truly acceptable to God. The hope of salvation, as it was the only cause of his entrance into that communion, so it can be the only reason of his stay there. For if afterwards he discover anything either erroneous in the doctrine or incongruous in the worship of that society to which he has joined himself, why should it not be as free for him to go out as it was to enter? No member of a religious society can be tied with any other bonds but what proceed from the certain expectation of eternal life. A church, then, is a society of members voluntarily uniting to this end.[26]

The interest of the state, on the other hand, was secular, having to do with the "life, liberty, health, and indolency of body; and the possession of outward things, such as money, lands, houses, furniture, and the like." The state or magistrate's function was "to secure unto all the people in general, and to every one of his subjects in particular, the just possession of these things belonging to this life."[27]

Locke maintained that force was necessary for the magistrate to perform his function, which included "the punishment of those that violated any other man's rights." Force, however, was alien to the performance of a church's function, according to Locke. This is evidenced by his emphasis on voluntary participation in the beliefs and worship of a church or religion in his definition of a church quoted above. Locke believed that force used to compel such participation was inappropriate because "True religion consists in the *inward* and full persuasion of the mind" as respects profession of beliefs and what we are "fully satisfied *in* our mind . . . is well pleasing unto God" as respects worship (emphasis added). He maintained that if men were forced to profess outwardly what they were not persuaded *in* their minds was true, and to worship in a form they deemed unacceptable to God, they were adding to their "other sins those also of hypocrisy," which precluded the attainment of salvation. Only faith would lead to salvation, not hypocrisy, or as Locke put it, "Faith only, and inward sincerity, are the things that procure acceptance with God." Jefferson's agreement that a hypocritical profession of faith and practice of worship were ineffectual in attaining salvation is found in his 1776 notes on religion, where he paraphrased this statement from Locke: "I may grow rich by an art that I take not delight in, I may be cured of some disease by remedies that I have not faith in; but I cannot be saved by a religion that I distrust, and by a worship that I abhor."[28]

Locke was also of the opinion that in matters of religion, individuals could not help but believe *in* their minds what conformed to the evidence as they perceived that evidence with their own reason. Therefore he stated, "Only light [reason] and evidence can work a change in men's opinions." Force, Locke maintained, was incapable of changing religious views. This is seen in his statement that "no man can, if he would, conform his faith to the dictates of another. . . . Confiscation of estate, imprisonment, torments, nothing of that nature can have any such efficacy as to make men change the *inward* judgement that they have framed of things" (emphasis added).[29]

Compulsion in religion was not only an ineffective way to change persons' minds and help them attain salvation; it was also a corrupting influence, according to Locke. It corrupted individuals by making them hypocritically profess what they did not inwardly believe. It corrupted true religion or the true church, which was "not instituted" for "the exercising of compulsive force," by making men profess what it deemed to be truth but which they did not believe. Finally, it corrupted government. When government used force in religion, it involved itself in a realm where it did not belong, since government "relates only to men's civil interests," which are "confined to the care of the things of this world" and have "nothing to do with the world to come."[30] Therefore, preventing state power from being used as compulsion in religion benefited not only religious freedom but also the integrity of the individual, the integrity of the church, and the integrity of the state.

Jefferson utilized these ideas contained in Locke's *Letter concerning Toleration* in his Virginia Statute for Religious Freedom and stressed there the *Letter*'s view that it was each individual's responsibility to find a true religion or way to salvation according to his own perception. Jefferson paraphrased the *Letter*'s statement on this responsibility, "The care . . . of every man's soul belongs unto himself," in his notes on religion made in 1776 prior to his legislative efforts on religious freedom.[31] Locke was convinced there was no alternative to this "care" on the part of the individual, given the unreliability of both magistrates and ecclesiastical authorities for this care. In his 1776 notes Jefferson paraphrased Locke's statement that the magistrate "may probably be as ignorant of the way [to salvation] as myself."[32] The church was similarly unreliable, according to Locke: "Who sees not how frequently the name of the church, which was venerable in the time of the apostles, has been made use of to throw dust in people's eyes, in following ages?" Although he was speaking here of the Roman Catholic Church, he maintained that unreliability and obscurantism extended to the doctrine and worship of Protestantism as well. He stated this when he said he was "doubtful concerning the doctrines of the Socinians" and "suspicious of the way of worship practiced by the . . . Lutherans."[33] Jefferson, consistent with these Lockean views, was critical not only of Catholicism's but also of Protestantism's errors and departure from the original teachings of Christianity, since he maintained that ideas common to both—that Jesus was God and scripture the revealed word of God—were imposture (see chapter 4).

Religious Freedom, Nature's God, and Reason

Jefferson's indebtedness to *A Letter concerning Toleration* for the ideas found in the Virginia Statute for Religious Freedom is seen throughout that statute. The preamble began by stating Locke's view that men's minds could not help but believe what was in accordance with the evidence born of their perceptions: "Well aware that the opinions and belief of men depend not on their own will, but follow involuntarily the evidence proposed to their minds."[34] The statute then went on to say that the mind was created free. This was not a contradiction to the mind's involuntary following of the evidence it perceived. Jefferson was merely emphasizing that external authoritarian compulsions and restraints could not alter the inner judgments of the mind on religious truth that were based on the evidence it perceived. Jefferson's language in the preamble to this effect was "Almighty God hath created the mind free, *and manifested his supreme will that free it shall remain by making it altogether insusceptible of restraint.*"[35] In other words, the mind was created free to make its own inner judgments on religious truth on the basis of the evidence it perceived, but it was not free to alienate those inner judgments in the sense of going against or altering them, even though force could make an individual hypocritically profess something different from what his mind inwardly judged to be true. This would seem to be the reason Jefferson described the right of religious freedom as an "inalienable" right, an interpretation in accord with Jefferson's use of "inalienable" in his rough draft of the Declaration (see chapter 6).[36] Consistent with this meaning of the inalienable right of religious freedom, Jefferson's preamble then recapitulated Locke's view that force and violence made men hypocritically profess views different from what they really believed in their minds. He did this by stating, "All attempts to influence it [the mind] by temporal punishments, or burthens, or by civil incapacitations, tend only to beget habits of hypocrisy and meanness."[37]

In the succeeding passage Jefferson stated that such force in religion was "a departure from the plan of the holy author of our religion, who being lord both of body and mind, yet chose not to propagate it by coercions on either, as was in his Almighty power to do, but to extend it by its influence on reason alone."[38] Garry Wills interprets the phrase "our religion" as a reference to Protestantism apart from not only Catholicism but also Anglicanism. Indeed, Wills seems to believe that Jefferson suffered from an anti-Catholic and anti-Anglican bias but was willing to aid certain Protestant denominations such as Presbyterian and Quaker.[39] But this does not seem to have been Jefferson's disposition toward religion when he drafted the Virginia Statute for Religious Freedom or the Declaration of Independence. His bias against institutionalized Christianity at that time extended to all Protestantism, especially Presbyterianism, as well as Catholicism and Anglicanism. This is evident in his criticism of the Presbyterians for being power-oriented. In his notes for arguments to the Virginia assembly in 1776, he specifically stated that Presbyterians did not want freedom of religion for all sects; they merely wanted toleration under the law of Virginia opened "just wide enough" for themselves.[40] The Presbyterians and their clergy were therefore alien to Jefferson's ideal of religious freedom for all as well as to his heretical heterodox theology, which denied the Trinity, the divinity of Jesus, the divine inspiration of the Christian scriptures, predestination, grace, and the fall of man. In addition, Presbyterians, like Catholics, subscribed to a catechism and were controlled doctrinally by a central authority (see chapter 1).[41] A minister of that denomination and his congregation were under that control, which was alien to the freedom of individual reason in religion championed by Jefferson.

In fact, most of the predominating Protestant denominations in America—or the world, for that matter—were under some doctrinal authority and thus no more free to express what their minds believed according to the evidence they perceived than were Catholics. Thus the "tyranny over the mind of man" that Jefferson decried in his letter to Benjamin Rush, and against which he swore an oath of hostility early in life (see chapter 5), was as much a part of Protestantism as of Catholicism. Jefferson's letter to Rush specifically referred to the tyranny of Episcopalianism and Congregationalism, and Congregationalism was a cousin of Presbyterianism in subscribing to a similar doctrinal authority.[42] Further, in his letter to Rush, Jefferson significantly stated he was opposed to "*every* form of tyranny over the mind of man" (emphasis added) and thus in effect condemned *all* institutionalized Christian denominations that claimed authority in matters of truth over the reason of man, Catholic or Protestant.[43] Jefferson thereby subscribed fully to Locke's contention in *A Letter concerning Toleration* that "ecclesiastical authority, whether it be administered by the hands of a single person or many, is everywhere the same."[44]

Therefore, when Jefferson wrote of the "holy author of *our religion*" (emphasis added) in the Virginia Statute for Religious Freedom, he was referring not to the Protestant religion or God, as Wills suggests, but to Bolingbroke's deistic God of natural theology and His natural religion discovered through reason. This interpretation is supported by the statement in Jefferson's statute that the "holy author of our religion" did not use His power to propagate the religion He authored but rather "chose" to "extend it by its influence on *reason alone"* (emphasis added). Certainly Jefferson's denial of the Trinity precluded the inspiration of reason by the Holy Spirit as God's method of disseminating His religion through reason. Therefore, it seems safe to conclude that by saying God used "reason alone" to extend the influence of His religion, Jefferson meant that the "holy author" referred to in his statute appealed to the reason of each individual as the authority in religion and let that reason decide what the "holy author's" religion was, based on the evidence perceived by that individual. The fact that Jefferson argued in favor of individual reason in religion in his 1776 notes—"b[u]t wh[at] m[an's] reas[o]n [can] step int[o the] j[u]d[g]m[en]t seat of yours?"[45]—supports this conclusion.

This God of the Virginia statute, who used not force but reason in religion, is consistent with the concept (mentioned in the Declaration) of a deistic God who would not interfere with the freedom or liberty He gave to each individual at the time of his creation (see chapter 6). In addition, the "reason alone" method of the Virginia statute's God to extend the influence of His religion excluded both the Protestant authority of scripture and the Catholic authority of tradition as means to extend that influence. There seems little doubt, therefore, that in his statute Jefferson was referring to the deistic "Nature's God" and the natural religion reflected in the Declaration, and that he was using the statute to promote that God and the theology of the Declaration of Independence.

By making individual reason the sole means of determining religious truth with his "Nature's God" of the Declaration and the Virginia Statute for Religious Freedom, Jefferson eliminated all intermediate authorities between God and man as the source of religious truth, such as exclusive revelation or scripture, church or tradition, and most of all, the clergy. To Jefferson, the elimination of such intermediaries was a blessing, because he maintained that they caused theological exclusivism and sectarian bigotry. He expressed his ideas on unmediated religion when he said, "I have ever thought religion a concern purely between our God and our consciences, for which we are accountable to Him, and not to the priests."[46] This comment was made in 1816, but the phrase "I have ever thought" or held the view expressed in this comment indicates that it was a view he had held from his early years. It would seem that Jefferson's "reason alone" approach to religion in his Statute for Religious Freedom must have sounded too natural theological or deistic to the Virginia assemblymen. When they finally passed his statute in 1786, they kept the phrase "the holy author of our religion" but edited away the idea that He chose to extend His religion's influence exclusively with reason by deleting the phrase "but to extend it by its influence on reason alone."[47]

In the preamble of the statute Jefferson also mentioned the corruption of religion and religious truth by men in church and state who claimed infallibility in matters of religion and who used force rather than reason to make others accept their views. Such men, he believed, were suffering from delusions and illusions. They were deluded in thinking they were infallible, and they were living in illusion as a result of thinking their views on religion were true when in fact they were false.[48] They were also impious because they went against God, who was pro-reason and anti-force in religion. In addition they imposed false religions on mankind by their use of force. As Jefferson put it, "The impious presumption of legislators and rulers, civil as well as ecclesiastical, who, being themselves but fallible and uninspired men, have assumed dominion over the faith of others, setting up their own opinions and modes of thinking as the only true and infallible, and as such endeavoring to impose them on others, hath established and maintained false religions over the greatest part of the world and through all time."[49]

Wills believes that Jefferson tailored the argument in this passage to appeal to a Protestant audience because established religion that was enforced and therefore false in the Christian world was for the most part Catholic.[50] But surely Jefferson's argument would more likely insult and inflame rather than appeal to a Protestant audience, especially the one to which it was addressed. Jefferson's language stated that all those who successfully used force in religion establish and maintain false religions. Presbyterians were one of the largest sects in Virginia when Jefferson drafted the statute, and the Scotch Irish Presbyterians of that state were certainly aware that Presbyterianism was the established or government-enforced religion of Scotland.[51] Likewise, Anglicanism was still the enforced religion of Virginia. Therefore Jefferson, via the language presented to the Presbyterians and Anglicans of Virginia and its assembly, blatantly branded both religions false. The fact that this passage did not target any specific religion or sect but pronounced all that used force as false, plus the religious liberalism of some members of the Virginia assembly, seem to be the reasons that Jefferson's affront to the principal churches of Virginia was tolerated.

Wills also believes that in speaking of "false religions," Jefferson claimed to know the true one and was thus not a relativist as respects religious truth.[52] Once again this does not seem to be the case. The religions Jefferson deemed false that were forced on others were ones that placed certain authorities such as revelation and tradition over individual reason; further, they were religions caught in superstitions. Like Bolingbroke, Jefferson thought that the truth claims of such religions and authorities could not withstand the test of rational scrutiny. To Jefferson only unlimited rational scrutiny born of "reason alone," or reason without any restraints, could determine truth in religion. He maintained in his 1776 notes on religion, therefore, that there was no alternative to each individual's reliance on "h[i]s own Und[er]st[andin]g, wh[ether] mo[re] or less judic[iou]s," even if "oth[er] mens Und[er]-st[andin]g[s] [were] *better*."⁵³ Yet he also maintained that the structural differences between the minds or rational faculties of different individuals resulted in different perceptions of religious truth, an idea he adopted early in life (see chapter 5).

Truth in religion *was,* therefore, relative to Jefferson. Moreover, he was tentative in his approach to religious truth, believing that no one could be certain of having arrived at correct rational determinations of that truth. He mentioned this idea to Miles King in a way that demonstrated his relativism: "Our particular principles of religion are a subject of accountability to our God alone, I enquire after no man's, and trouble none with mine; nor is it given to us in this life to know whether yours or mine, our friends or our foes, are exactly the right."⁵⁴ King claimed to have had a revelation from God, and Jefferson's response to that claim spelled out his ideas on individual reason in religion:

> Whether the particular revelation which you suppose to have been made to yourself were real or imaginary, your reason alone is the competent judge. For dispute as long as we will on religious tenets, our reason at last must ultimately decide, as it is the only oracle which God has given us to determine between what really comes from Him and the phantasms of a disordered or deluded imagination. When He means to make a personal revelation, He carries conviction of its authenticity to the reason He has bestowed as the umpire of truth. You believe you have been favored with such a special communication. Your reason, not mine, is to judge of this; and if it shall be His pleasure to favor me with a like admonition, I shall obey it with the same fidelity with which I would obey His known will in all cases. Hitherto I have been under the guidance of that portion of reason which He has thought proper to deal out to me. I have followed it faithfully in all important cases, to such a degree at least as leaves me without uneasiness; and if on minor occasions I have erred from its dictates, I have trust in Him who made us what we are, and know it was not His plan to make us always unerring.⁵⁵

These comments, although made in 1814, were retrospective about Jefferson's use of reason, as is evidenced by his statement that "hitherto" he had "followed" it "faithfully in all important cases." The text of the King letter thus indicates Jefferson's commitment to reason as a guide in his life since the early years of his adulthood, especially in matters of religion. He significantly acknowledged the limitations of that guide when he described his rational faculty as "that portion of reason" which God had given him. The overall thrust of his comments to King was that he could not be certain of the determinations of truth about God and religion made by his reason, nor could any others be certain of theirs. Contrary to Wills's view, therefore, Jefferson was never assertive about his own determinations of religious truth. His comment to King, "I trouble none with mine," in reference to his determinations of truth in religion is evidence of his lack of assertiveness. Yet, notwithstanding the uncertainty of individual rational determinations of religious truth, Jefferson affirmed to King that each man had no alternative to the use of his reason in religion, since it was "the only oracle which God has given us" in matters of religion. His letter to King thereby reiterated a theme stressed in his 1776 notes on religion, when he said that there was no alternative to each individual's reliance on "h[i]s own Und[er]st[andin]g, wh[ether] mo[re] or less judic[iou]s" when it came to finding religious truth.

Statutory Separation of Church and State

A vital part of the Virginia Statute for Religious Freedom was the Lockean idea of separating church and state functions. This is seen in a provision deleted by the assembly that stated, "The opinions of men are not the object of civil government, nor under its jurisdiction."[56] Jefferson, however, used similiar language, which was not deleted and conveyed a separation of church and state meaning, when he mentioned implicitly the Lockean idea that force or coercion exercised by government in religion corrupts government. That language is found in the preamble in the passage referring to the Virginia law that subjected those who did not believe in God, the Trinity, the truth of Christianity, or the divine authority of scripture to an "incapacity to hold any office."[57] It states: "Our civil rights have no dependence on our religious opinions, any more than our opinions in physics or geometry; that therefore the proscribing any citizen as unworthy the public confidence by laying upon him an incapacity of being called to offices of trust and emolument, unless he profess or renounce this or that religious opinion, is depriving him injuriously of those privileges and advantages to which, in common with his fellow citizens, he has a natural right." Locke said that government was corrupted when it entered an area where it did not belong by coercing religious opinion, as did the Virginia law referred to in this passage. According to Jefferson, this law was also a bribe and therefore a corruption on the part of government. It bribed those seeking public office to subscribe to certain religious beliefs. Jefferson then chastised the corrupting influence of such law on both the bribed and the briber in the preamble by stating that "though indeed these are criminal who do not withstand such temptation, yet neither are those innocent who lay the bait in their way." In the succeeding clause he added that religion too was tainted by this bribe. He did so in a way that reflected Locke's belief that hypocrisy, which precluded salvation and was the result of using force in religion, vitiated religion's function, which was the salvation of souls, by stating "that it tends also to corrupt the principles of that *very* religion it is meant to encourage, by bribing, with a monopoly of worldly honours and emoluments, those who will externally profess and conform to it."[58]

Jefferson concluded his preamble with the idea in Locke's *Letter* that force, in addition to being alien to the function of church or religion, was unnecessary to disseminate religious truth. As Locke put it, "Truth certainly would do well enough if she were once left to shift for herself" without the use of force.[59] The preamble stated: "Truth is great and will prevail if left to herself; that she is the proper and sufficient antagonist to error, and has nothing to fear from the conflict unless by human interposition disarmed of her natural weapons, free argument and debate; errors ceasing to be dangerous when it is permitted freely to contradict them."[60] As long as reason and "arguments and debate" born of reason were "free," or unobstructed by authority or force that compromised their efficacy, Jefferson believed they would eventually perceive and reject error as well as perceive and accept truth. Truth would thereby emerge triumphant. To Jefferson, truth and free reason were two sides of the same coin. Therefore, when authorities such as scripture, tradition, or government force were used to control reason and dictate truth in religion, the result was error. Although truth could take care of itself, errors needed some nonrational authority or force to sustain them, according to Jefferson. He mentioned this when he said, "It is error alone that needs the support of government," reflecting a similar statement from Locke in his *Letter,* "Errors indeed prevail by the assistance of foreign and borrowed succours."[61]

In the enacting passage of the Virginia Statute for Religious Freedom, immediately following its preamble, Jefferson proscribed all use of force in religion: "No man shall be compelled to frequent or support any religious worship, place, or ministry whatsoever, nor shall be enforced, restrained, molested, or burthened in his body or goods, nor shall otherwise suffer, on account of his religious opinions or belief; but that all men shall be free to profess, and by argument to maintain, their opinions in matters of religion, and that the same shall in no wise diminish, enlarge, or affect their civil capacities."[62] He thereby put into law Locke's idea that the functions of church and state were separate and that the use of force in religion was no part of either of those functions. This legal prohibition of the use of force in religion not only protected all individuals from persecution for their religious perceptions and beliefs but also made all religions and sects equal in the eyes of the law. Jefferson mentioned this Lockean principle of legal equality to an American Jew when he wrote: "Our laws have applied the only antidote to this vice [intolerance], protecting our religions, as they do our civil rights, by putting all on equal footing."[63]

The principle of equality before the law brought the laws of Virginia into accord with the God of the Declaration of Independence. That God gave no religion, no people, and no individual special favor by choosing one over others. Every person, no matter what his religious views, was treated equally by Him (see chapter 3). As the God of the Declaration did not exclude or favor any person or religion, neither did the language of the enacting passage of the Virginia Statute for Religious Freedom. All persons and religions were equally protected by that passage. This was no doubt Jefferson's intent when he drafted it. Evidence of this intent may be seen in his 1776 notes on *A Letter concerning Toleration:* observing that Locke excluded Catholics and atheists from toleration, Jefferson stated, "Where he stopped short, we may go on."[64]

Despite Jefferson's intent and language in the statute, an attempt was made in the assembly to restrict its protection to Christian sects only: a proposed amendment would have changed the words of the preamble to read "Jesus Christ, the holy author of our religion." As Jefferson recalled, that attempt "was rejected by a great majority in proof that they meant to comprehend, within the mantle of its [the law's] protection, the Jew and the Gentile, the Christian and Mohametan, the Hindoo and Infidel of every denomination."[65]

Legal protection of all individuals, religions, and sects from persecution by law had limitations in any government—including democracy—according to Jefferson. These limitations existed because the moment any religion or sect that believed it was true and others false was favored by the state, it would use that favor to persecute other religions and sects, despite the fact that without such favor it would be peaceful and even promote tolerance. This idea too came from Locke, who said that where religions and sects "have not the power to carry on persecution and to become masters, there they . . . preach up toleration," but "so soon as ever court favour has given them the better end of the staff, . . . then presently peace and charity are to be laid aside." A religion or sect with power born of government favor, Locke maintained, became "the most violent of these defenders of the truth, the oppressors of errors, the exclaimers against schism."[66] Jefferson echoed these ideas in the aforementioned letter to a Jew: "Your sect by its sufferings has furnished a remarkable proof of the universal spirit of religious intolerance inherent in every sect, disclaimed by all while feeble and practiced by all while in power."[67]

Well aware that power in a democracy belonged to the majority, Jefferson feared the day when any one religious group obtained a majority in Virginia. It would then control the legislature and could overturn the statute for religious freedom and pass laws legalizing persecution of those holding other religious beliefs. In an attempt to provide a sanction against any majority that might be tempted to do this, he added a final clause to his statute that affirmed his belief that religious freedom was a natural right.

> And though we well know that this assembly, elected by the people for the ordinary purposes of legislation only, have no power to restrain the acts of succeeding Assemblies, constituted with powers equal to our own, and that therefore to declare this act irrevocable would be of no effect in law; yet we are free to declare, and do declare, that the rights hereby asserted are of the natural rights of mankind, and that if any act shall be hereafter passed to repeal the present or to narrow its operation, such act will be an infringement of natural right.[68]

The Virginia statute's protection of the right of religious freedom via the Lockean principle of separating church and state became law in the United States Constitution, and Jefferson played a part in establishing that law. James Madison, though no less a champion of religious freedom than Jefferson,[69] did not include safeguards for the right of religious freedom, or any other right, in his draft of the Constitution. Jefferson wrote to Madison as soon as he read the Constitution that he did not like "the omission of a bill of rights" and listed both freedom of religion and freedom of the press among the rights he believed should be included in such a bill. He then recommended that a bill of rights be added to the Constitution. "A bill of rights," he said, "is what the people are entitled to against every government on earth, general or particular; and what no just government should refuse, or rest on inference."[70] In 1791 the Bill of Rights, originally drafted by Madison, was made part of the Constitution, and the first of its ten amendments read, "Congress shall make no law respecting an establishment of religion, or prohibiting the free exercise thereof; or abridging the freedom of speech or of the press; or the right of the people peaceably to assemble and to petition the Government for a redress of grievances."[71] The force of government was thereby precluded from being used in church or religion. Jefferson regarded the First Amendment with "sovereign reverence" because, as he stated, it constructed "a wall of separation between Church and State," an idea he obtained from Locke's *Letter concerning Toleration.*[72]

By specifying the "free exercise" of religion, the First Amendment guaranteed freedom of worship, thought, speech, and assembly in religious matters, as did the Virginia Statute for Religious Freedom. By specifying freedom of speech, freedom of the press, and peaceful assembly in political matters, the amendment extended the spirit of Jefferson's Virginia Statute for Religious Freedom, which included freedom for atheists and secular thought, to politics. Finally, in qualifying the right of political assembly by the word "peaceable," the First Amendment ruled out the use of force in politics as it did in religion, leaving political disputes to be decided peacefully by the will or "consent" of the people via the ballot. Thus American constitutional law provided the means to maintain political peace as well as religious peace within a nation, two of John Locke's aims in the seventeenth century.[73] In enforcing that law, governmental power would come to be used against those who disrupted peace by applying force in religion or politics.[74]

Public Argument and Individual Judgment

Jefferson had emphasized freedom of speech and assembly in the Virginia Statute for Religious Freedom's enacting passage when he wrote, "All men shall be free to profess, and by argument to maintain, their opinions in matters of religion."[75] This of course gave individuals the right to express their religious views publicly and to maintain those views by reason or argument in conjunction with their public expression. This passage reveals Jefferson's disposition toward religion. To him it was not sufficient to state "I believe" and merely recite religious opinions without any rational justification. Such affirmations were the method of faith, and Jefferson, as an advocate of reason, thought that religious opinion should be justified by arguments born of reason. Since the statute gave all men the freedom to profess and argue their religious views, they could publicly examine and criticize one another's professed opinions. Thus, an open forum of different religious views would emerge if the right of professing and arguing religious opinions was exercised as a result of Jefferson's statute. In such a forum only well-argued beliefs based on substantial evidence could be expected to be "by argument" maintained and thereby survive.

The source of Jefferson's ideas on the open-forum approach to religion is found in the 1776 notes he made from Shaftesbury's *Characteristics,* idealizing the open forum of the Greeks: "The antients tolerated visionaries & enthusiasts of all kinds so they permitted a free scope to philosophy as a balance. as the Pythagoreans & latter Platonicks joined with the superstition of the times the Epicurians & Academicks were allowed all the use of wit & raillery against it. thus matters were balanced; reason had [full] play & science flourished. these contrarieties produced harmony. superstition & enthusiasm thus let alone never raged to bloodshed persecution &c." Shaftesbury's theme of using "wit & raillery" to tame the excessive and unproved claims of religion is expanded in a further Jeffersonian paraphrase: "Nothing but free argument, raillery, & even ridicule will preserve the purity of religion."[76] Falsity in religion could withstand solemn and serious criticism but not lighthearted, good-natured, humorous criticism in the form of wit and raillery, according to Shaftesbury. Of the former type he stated, "*That Imposture* shou'd dare sustain the *Encounter* of a *grave* Enemy, is no wonder. A solemn Attack, she knows, is not of such danger to her." Of the latter type he said, "There is nothing she [imposture] abhors or dreads like Pleasantness and *good Humor,*" because imposture would be "detected and expos'd" by criticism in the form of good-natured wit and raillery.[77] Echoing Shaftesbury, Jefferson cited an example of the effectiveness of wit and raillery as an antidote to the excessive and erroneous claims of religion. In his *Notes on the State of Virginia,* when discussing the freedom of religion practiced in Pennsylvania and New York, he wrote, "If a sect arises, whose tenets would subvert morals, good sense has fair play, and reasons and laughs it out doors."[78]

Multiple competing religions and sects would be conducive to the effectiveness of an open forum, since each one or a combination of several could and would tame the abuses of another or several others, according to Jefferson. As he expressed this idea in *Notes,* "Difference of opinion is advantageous in religion. The several sects perform the office of a Censor morum over each other."[79] Given this comment and the statement in the enacting clause "that men shall be free to profess and by argument to maintain" their views on religion, it is clear that Jefferson intended the Virginia Statute for Religious Freedom to provide an open forum in matters of religion through encouraging the use of individual reason and freedom of expression in religion. Indeed, the right of individuals to argue their religious beliefs and criticize those of others in such a forum, provided by Jefferson's statute, brought legal protection to his idea that individual reason should be exercised in an unlimited way in religion. That right enabled individuals to inject their reason without any restrictions in religion, which was heretofore largely the domain of faith and belief, a domain that claimed the authority of scripture and tradition over individual reason.

In providing an environment conducive to the use of individual reason in religion, Jefferson's Virginia statute brought religion into accord with the politics of the Declaration of Independence and the *Second Treatise.* Lockean political theory rested on the principle that individuals had the capacity and right to judge the morality of their government and accept or reject that government on the basis of their judgments. Institutionalized Christian religions, however, because of their belief in the fall of man and their moral authority over their congregations, had often denied that individuals had either the capacity or the right to judge their churches and clergymen. On the contrary, institutionalized religions and their ecclesiastical authorities claimed the moral authority to judge their congregations and anyone in them. Instead of the people having moral control and authority over their religious leaders, those leaders, especially in colonial America (see chapter 1), assumed some form of moral authority over the people.

Jefferson's argument in the preamble of the Statute for Religious Freedom took a very different approach. It turned the moral authority of religion upside down. Of voluntary as compared to forced financial support of the clergy by the individual, Jefferson stated, "Forcing him to support this or that teacher of his own religious persuasion, is depriving him of the comfortable liberty of giving his contributions to the particular pastor whose morals he would make his pattern, and whose powers he feels most persuasive to righteousness."[80] The premise underlying this statement is that each man has knowledge of morality and therefore the capacity to judge not only the "pastor whose morals he would make his pattern" but all clergymen. He could reject any one or all of them if they performed or encouraged action that he deemed immoral. Further, he could exercise a powerful sanction against those he judged adversely after the passage of the Virginia Statute for Religious Freedom; he could withhold financial support. In fact, the voluntary financial support of religion had great potential to democ-ratize the religions of America, as the Unitarian clergymen of Massa-chusetts recognized. When their state repealed its laws enforcing fi-nancial support of religion in the early 1820s, they not only lamented the financial loss but believed their congregations would, as a result of controlling the purse strings of their church, inevitably dictate what was heard from the pulpit.[81]

Jefferson's statute thus placed individual human beings in a posi-tion vis-à-vis their religion and its leaders similar to the one they held vis-à-vis their government and its leaders in Lockean politics. They could exercise moral control over religion and ecclesiastical authority just as they did over their leaders in government and governmental authority. As a result, religion would not become, or at least would have difficulty in becoming or remaining, a tyrannizing force in the lives of the people, just as government would in Lockean politics.

The State and Religious Pluralism

One effect of the Virginia Statute for Religious Freedom and the Bill of Rights of the federal Constitution was religious pluralism. This out-come was not universally approved, for some held that one religion, established, supported, and enforced by the government, was a neces-sary element of a state. It encouraged the people to support the gov-ernment and uphold its laws, and provided a cohesive force to mold the people into a national unit in a time of crisis. Freedom of religion resulted in divergent religious opinions, and those who subscribed to the one-religion theory feared that this diversity would disrupt na-tional unity, make the people apathetic to the laws of the land, and lead eventually to anarchy. Cicero, whom Jefferson had read before he drafted the Declaration of Independence, argued that a state religion was of such vital importance to an effective government and a healthy state that it should be preserved by force even if false.[82] Conyers Middleton, whom Jefferson read in 1776 and who wrote on Cicero, argued similarly in *A Letter to Dr Waterland,* where he mentioned Cicero's views.[83]

Locke, however, in his *Letter concerning Toleration,* maintained that all efforts to attain uniformity of religious opinion by force were futile because "diversity" of religious views "cannot be avoided."[84]

Jefferson agreed. He believed that differences in the structures of the minds of individuals caused them to come to different conclusions about the nature of God and religion, as evidenced by the fact that religious pluralism existed despite all efforts to attain religious uniformity by force. In his 1776 notes on his arguments to the Virginia assembly, after asking, "Is *Unif[or]m[i]ty Attainable*" in religion, he answered, "Mill[io]ns. burnt-tort[ure]d.-fin[e]d-impris[one]d. yet men *differ.*"[85] In *Notes on the State of Virginia* he expanded the point, added an indictment of Christian religious persecution, and reiterated the Lockean idea that force in religion leads to hypocrisy and error: "Is uniformity attainable? Millions of innocent men, women, and children, since the introduction of Christianity, have been burnt, tortured, fined, imprisoned; yet we have not advanced one inch toward uniformity. What has been the effect of coercion? To make one half of the world fools, and the other half hypocrites. To support roguery and error all over the earth."[86]

Apart from his view that diversity in religion was unavoidable, Locke asserted, contrary to Cicero, that if all religions were made equal before the law and allowed free expression of their different views, the result would be widespread citizen support of government. Conversely, he implied, if the law favored one religion and persecuted others in order to attain religious uniformity, it would cause some of those persecuted not to support or even to turn against the government. He expressed these ideas in *A Letter concerning Toleration:*

> Take away the penalties unto which they [those who had religious
> views different from the magistrate's] are subjected, and all things will
> immediately become safe and peaceable. Nay, those that are averse to
> the religion of the magistrate will think themselves so much the more
> bound to maintain the peace of the commonwealth as their condition
> is better in that place than elsewhere; and all the several separate
> congregations, like so many guardians of the public peace, will watch
> one another, that nothing may be innovated or changed in the form of
> the government, because they can hope for nothing better than what
> they already enjoy; . . . how much greater will be the security of
> government where all good subjects, of whatsoever church they be,
> without any distinction upon account of religion, enjoying the same
> favour of the prince and the same benefit of the laws, shall become
> the common support and guard of it, and where none will have any
> occasion to fear the severity of the laws but those that do injuries to
> their neighbors and offend against the civil peace?[87]

There seems little doubt that this was Jefferson's source for the prin-

ciple, used in his Virginia Statute for Religious Freedom, that all religions and persons are equal before the law regardless of their religious
beliefs.

Approximately twenty years after the United States Constitution
and Bill of Rights became law, Jefferson stated that the American experiment with religious freedom and religious equality before the
law had demonstrated that Locke was right and men like Cicero wrong.
Not only New York and Pennsylvania, which had practiced Locke's
ideas on religion before and during the Revolutionary War, but also
Virginia and the United States as well by that time had proved that
religious freedom and equality before the law, resulting in religious
pluralism, was the "best support" of government and its laws, as Locke
had said.[88] Far from being detrimental to the state, freedom of religion
had improved and enhanced it, according to Jefferson, who, sounding
much like Locke, asserted in 1808: "We have solved by fair experiment, the great and interesting question whether freedom of religion is
compatible with order in government, and obedience to the laws. And
we have experienced the quiet as well the comfort which results from
leaving every one to profess freely and openly those principles of religion which are the inductions of his own reason, and the serious convictions of his own inquiries."[89] When he spoke of "leaving every one
to profess freely and openly" their religious views in this passage,
Jefferson echoed the language he had used in the enacting clause of the
Virginia Statute for Religious Freedom. He also affirmed, as he did in
that statute, that views professed should be based on an individual's
"own reason." He even stated the type of reason to be used: "the
inductions of his own reason, and the serious convictions of his own
inquiries." This reference to inductive reason and inquiry demonstrates
that Jefferson adhered to the use of a sense-based critical reason in
religion, the Bolingbrokean or Lockean type that he had adopted in
the years prior to the Declaration that gave rise to the natural religion
and natural theology of the Declaration of Independence.

From Jefferson's perspective as a proponent of democratic Lockean
politics, an obvious benefit of religious pluralism, fostered by legally
protected freedom of religion, was that it prevented a particular religion from having a majority. The absence of such a majority prevented
any religion not only from using the power of government to enhance
its own position and persecute others, but also from taking complete
control of political power. This prevention applied to all religions including those in which the clergy or ecclesiastical authority dominated
the minds of its followers. If such a religion ever did gain a majority

and thereby control the government, its ecclesiastical authority would dictate the normative direction of the government and its laws, backed by unthinking followers who would have the political power to carry out the dictates of their clergy.[90] Thus, a majority of unthinking followers of ecclesiastical authority could nullify a Lockean democracy in which the people were supposed to provide the normative content of and pass moral judgment upon their government. To put it another way, a majority of unthinking followers of an authoritarian church could transform a democratic government into a de facto monarchy or oligarchy, depending on the nature of the ecclesiastical authority of their church.

This disastrous impact of authoritarian faith religions on the minds of men, which resulted in mental tyranny and the linkage of such tyranny to political tyranny, was mentioned by Jefferson in a letter to John Adams in 1818, when he wrote, "The revolution in South America will succeed against Spain. But the dangerous enemy is within their own breasts. Ignorance and superstition will chain their minds and bodies under religious and military despotism."[91]

Considering the fact that most institutionalized religions in America in the eighteenth century were based on faith and were sectarian in the sense of being founded on authoritarian theological or ecclesiastical exclusivism rather than the free unlimited reason of the individual, the minds of their followers were or had the potential to be dominated by their clergy. Therefore, the religious pluralism fostered by American religious law protected not only religious freedom but also political freedom. Jefferson was aware of this protection because *A Letter concerning Toleration,* which he had read carefully, contained the foregoing passage, which stated, "The several separate congregations" were "like so many guardians of the public peace," and they "will watch one another that nothing may be innovated or changed in the form of government." In other words, religious pluralism "performed the office of a Censor morum over each other [religion]" that protected the state as well as other religions from being dominated by one religion's ecclesiastical authority. Only if a balance of political power existed between different and conflicting religions would the state be safe from domination by the moral or doctrinal authority of one religious institution. As long as religious pluralism existed, any attempt by one religion to obtain dominion in politics over all others would be in the mutual interest of all others to block since none wanted to be dominated by another. Therefore, if one religion did attempt to dominate politically, all or most others would form an alliance to defeat that religion.

Unitarianism and the Declaration's Theology

A politics based on individual reason was best served and preserved by a religion similarly based, as the young Jefferson had learned from reading Bolingbroke (see chapter 5). This knowledge must have worried Jefferson, since he was painfully aware of the disparity between the individual reason-based politics of the new United States and its predominantly faith-based religions. Adding to his worries was his knowledge that maintaining a legal balance of power among faith-based authoritarian religions was a precarious method of preserving religious and political freedom, because all such balances could be altered and thereby destroyed. In his native Virginia before 1776 he had witnessed how large immigrations of people of a similar faith could disrupt the stability of political power between religions.[92] In the long run, he believed, the best safeguard against the potential for tyranny in both religion and politics of sectarian faith-based religions was education (see chapter 5). Through education individuals would be liberated from religious superstition and clerical domination and learn to reason for themselves, an outcome conducive to both religious and political freedom. But an intermediate or "more proximate" remedy to the dangers posed by authoritarian religions emerged after passage of the Virginia Statute for Religious Freedom and the federal Bill of Rights, according to Jefferson. That remedy was "Unitarianism," which he had "no doubt" would "ere long, be the religion of the majority from north and south."[93]

The basic tenets of Unitarianism were a denial of the Trinity and acceptance of the unity of God and the humanity of Jesus; a denial of original sin and a belief in the essential goodness of man; and a belief in man's perfectibility through rational humanitarian means.[94] More important, from Jefferson's perspective, Unitarians rejected any "universal, exclusive, or binding definition" of creed.[95] Unitarian Joseph Priestley—who had an impact on Jefferson's religious views[96] after he emigrated in 1794 to Philadelphia, where Jefferson attended his lectures—attributed this rejection to a belief that no doctrine or creed was necessary to attain salvation; rather, salvation was earned by moral actions and had nothing to do with either doctrinal faith or grace.[97] Jefferson feared, however, that Unitarians would "fall into the fatal error of fabricating formulas of creed and confessions of faith, the engines which so soon destroyed the religion of Jesus, and made of Christendom a mere Aceldama." He praised the Quakers for not falling into this error and added, "Be this the wisdom of Unitarians."[98]

To Jefferson, surrendering one's reason to a system of creedal doctrines, even by choice, was not only ineffective in attaining salvation and led to bigotry but also an offense to one's self. Such a surrender was using freedom to become unfree, for after pledging allegiance and obedience to a creed, the individual was bound to that creed, became a follower as well as an advocate of its system of beliefs, and thus suspended his critical reason with regard to those beliefs. Jefferson expressed these ideas in personal terms: "I never submitted the whole system of my opinions to the creed of any party of men whatever, in religion, in philosophy, in politics or in anything else, where I was capable of thinking for myself. Such an addiction, is the last degradation of a free and moral agent."[99]

The Unitarian Church, by not requiring any universal or binding creedal commitment, allowed individuals to maintain the freedom of their critical reason and moral choice in religion and still be members. As a result, Unitarians were without any binding ecclesiastical or clerical authority that told them what to believe and what was right and wrong, which allowed for religious pluralism within the Unitarian Church. To Jefferson, the political implications of this were extremely important. It left Unitarians free to make moral and rational decisions in politics, decisions the ecclesiastical and clerical authority of most orthodox colonial denominations claimed the moral authority to make for their congregations (see chapter 1). Consequently, Unitarianism was consistent with Jefferson's liberal religious and political views. Jefferson in effect said this, along with his opinion that Unitarianism was an emergent religion that would soon become dominant in America as a result of the practice of free religious inquiry fostered by American law, in a statement he made in 1822: "I rejoice that in this blessed country of free enquiry and belief, which has surrendered its creed and conscience to neither kings nor priests, the genuine doctrine of one only God is reviving, and I trust there is not a young man now living in the United States who will not die an Unitarian."[100]

Unitarianism was not only in accord with the use of individual critical reason in religion as espoused and put into practice by the Enlightenment and Jefferson; it was a product of the Enlightenment and critical reason.[101] It would seem, therefore, that Jefferson regarded it as the religious counterpart of the University of Virginia, which Charles Sanford described as "an institution that would foster the development of the ideals of the Enlightenment by which he had lived all his life."[102] Indeed, Unitarianism was perceived by Jefferson as a religion that corresponded generally with the theology of the Declaration of

Independence and one that, like that theology, was conducive to the efficacy of the political theory of that document. As a religion based on individual reason and judgment, it served and preserved the similarly based politics of the Declaration. It was thereby a religion in accord with what Jefferson as a young man had learned from Bolingbroke.

Conclusion

It should now be clear that Thomas Jefferson was very much the eclectic. Many thinkers contributed to his worldview, principally Henry St. John, Lord Viscount Bolingbroke; John Locke; Henry Home, Lord Kames; and Thomas Reid. Bolingbroke gave Jefferson his heterodox views on religion, which emphasized a deistic, universal, impartial God of natural religion whom Jefferson referred to in the Declaration of Independence as "Nature's God." Locke contributed the political theory of the Declaration and added an egalitarian element to the God of that document, a God who created all men equal. He and Bolingbroke also contributed to Jefferson's ideas on reason without restraint in the search for truth, including religious truth.

Jefferson's ideas on religious freedom and their relation to political freedom were predominantly Lockean as well. Jefferson did not go along with Locke's epistemology, however. Locke's political philosophy depended on the ability of the reason of each individual to find the moral laws of nature easily and independently, yet Locke said that these laws were not easily found with reason, using the epistemolgy he promulgated. For Jefferson, it was Kames who bridged this gap between Lockean political thought and epistemology with his concept of man as a being who could independently and easily find the moral laws of nature by using his moral sense and a minimal amount of reason.

Reid's contribution was to rescue the senses and reason of man, faculties precious to Jefferson as an apostle of reason, from the onslaught of philosophical skepticism. Reid claimed that Locke's epistemology—which stated that ideas of objects perceived by the senses mediated in the mind between the object perceived and the perceiver—was a principal cause of philosophical skepticism. Reid's commonsense philosophy rejected the notion of such mediating ideas in the process of perceiving truth. Kames also contributed to the defeat of philosophical skepticism, especially as respects the self of man, and also to the meaning of "self-evident" that Jefferson used in the Declaration. Jefferson's political thought as stated in the Declaration, therefore, did not derive exclusively from Locke or the Scottish Enlightenment thinkers, as Carl Becker and Garry Wills have maintained.

Some revisionist scholars, such as Garry Wills, perceive a communitarian element in Jefferson and the Declaration; others, such as J.G.A. Pocock, though acknowledging an element of Lockean individual rights in the Declaration, maintain that it was a useful but short-lived aspect of Jeffersonian thought, giving way to a communitarian perspective after 1776. The Lockean ideas stated in the Declaration, however, as well as Jefferson's subsequent emphasis on individual rights and Kamesean moral sense, are irreconcilable with the conclusions of either category of revisionists. Jefferson later emphasized individual rights to the extent of believing that if the community claimed rights superseding those of the individual, the result would be slavery. This anticommunitarian idea may have been implicit in Lockean theory contained in the Declaration, but Jefferson expressed it explicitly in 1782: "If we are made in some degree for others, yet in a greater are we made for ourselves. It were contrary to feeling and indeed ridiculous to suppose a man had less right in himself than one of his neighbors or all of them put together. This would be slavery and not that liberty which the bill of rights has made inviolable and for the preservation of which our government has been changed."[1]

Not only Locke's stress on individual rights but Kames's moral-sense concept of man upheld the ideas Jefferson expressed in this statement. Kames believed that benevolence, or the performance of actions that benefited others, was not always a duty; if it were, individuals would be bound to live their lives for the benefit of others, making each one a slave to actions on behalf of "one of his neighbors or all of them put together." Thus, benevolence seen as always a duty would have a similar impact on the individual as would community rights that superseded those of the individual. To Kames, however, only justice, or refraining from acts that harmed others, was always a duty. God, he believed, made justice a duty in man via the moral sense because He made man sociable by nature, and if men harmed one another they could not be sociable. Benevolence, though also part of Kames's moral philosophy, was not always a duty because society could exist without it.

I have argued that Kames's ideas on the moral sense were held by Jefferson during the writing of the Declaration and that he continued to hold these ideas during his later years. This continuity is substantiated in a letter Jefferson wrote in 1816: "Assuming the fact, that the earth has been created in time, and consequently the dogma of final causes, we yield, of course, to this short syllogism. Man was created for social intercourse; but social intercourse cannot be maintained without a sense of justice; then man must have been created with a sense of justice."[2]

Even if benevolent acts were not always a duty, the heterodox theology of Jefferson and the Declaration nevertheless provided a powerful inducement to their performance—apart from their giving pleasure to the performer, which Kames said was an effect of such acts. Salvation, according to that theology, was earned by individuals through the performance of moral actions, which included benevolent acts. In this way the theology of Jefferson and the Declaration, to borrow a phrase used by Thomas Pangle about Locke's ideas, "narrowed the gap between individual self-interest and communal welfare"—even though it did not close it.[3]

Kames's concept of man was the cornerstone of Jefferson's Lockean political theory as stated in the Declaration, whereas the Christian view of fallen man and original sin was antithetical to that theory. Kamesean man was able to provide his own moral direction independent of scripture, church, and clergy. He could therefore be trusted to provide moral direction to his government and, consequently, to have authority over that government. According to Jefferson, the political implication of the Christian original sin concept of man was to give scripture, church, and clergy moral authority over government. Morality supplied this way was needed by government for its moral direction, since men tainted by original sin could not be trusted to supply that direction. The Christian concept of man thereby precluded the Lockean democracy specified in the Declaration, where the people had moral authority over their government because they were able to supply its moral direction independent of scripture, church, and clergy. Indeed, the Christian concept of man had frequently resulted in the establishment of authoritarian rule said to be divinely ordained, with the people having no authority over their government at all.

The importance of Kames's moral-sense concept of man to the efficacy of the Declaration's political theory was expressed by Jefferson in a letter to David Hartley in 1787. In the United States, he said, "we shall have the difference between a light and a heavy government, as clear gain. I have no fear, but that the result of our experiment will be, that men may be trusted to govern themselves without a master. Could the contrary of this be proved, I should conclude, either that there is no God, or that he is a malevolent being."[4] Here Jefferson defined a "heavy" government as "a master" having absolute authority over its subjects, and a "light" government as one that gives the people authority over their government because they are able, and therefore "trusted," to supply its moral direction.

A moral breakdown of society under a "light" government would prove the people incapable of supplying its moral direction—but Jefferson confidently maintained in his letter to Hartley that this would not happen. If it did, there were two implications: either "there is no God" or "he is a malevolent being." A God who created persons as social yet simultaneously morally defective beings, as did the Christian God, who created men who would fall and thereby become morally tainted, would be "malevolent." Persons with God-given social instincts and God-given moral deficiency would be unable to refrain from inflicting harm and pain on each other unless they were under the dominion of a "master," a government having absolute authority. But authoritarian governments too inflicted pain on their subjects, the pain of tyranny and despotism, as Jefferson specified in the Declaration. Therefore, his statement to Hartley implied, the Christian concept of original sin, if proved true, left human beings in a cruel and painful dilemma: they could suffer in a democracy at the hands of one another because they and the government they controlled lacked moral direction because men were morally tainted, or they could suffer the tyranny of a Leviathan repressing and oppressing them. In a democracy, people would inflict suffering horizontally on one another; under authoritarian rule, government would inflict suffering vertically on the people from its position of absolute authority over them.

Jefferson implied, in this statement to Hartley, that a benevolent God would not manifest the cruelty or malevolence of placing humans in this painful dilemma by creating them as social and yet simultaneously morally deficient beings, as did the Christian God of revelation. The dilemma was avoided by Jefferson's rationally known "Nature's God" who created men as both social *and* moral beings, like those Kames described. The moral men of Jefferson's and the Declaration's theology, unlike the morally tainted men of Christianity, would be able to earn their salvation by their own moral actions and to govern themselves in a Lockean democracy to which they supplied moral direction, independent of scripture, church, and clergy.

Late in his life, Jefferson did not waver in his commitment to the heterodox theology and Lockean liberal political theory of the Declaration. Not long before his death in 1826, he designed his own tombstone with an inscription that listed the three achievements for which he wanted to be remembered: "Here was buried Thomas Jefferson—Author Of the Declaration of American Independence—Of The Statute of Virginia for Religious Freedom, and—Father of the University of Virginia."[5] In the first of these achievements Jefferson stated his heterodox theology and Lockean political theory. In the second he protected that theology and theory from authoritarian sectarian orthodoxy. In the third he provided for the actualization of the reason of each individual and encouraged its unlimited use, which he believed would liberate mankind from what he regarded as the false claims of revelation and the scriptural and ecclesiastical authority that resulted from those claims. This actualization of reason, he believed, would cause individuals to look to their own reason and moral sense in both religion and politics.

Perhaps the greatest testimony to his lasting commitment to the Declaration's political theory and heterodox theology is to be found in a statement made just ten days before his death. Commemorating the document's fiftieth anniversary, he wrote:

> May it [the Declaration] be to the world, what I believe it will be, (to some parts sooner, to others later, but finally to all,) the signal of arousing men to burst the chains under which monkish ignorance and superstition had persuaded them to bind themselves, and to assume the blessings and security of self-government. That form which we have substituted, restores the free right to the unbounded exercise of reason and freedom of opinion. All eyes are opened, or opening, to the rights of man. The general spread of the light of science has already laid open to every view the palpable truth, that the mass of mankind has not been born with saddles on their backs, nor a favored few booted and spurred, ready to ride them legitimately, by the grace of God. These are grounds of hope for others.[6]

Significantly, Jefferson here indicted orthodox Christian authorities for their offenses against the freedom and rights of man. Among these were the bondage of "chains under which monkish ignorance and superstition had persuaded them [men] to bind themselves." He also repudiated "the grace of God" as an offense. From the time of his extracts of Bolingbroke's writings, Judeo-Christian "grace" to Jefferson meant privilege or partiality extended by God to some men over others. Grace was thus alien to the impartial, universal, and egalitarian "Nature's God" of Bolingbroke, Locke, and the Declaration; it was a tool used by some men to claim privilege and authority over "the mass of mankind," who, under the spell of "monkish ignorance and superstition," accepted those claims. That acceptance destroyed or restricted the people's freedom, their equality, their reason, and their rights. As Jefferson put it, "a favored few," as a result of grace, were "booted and spurred" and rode "the mass of mankind," who were taught to believe they were "born with saddles on their backs" and therefore accepted the privilege and authority claims of the "favored few."

Liberation from the offenses committed by orthodox religious authority and belief could be found in the ideas and ideals of the Declaration. Its democratic political theory would assure "the blessings . . . of self-government" and "the rights of man"—provided that "all eyes were opened" and people freed themselves from "monkish ignorance and superstition." What would open the eyes of the people? Jefferson's answer affirmed a long-held view: "the unbounded exercise of reason and freedom of opinion." Here Jefferson rejected, as he had while a student, any boundaries or restraints on individual reason, such as the scholasticism that restrained reason with ecclesiastical authority and tradition in Catholicism, or scripture and ecclesiastical authority in Protestantism.

Implicit in this final statement of Jefferson on the Declaration is an affirmation of the heterodox theology of that document, since that theology rejected and opposed monkish ignorance, superstition, grace, and any restraints on individual reason, as Jefferson did in this statement. Indeed, when he said of the Declaration, "May it be to the world, . . . the signal of arousing men to burst the chains under which monkish ingnorance and superstition had persuaded them to bind themselves, and assume the blessings and security of self-government," he stated both the political theory and the theological parts of the Declaration. Significantly, he did this in a manner that made the Declaration's theology, which rejected the authority of orthodoxy, a prerequisite to the efficacy of its political theory. He did this by first mentioning his hope that men would be aroused by the Declaration to "burst the chains under which monkish ignorance and superstition had persuaded them to bind themselves." The theology of "Nature's God" in the Declaration, with its emphasis on the authority of individual reason in religion, would accomplish this bursting. Then, in their newfound freedom, he mentioned his hope that men would "assume the blessings and security of self-government" as described in the Declaration. Thus, the Declaration of Independence with its Lockean democratic political theory and theology born of "Nature's God" attacked two claims of absolute authority—that of any government over its subjects and that of any religion over the minds of men as respects religious and moral truth—by putting the authority of both government and religion in the hands of the individual human beings that make up the populace.

The Declaration of Independence

When in the Course of human events, it becomes necessary for one People to dissolve the Political Bands which have connected them with another, and to assume among the Powers of the Earth, the separate and equal Station to which the Laws of Nature and of Nature's God entitle them, a decent Respect to the Opinions of Mankind requires that they should declare the causes which impel them to the Separation.

We hold these Truths to be self-evident, that all Men are created equal, that they are endowed by their Creator with certain unalienable Rights, that among these are Life, Liberty, and the Pursuit of Happiness. That to secure these Rights, Governments are instituted among Men, deriving their just Powers from the Consent of the Governed, that whenever any Form of Government becomes destructive of these Ends, it is the Right of the People to alter or to abolish it, and to institute new Government, laying its Foundation on such Principles and organizing its Powers in such Form, as to Them shall seem most likely to effect their Safety and Happiness. Prudence, indeed, will dictate that Governments long established should not be changed for light and transient Causes; and accordingly all Experience hath shewn, that Mankind are more disposed to suffer, while Evils are suferable, than to right themselves by abolishing the Forms to which they are accustomed. But when a long Train of Abuses and Usurpations, pursuing invariably the same Object, evinces a design to reduce them under absolute Despotism, it is their Right, it is their Duty, to throw off such Government, and to provide new Guards for their future Security. Such has been the patient Sufferance of these Colonies; and such is now the Necessity which constrains them to alter their former systems of Government. The History of the present King of Great-Britain is a History of repeated Injuries and Usurpations, all having in direct Object the Establishment of an absolute Tyranny over these States. To prove this, let Facts be submitted to a candid World.

He has refused his Assent to Laws, the most wholesome and necessary for the public good.

He has forbidden his Governors to pass Laws of immediate and pressing Importance, unless suspended in their Operation till his Assent should be obtained; and when so suspended, he has utterly neglected to attend to them.

He has refused to pass other Laws for the Accommodation of large Districts of People, unless those People would relinquish the right of Representation in the Legislature, a Right inestimable to them and formidable to Tyrants only.

He has called together Legislative Bodies at Places unusual, uncomfortable, and distant from the Depository of their public Records, for the sole Purpose of fatiguing them into Compliance with his Measures.

He has dissolved Representive Houses repeatedly, for opposing with manly Firmness his Invasions on the Rights of the People.

He has refused for a Long Time, after such Dissolutions, to cause others to be elected; whereby the Legislative Powers, incapable of Annihilation, have returned to the People at large for their exercise; the State remaining in the mean time exposed to all the Dangers of Invasion from without, and Convulsions within.

He has endeavored to prevent the Population of these States; for that Purpose obstructing the Laws for Naturalization of Foreigners; refusing to pass others to encourage their Migrations hither, and raising the Conditions of new Appropriations of Lands.

He has obstructed the Administration of Justice, by refusing his Assent to Laws for establishing Judiciary Powers.

He has made Judges dependent of his Will alone, for the Tenure of their Offices, and the Amount and Payment of their Salaries.

He has erected a Multitude of new Offices, and sent hither Swarms of Officers to harass our People, and eat out their Substance.

He has kept among us, in Times of Peace, Standing Armies, without the Consent of our Legislatures.

He has affected to render the Military independent of and superior to the Civil Power.

He has combined with others to subject us to a Jurisdiction foreign to our Constitution, and unacknowledged by our Laws; giving his Assent to their Acts of pretended Legislation:

For quartering Large Bodies of Armed Troops among us:

For protecting them, by a mock Trial, from Punishment for any Murders which they should commit on the Inhabitants of these States:

For cutting off our Trade with all Parts of the world:

For imposing Taxes on us without our Consent:

For depriving us, in many Cases, of the Benefits of Trial by Jury:

For transporting us beyond Seas to be tried for pretended Offences:

For abolishing the free System of English Laws in a neighboring Province, establishing therein an arbitrary Government, and enlarging its Boundaries, so as to render it at once an Example and fit Instrument for introducing the same absolute Rule into these Colonies:

For taking away our Charters, abolishing our most valuable Laws, and altering fundamentally the Forms of our Governments:

For suspending our own Legislatures, and declaring themselves invested with Power to legislate for us in all Cases whatsoever.

He has abdicated Government here, by declaring us out of his Protection and waging War against us.

He has plundered our Seas, ravaged our Coasts, burnt our Towns, and destroyed the Lives of our People.

He is, at this Time, transporting large Armies of foreign Mercenies to compleat the Works of Death, Desolution, and Tyranny, already begun with circumstances of Cruelty and Perfidy, scarcely paralleled in the most barbarous Ages, and totally unworthy the Head of a civilized Nation.

He has constrained our fellow Citizens taken Captive on the high Seas to bear Arms against their Country, to become the Executioners of their Friends and Brethren, or to fall themselves by their Hands.

He has excited domestic Insurrections amongst us, and has endeavored to bring on the Inhabitants of our Frontiers, the merciless Indian Savages, whose known Rule of Warfare, is an undistinguished Destruction, of all Ages, Sexes and Conditions.

In every stage of these Oppressions We have Petitioned for Redress in the most humble Terms: Our repeated Petitions have been answered only by repeated Injury. A Prince, whose character is thus marked by every act which may define a Tyrant, is unfit to be the Ruler of a free People.

Nor have We been wanting in Attention to our British Brethren. We have warned them from Time to Time of Attempts by their Legislature to extend an unwarrantable Jurisdiction over us. We have reminded them of the Circumstance of our Emigration and Settlement here. We have appealed to their native Justice and Magnanimity, and we have conjured them by the Ties of our common Kindred to disavow these Usurpations, which, would inevitably interrupt our Connections and Correspondence. They too have been deaf to the Voice of Justice and of Consanguinity. We must, therefore, acquiesce in the Necessity, which denounces our Separation, and hold them, as we hold the rest of Mankind, Enemies in War, in Peace, Friends.

We, therefore, the Representatives of the UNITED STATES OF AMERICA, in GENERAL CONGRESS, Assembled, appealing to the Supreme Judge of the World for the Rectitude of our Intentions, do, in the Name, and by Authority of the good People of these Colonies, solemnly Publish and Declare, That these United Colonies are, and of Right ought to be, FREE AND INDEPENDENT STATES; that they are absolved from all Allegiance to the British Crown, and that all political Connection between them and the State of Great-Britain, is and ought to be totally dissolved; and that as FREE AND INDEPENDENT STATES, they have full Power to levy War, conclude Peace, contract Alliances, establish Commerce, and to do all other Acts and Things which INDEPENDENT STATES may of right do. And for the support of this Declaration, with a firm Reliance on the Protection of divine Providence, we mutually pledge to each other our Lives, our Fortunes, and our sacred Honor.*

---

*The text used here is "The First Printing of the Declaration of Independence, as inserted in the Rough Journal of Congress," from Julian P. Boyd, *The Declaration of Independence: The Evolution of the Text* (Washington, 1943), Plate X. In his 1945 edition of this work, Boyd refers to this document as "The First Official Text of the Declaration of Independence."

Notes

Full information for the sources cited here in brief may be found in the Bibliography.

Introduction

1. Perry, *Puritanism and Democracy*, p. 133.

2. See Jefferson to James Madison, 30 August 1823, and to Henry Lee, 8 May 1825, in *The Writings of Thomas Jefferson*, ed. Paul Leicester Ford, 10:266, 343. This edition is cited hereafter as *Writings* (Ford).

3. See Macpherson, *The Political Theory of Possessive Individualism*, pp. 263–64, 269–70; and Macpherson, *Democratic Theory*, p. 199.

4. See, e.g., Dworetz, *The Unvarnished Doctrine*, pp. 31–35; and Dunn, *The Political Thought of John Locke*.

5. Spragens, "Communitarianism and the Liberal Tradition," p. 15.

6. Becker, *The Declaration of Independence*, p. 79.

7. See Wiltse, *The Jeffersonian Tradition in American Democracy*, pp. 36, 38; A. Koch, *The Philosophy of Thomas Jefferson*, p. 196; Boorstin, *The Lost World of Thomas Jefferson*, p. 196; Boyd, *Declaration of Independence* (1943), p. 12; J. Miller, *The Origins of the American Revolution*, pp. 491–92; Dumbauld, *The Declaration of Independence and What It Means Today*, p. 42; Wishy, "John Locke and the Spirit of 76," p. 413; Hawke, *A Transaction of Free Men*, p. 151; Commager, "The Declaration of Independence," pp. 179–87; Malone, *Jefferson and His Time*, 1:175, 227; Chinard, *Thomas Jefferson, the Apostle of Americanism*, p. 72; and White, *The Philosophy of the American Revolution*, p. 48. For the general influence of Locke on America, see Hartz, *The Liberal Tradition in America*, p. 140.

8. Kramnick, *Republicanism and Bourgeois Radicalism*, p. 3.

9. Robbins, *The Eighteenth-Century Commonwealthman*, pp. 190, 105, 370, 34–35, 41–45.

10. Bailyn, *The Ideological Origins of the American Revolution*, pp. 25, 48–50.

11. Pocock, "Virtue and Commerce in the Eighteenth Century," pp. 120–21.

12. Ibid., pp. 120–21.

13. Pocock, *The Machiavellian Moment,* pp. 545–48. See also Pocock, "The Myth of John Locke and the Obsession with Liberalism," pp. 1–24.

14. Pocock, *Virtue, Commerce, and History,* p. 266.

15. Ibid., p. 267.

16. See G. Wood, *The Creation of the American Republic,* pp. 283, 475–508; Banning, *The Jeffersonian Persuasion,* pp. 273–77; McDonald, *The Presidency of Thomas Jefferson,* pp. 17–22, 161–69; and Murrin, "The Great Inversion, or Court versus Country," pp. 382–83, 410–11, 414.

17. Wills, *Inventing America,* pp. 173–74 and esp. chaps. 11–23.

18. Ibid., pp. 215–16.

19. Ibid., pp. 239, 201–5.

20. Mathews, *The Radical Politics of Thomas Jefferson,* pp. 18, 125–26.

21. Ibid., pp. 123, 17–18.

22. O'Brien, *The Long Affair,* pp. 302–18; and Jefferson to Dumas, 10 September 1787, in *The Writings of Thomas Jefferson,* ed. Andrew A. Lipscomb and Albert Ellery Bergh, 6:295. This edition is cited hereafter as *Writings* (Lipscomb and Bergh).

23. See Kramnick, "Republican Revisionism Revisited," pp. 633, 651, 660, 662; Kramnick, *Republicanism and Bourgois Radicalism,* p. 168; Appleby, "What Is Still American in the Political Philosophy of Thomas Jefferson," pp. 289, 293–96; Appleby, "Commercial Farming and the 'Agrarian Myth' in the Early Republic," pp. 844–45; Diggins, *The Lost Soul of American Politics,* pp. 5, 7–9, 16–17, 19–20, 30–32; Pangle, *The Spirit of Modern Republicanism,* pp. 36, 99, 101–2, 209, 211, 258–60; Dworetz, *The Unvarnished Doctrine,* pp. 31, 35, 70–72; Sheldon, *The Political Philosophy of Thomas Jefferson,* pp. 46–47.

24. Shain, *The Myth of American Individualism,* pp. 246–50.

25. Conkin, "The Religious Pilgrimage of Thomas Jefferson," p. 35.

26. Mark Goldie, "The Reception of Hobbes," p. 590.

Chapter 1. The Theological Context

1. Perry, *Puritanism and Democracy,* p. 80; Ahlstrom, *A Religious History of the American People,* pp. 245–46.

2. Burns, *The Vineyard of Liberty,* p. 7.

3. See Locke, *The Second Treatise on Government and A Letter Concerning Toleration,* p. 135 (hereafter cited as *Treatise and Letter*); Harris, *The Mind of John Locke,* p. 187.

4. Jefferson to Thomas B. Parker, 15 May 1819, Jefferson Papers, 38400, S1 R150. Jefferson made a similiar comment to Charles Clay, Esq., on 29 January 1815; see *Writings* (Lipscomb and Bergh), 16:232.

5. Maimonides, "Epistle to Yemen," 1:104. For Maimonides' contribution to Christian as well as Judaic scholasticism, see Julius Guttmann's introduction to Maimonides, *The Guide of the Perplexed,* pp. 1–7.

6. All biblical quotations are taken from the King James Version.

7. Dillenberger and Welch, *Protestant Christianity*, pp. 88–89.

8. Wood, *The Arrogance of Faith*, pp. 39, 58.

9. Maimonedes, "Epistle to Yemen," 1:106.

10. Aquinas, *Basic Writings*, 1:239, 240–41, 243–44.

11. Loyola, *Spiritual Exercises*, pp. 574–75.

12. Luther, *Works*, 25:374, 371.

13. Zwingli, *The Latin Works*, 2:20.

14. Calvin, *Institutes*, 21:926-27.

15. Maimonedes, "Epistle to Yemen," pp. 105, 109–10.

16. Calvin, *Institutes*, 21:927, quoted also Exodus 32:9, which refers to the "stiffnecked" or stubborn characteristic of the Jewish people as a demerit.

17. Ibid., pp. 921–22.

18. Ibid., pp. 934–35.

19. Ibid., p. 929.

20. Augustine, *The Enchiridion*, pp. 242–43.

21. For the effects of the fall, see Romans 7:19–25; Augustine, *Works*, 2:5; Aquinas, *Summa Theologica*, 7:415–16; Loyola, "Spiritual Exercises," pp. 116–17; Luther, *Works*, 25:299; Calvin, *Institutes*, 20:249–51; Zwingli, *Works*, 2:6, 10, 26–27; Ahlstrom, *A Religious History of the American People*, p. 34; and Bicknell, *A Theological Introduction to the Thirty-Nine Articles of the Church of England*, p. 181.

22. Augustine, *The Fathers of the Church*, p. 200.

23. Dillenberger and Welch, *Protestant Christianity*, pp. 12, 16.

24. H. Davis, *Moral and Pastoral Theology*, p. xxxi; Mourret, *A History of the Catholic Church*, 6:239.

25. Gaustad, *The Great Awakening in New England*, p. 5.

26. Dillenberger and Welch, *Protestant Christianity*, pp. 88–89, 40–44, 78–79.

27. F. Wood, *The Arrogance of Faith*, p. 250.

28. G.A. Koch, *Republican Religion*, p. 289.

29. Galloway, "The View from Outside," p. 21.

30. Buel, "Democracy and the American Revolution," p. 179; Morgan, "The Revolution as Intellectual Movement," pp. 11–33. See also Thornton, *The Pulpit of the American Revolution*, pp. 276–77.

Chapter 2. Bolingbroke and the Enlightenment

1. Malone, *Jefferson and His Time*, 1:42–45. Daniel J. Boorstin cautions about exaggerating the impact of the Enlightenment on Jefferson and other American Founding Fathers ("The Myth of an American Enlightenment," p. 72).

2. Ganter, "William Small, Jefferson's Beloved Teacher," p. 506. For the impact of the Scottish Enlightenment on its universities, see Cant, "Origins of the Enlightenment in Scotland," pp. 42–64.

3. Dos Passos, *The Head and Heart of Thomas Jefferson,* pp. 95, 101. For the intensity and scope of Jefferson's education, see Malone, "Jefferson Goes to School in Williamsburgh," pp. 481–96.

4. Jefferson, *Autobiography,* pp. 5–6.

5. Schofield, *The Lunar Society of Birmingham,* p. 36, notes two principal but limited sources of knowledge on William Small: Ganter, "William Small, Jefferson's Beloved Teacher," pp. 505–11; and Dos Passos, *The Head and Heart of Thomas Jefferson,* pp. 82–89.

6. Jefferson, *Autobiography,* p. 6.

7. Bolton and Wells, *The Lunar Society of Birmingham,* p. 6.

8. See *The Literary Bible of Thomas Jefferson: His Commonplace Book of Philosophers and Poets,* ed. Gilbert Chinard, hereafter cited as *Literary Commonplace Book* (Chinard).

9. *Jefferson's Literary Commonplace Book,* ed. Douglas L. Wilson, pp. 155–56, 195–98, 205. This edition of the same work edited by Chinard (see note 8) is cited hereafter as *Literary Commonplace Book* (Wilson). Wilson determined the chronology of the Bolingbroke extracts by comparing the handwriting with that of Jefferson's dated letters.

10. Kramnick, preface to *Lord Bolingbroke: Historical Writings,* pp. xii–xxi; Dickenson, *Bolingbroke,* p. 162; Hart, *Viscount Bolingbroke,* p. viii.

11. Gay, *The Enlightenment,* p. 130.

12. Cassirer, *The Philosphy of the Enlightenment,* pp. 234, 134.

13. *Literary Commonplace Book* (Wilson), p. 156.

14. Quoted in Dickenson, *Bolingbroke,* p. 298.

15. *Literary Commonplace Book* (Chinard), pp. 19, 20.

16. Jefferson to Francis Eppes, 19 January 1821, *Writings* (Lipscomb and Bergh), 15:305. Quentin Skinner puts forth the view that Bolingbroke used Whig ideas "to further his own cynical and self-interested ends" ("The Principles and Practice of Opposition," p. 126). Bolingbroke's political writings against Robert Walpole were used by Virginians as early as 1770 "to prove the responsibility of George III for preserving a balanced uncorrupt government," according to Duff, "The Case against the King," p. 392. Jefferson also commonplaced lengthy extracts from Montesquieu's *Spirit of the Laws,* but according to Schachner, *Thomas Jefferson: A Biography,* p. 391, he had reservations about the French philosopher's ideas.

17. Jefferson to Thomas Cooper, 10 February 1814, in *Writings* (Lipscomb and Bergh), 14:85.

18. Locke, *An Essay concerning Human Understanding,* p. 285 (hereafter cited as *Human Understanding*).

19. See Clark, "Thomas Jefferson and Science," pp. 193–203; R. Brown, "Jefferson's Contribution to Paleontology," pp. 257–59; Martin, *Thomas Jefferson, Scientist;* and Bedini, *Thomas Jefferson, Statesman of Science.*

20. *Literary Commonplace Book* (Chinard), pp. 70–71. (It is from Jefferson's extracts in this book that I take this and subsequent Bolingbroke quotations.)

21. Ibid., pp. 58–59.

22. Ibid., p. 44.

23. Dickinson, *Bolingbroke,* p. 163. The epistemology of the deistic movement was expounded by Locke, who was accused of being a deist, according to Yolton, *Locke and the Way of Ideas,* pp. 115, 171.

24. *Literary Commonplace Book* (Chinard), p. 60.

25. Spinoza, *Theologico-Politico Treatise,* p. 83: "It is plain that the universal laws of nature are decrees of God following from the necessity and perfection of the Divine nature. Hence, any [miraculous] event happening in nature which contravened nature's universal laws, would necessarily also contravene the Divine decree, nature, and understanding; or if anyone asserted that God acts in contravention to the laws of nature, he, *ipso facto,* would be compelled to assert that God acted against His own nature—an evident absurdity."

26. *Literary Commonplace Book* (Chinard), p. 49.

27. Spinoza, *Theologico-Politico Treatise,* pp. 85–86: "When we know that all things are ordained and ratified by God, that the operations of nature follow from the essence of God, and that the laws of nature are eternal decrees and volitions of God, we must perforce conclude that our knowledge of God and of God's will increases in proportion to our knowledge and clear understanding of nature, as we see how she depends on her primal cause, and how she works according to eternal law. Wherefore so far as our understanding goes, those phenomenae which we clearly and distinctly understand have much better right to be called works of God, and to be referred to the will of God than those about which we are entirely ignorant, although they appeal powerfully to the imagination and compel men's admiration."

28. For deism's reconciliation of science with God, see Savelle, *Seeds of Liberty,* pp. 167–69.

29. *Literary Commonplace Book* (Chinard), p. 44.

30. Ibid., p. 49. Toland wrote: "A Man may give his verbal Assent to he knows not what, out of Fear, Superstition, Indifference, Interest, and the like feeble and unfair Motives: but as long as he conceives not what he believes, he cannot sincerely acquiesce in it, and remains depriv'd of all solid Satisfaction" (*Christianity Not Mysterious,* p. 35).

31. Jefferson to John Adams, 8 April 1816; and Jefferson to Jared Sparks, 4 November 1820, both in *Writings* (Lipscomb and Bergh), 14:470, 15:288. See also S. Brown, "The Mind of Thomas Jefferson," p. 81, for Jefferson's distaste for metaphysics.

32. Dickenson, *Bolingbroke,* p. 163.

33. Jefferson to John Adams, 22 August 1813, in *Writings* (Lipscomb and Bergh), 13:350.

34. Jefferson to Justin Pierre Plumard Derieux, 25 July 1788, in *The Papers of Thomas Jefferson,* ed. Julian P. Boyd and Charles Cullen, 13:418. This edition is cited hereafter as *Papers* (Boyd and Cullen).

35. Jefferson to John Adams, ll April 1816, in *Writings* (Lipscomb and Bergh), 15:426–27.

36. *Literary Commonplace Book* (Chinard), pp. 62–63.

37. Ibid., p. 63. Bolingbroke's use of "theism" here to denote his natural theology with its deistic, universal, and impartial God was, some might say, an idiosyncratic use. On theism and deism, words often used to define different concepts of God during the Enlightenment, see Sanford, *The Religious Life of Thomas Jefferson,* p. 91.

38. *Literary Commonplace Book* (Chinard), p. 69.

39. Ibid., pp. 69–70.

40. Ibid., p. 54.

41. Ibid., pp.53–55.

42. Locke, *Human Understanding,* pp. 530–31: "If we will reflect on our own ways of Thinking, we shall find, that sometimes the Mind perceives the Agreement or Disagreement of two *Ideas* immediately by themselves, without the intervention of any other: And this, I think, we may call *intuitive knowledge.* For in this, the Mind is at no pains of proving or examining, but perceives the Truth, as the Eye doth light, only by being directed toward it. Thus the Mind perceives, that *White* is not *Black,* That a *Circle* is not a *Triangle,* That *Three* are more than *Two,* and equal to *One* and *Two.*"

43. In support of his client, Jefferson cited a case that had been reported by Sir Humphrey Winch. George Wythe, the lawyer opposing Jefferson, challenged the authority of Winch by pointing out that among the cases Winch reported was one that contained his own eulogy. Jefferson's response: "We might as well endeavor to destroy the authority of the Pentateuch, by observing, that all the chapters thereof were not written by Moses, because in one of them Deut. XXXIV . . . is a eulogy on himself, on occasion of his death" (Dumbauld, *Thomas Jefferson and the Law,* pp. 98, 100).

44. Jefferson, *Summary View,* p. 6.

45. Lieberman, *The Province of Legislation Determined,* pp. 36–38, 95–97. For the basis in natural law of Jefferson's legal philosophy, see Caldwell, "The Jurisprudence of Thomas Jefferson," pp. 192–213.

46. R. Ferguson, *Law and Letters in American Culture,* p. 52. For Jefferson's intensive and extensive studies and training for the legal profession, see J. Davis, "Thomas Jefferson, Attorney at Law," pp. 118–22; and Blackburn, *George Wythe of Williamsburg,* pp. 43–45.

47. *The Commonplace Book of Thomas Jefferson: A Repository of His Ideas on Government,* ed. Gilbert Chinard, pp. 351–56, 359–63 (hereafter cited as *Government Commonplace Book*). Chinard (pp. 11, 14) dates the opinion to 1776 because it appears in a part of the second commonplace book where the entries were made (and numbered consecutively) no later than that. The preceding entries were taken from materials dated 1775. There was no possibility that Jefferson could have rearranged the entries, since the pages in his commonplace book were written on both sides, and each entry began and ended in mid-page.

48. Ibid., pp. 354, 362.

49. Ibid., p. 351. Dumbauld, *Thomas Jefferson and the Law,* p. 77.

50. *Government Commonplace Book,* pp. 351–52.

51. Jefferson stated: "Thus we find this string of authorities when examined to the beginning all hanging on the same hook a perverted expression of Prisot's or on nothing, for they all quote Prisot, or one another, or nobody. Thus Finch quotes Prisot; Wingate also; Sheppard quotes Prisot, Finch and Wingate; Hale cites nobody; the court in Woolston's case cite Hale; Wood cites Woolston's case; Blackstone that and Hale; and Ld. Mansfield like Hale ventures it on his own authority" (*Government Commonplace Book,* p. 353).

52. Ibid., pp. 362–63. Dumbauld, in *Thomas Jefferson and the Law,* pp. 79, 210–12, writes that Justice Story and John Quincy Adams disagreed with Jefferson's opinion when it was later published and notes that Jefferson's views have been subsequently supported by Courtney Kenny in "The Evolution of the Law of Blasphemy," pp. 127–42.

53. Quoted by Dumbauld in *Thomas Jefferson and the Law,* p. 76, from Thomas Jefferson, "Reports of Cases Determined in the General Courts of Virginia" (1829), p. vi.

54. *Literary Commonplace Book* (Chinard), p. 66.

55. Ibid., p. 49.

56. Ibid., pp. 65–67.

57. Ibid., pp. 67–68.

58. Ibid., p. 69.

59. Ibid., pp. 46–48.

60. Jefferson to Peter Carr, 10 August 1787, *Writings* (Lipscomb and Bergh), 6:261.

61. Jefferson to William Short, 4 August 1820, in ibid., 15:257.

62. Jefferson to John Adams, 24 January 1824, and 11 April 1823, both in ibid., 14:71–72, 15:430.

63. *Literary Commonplace Book* (Chinard), p. 63.

64. Frend, *The Rise of Christianity,* pp. 93–104.

65. *Literary Commonplace Book* (Chinard), pp. 50–51.

66. Ibid., p. 51.

67. Ibid., pp. 56–57.

68. Ibid., p. 57.

69. Socinus wrote: "Indeed no man of judgement and piety ought to entertain the idea of a SATISFACTION for sin; since it plainly does very much derogate from the power and authority, or goodness of God. . . . Nay, it neither ever has nor ever can be the case that any one should be delivered from the punishment of his sins, by the efficacy of SATISFACTION. . . . Hence it appears . . . to be repugnant to divine justice itself, that one should suffer punishment (and death is the greatest penalty) for the sins of another. . . . It is evidently impeaching the Majesty of God to suppose that he cannot, that is, hath not the right to forgive sin freely; for thus he would possess less authority than any man does, as there is no one who cannot justly pardon any offences committed against him. And what are our sins, but offences committed against the Divine Being? To say God is unwilling to do this, doth

most evidently deprecate, if not entirely destroy his goodness" (in Toulmin, *Memoirs of the Life, Character, Sentiments, and Writings of Faustus Socinus*, pp. 186–87). For Jefferson's reference, see *Papers* (Boyd and Cullen), 1:554.

70. *Literary Commonplace Book* (Chinard), p. 57; Becker, "What Is Still Living in the Political Philosophy of Thomas Jefferson?" p. 46. Jefferson's objection to the doctrines of the fall and the atonement was that both caused men to distrust their reason and rely on that of others. Both were responsible for what he described as "awing the human mind by stories of raw-head and bloody bones to a distrust of its own vision, and to repose implicitly on that of others" (to Elbridge Gerry, 26 January 1799, in *Writings* (Lipscomb and Bergh), 10:78.

71. *Literary Commonplace Book* (Chinard), p. 64.

72. Jefferson to William Short, 4 August 1820, in *Writings* (Lipscomb and Bergh), 15:260–61.

73. *Literary Commonplace Book* (Chinard), p. 64.

74. Jefferson to Benjamin Waterhouse, 26 June 1822, in ibid., 10:384.

75. *Of Predestination and Election* reads: "Predestination to Life is the everlasting purpose of God, whereby (before the foundations of the world were laid) he hath constantly decreed by his counsel secret to us, to deliver from curse and damnation those whom he hath chosen in Christ out of mankind, and to bring them by Christ to everlasting salvation, as vessels made to honour. Wherefore, they which be endued with so excellent a benefit of God be called according to God's purpose by his Spirit working in due season: they through Grace obey the calling: they be justified freely: they be made sons of God by adoption: they be made like the image of his only begotten Son Jesus Christ: they walk religiously in good works, and at length, by God's mercy, they attain to everlasting felicity.

"As the godly consideration of Predestination, and our Election in Christ, is full of sweet, pleasant, and unspeakable comfort to godly persons, and such as feel in themselves the working of the Spirit of Christ, mortifying the works of the flesh, and their earthly members, and drawing up their mind to high and heavenly things, as well because it doth greatly establish and confirm their faith of eternal Salvation to be enjoyed through Christ, as because it doth fervently kindle their love towards God: So, for curious and carnal persons, lacking the Spirit of Christ, to have continually before their eyes the sentence of God's Predestination, is a most dangerous downfall, whereby the Devil doth thrust them either into desperation, or into wretchedness of most unclean living, no less perilous than desperation.

"Furthermore, we must receive God's promises in such wise, as they be generally set forth to us in holy Scripture: and, in our doings, that Will of God is to be followed, which we have expressly declared unto us in the Word of God." (See Bicknell, *A Theological Introduction to the Thirty-Nine Articles of the Church of England*, pp. 218–19).

76. Jefferson to John Adams, 11 April 1823, in Jefferson, Adams, and Adams, *The Adams-Jefferson Letters*, 2:591.

77. Chinard in *Literary Commonplace Book* (Chinard), p. 20.

78. See note 37, above.

79. The language in this paragraph is taken from the first printed copy as approved by the Continental Congress. It was probably Jefferson's, according to Julian Boyd, since the changes it contains from Jefferson's original rough draft were marked in that draft in Jefferson's handwriting before it went to the Congress for approval. In fact, Jefferson stated that none of these changes were made by the Congress, nor were they among those credited by him to John Adams or Benjamin Franklin. Further, John Adams, in his letter to Timothy Pickering, attributed none of the alterations to himself, Benjamin Franklin, or the committee of which they were members. The major change was from "advance from that subordination in which they have hitherto remained" to "dissolve the political bands which have connected them with another." "Equal and independent" and "the change" were altered to "separate and equal" and "to like separation," respectively. See Boyd, *Declaration of Independence* (1943), plate 10, p. 1 of plate 5, and p. 32.

80. Curti, *Human Nature in American Thought*, p. 88.

81. Brodie, *Thomas Jefferson: An Intimate History*, p. 81; Jefferson to Robert Skipwith, 31 August 1771, in *Papers* (Boyd and Cullen), 1:80.

82. See Dodsley, *The Oeconomy of Human Life*, title page.

83. Sowerby, *Catalogue*, 2:47.

84. This is particularly true of the nonfiction works that Jefferson regarded as providing rudimentary knowledge of their subjects, according to the 31 August 1771 letter that accompanied his list of book recommendations to Skipwith (*Writings* [Lipscomb and Bergh], 4:239).

85. Quoted in Sowerby, *Catalogue*, 2:47.

86. Dodsley, *Oeconomy of Human Life*, p. 25.

87. Jefferson to Thomas Law, Esq., 13 June 1814, in *Writings* (Lipscomb and Bergh), 14:142: "The Creator would indeed have been a bungling artist, had he intended man for a social animal, without planting in him social dispositions."

88. Jefferson to Thomas B. Parker, 15 May 1819, Jefferson Papers, 38400, S1 R150.

89. Calvin, *Institutes*, 21:935, 967–68.

90. A. Koch, *The Philosophy of Thomas Jefferson*, p. 136.

Chapter 3. Locke and the Declaration

1. See Becker, *The Declaration of Independence*; and White, *The Philosophy of the American Revolution*.

2. Mathews, *The Radical Politics of Thomas Jefferson*.

3. *Papers* (Boyd and Cullen), 1:33–34; Malone, *Jefferson and His Time*, 1:125–26.

4. *Government Commonplace Book*, pp. 13–14.

5. Wills, *Inventing America*, pp. 173–74.

6. *Government Commonplace Book*, pp. 213–29. For Jefferson's appli-

cation of his knowledge of history, see Colbourn, "Thomas Jefferson's Use of the Past," pp. 56–70.

7. *Government Commonplace Book*, pp. 213–14.

8. Ibid., pp. 215–17.

9. Ibid., p. 214.

10. Locke, *Two Treatises*, pp. 362–63.

11. Jefferson, *Notes*, p. 84.

12. Locke, *Two Treatises*, p. 356.

13. Ibid., pp. 407–8.

14. The legal date of separation from Great Britain by the colonies was 2 July 1776, when the Continental Congress passed the Richard Henry Lee resolution "that these United Colonies are, and of right ought to be, free and independent States, that they are absolved from all allegiance to the British Crown, and that all political connection between them and the State of Great Britain is and ought to be totally dissolved" (see Chitwood, *Richard Henry Lee: Statesman of the Revolution*, p. 95). John Adams thought that 2 July would be the date celebrated rather than 4 July (*Letters of Members of the Continental Congress*, 1:526).

15. The word "repeated," used in the first printing of the Declaration in the Rough Journal of Congress, had been "unremitting" in the rough draft copy. (See Boyd, *Declaration of Independence* (1943), plate 10 and p. 1 of plate 5.

16. This language is identical with that of the rough draft (ibid.).

17. Locke, *Two Treatises*, p. 405.

18. "One People" was "a people" in the rough draft (Boyd, *Declaration of Independence* (1943), plate 10 and p. 1 of plate 5).

19. The phrase "under absolute Despotism" was "arbitrary power" in the rough draft (ibid.). Boyd (pp. 25–26) believes that Jefferson changed "arbitrary power" to "under absolute power" and that perhaps Benjamin Franklin inserted "Despotism" in place of "power." Neither alteration changes the meaning in a Lockean context, since despotism, which consists of *"Despotical Power,"* according to Locke, was "Absolute, Arbitrary Power" (Locke, *Two Treatises*, pp. 382–83).

20. Laslett, introduction to Locke, *Two Treatises*, p. 55 (Wills mentions in *Inventing America*, pp. 172–73, this similarity but does not think it significant); Locke, *Two Treatises*, p. 415.

21. The same language was used in the rough draft (Boyd, *Declaration of Independence* (1943), plate 10 and p. 1 of plate 5).

22. The phrase "a free people" was "a people who mean to be free" in the rough draft (ibid., plate 10 and p. 3 of plate 5).

23. Locke, *Two Treatises*, pp. 382, 358, 271, 380.

24. This language is identical with that of the rough draft except for the words "under absolute Despotism," discussed in note 19.

25. Locke, *Two Treatises*, pp. 379–80: "For the Rulers, in such attempts, exercising a Power the People never put into their hands (who can never be supposed to consent, that any body should rule over them for their harm) do

that, which they have not a right to do. And where the Body of the People, or any single Man, is deprived of their Right, or is under the Exercise of a power without right, and have no Appeal on Earth, there they have a liberty to appeal to Heaven, whenever they judge the Cause of sufficient moment. And therefore, tho' the *People* cannot be *Judge,* so as to have by the Constitution of that Society any Superior power, to determine and give effective Sentence in the case; yet they have, by a Law antecedent and paramount to all positive Laws of men, reserv'd that ultimate Determination to themselves, which belongs to all Mankind, where there lies no Appeal on Earth, *viz.* to judge whether they have just Cause to make their Appeal to Heaven. And this judgement they cannot part with."

26. Ibid., pp. 380, 414.

27. The same language was used in the rough draft (Boyd, *Declaration of Independence* (1943), plate 10 and p. 1 of plate 5).

28. On the veracity of the abuses alleged by the Declaration, see Fisher, "The Accusations," pp. 127–35. For a 1776 ridicule of the Declaration's abuses, see Lind, "An Answer to the Declaration," pp. 9–17.

29. The same language was used in the rough draft (Boyd, *Declaration of Independence* (1943), plate 10 and p. 2 of plate 5).

30. Locke stated, "The *first and fundamental natural Law,* which is to govern even the Legislative it self, is *the preservation of the Society,* and (as far as will consist with the public good) of every person in it." As respects laws passed by the legislative Locke said, "These *Laws* also ought to be designed *for* no other end ultimately but *the good of the People*" (Locke, *Two Treatises,* pp. 355–56, 363).

31. Ibid., p. 367.

32. The same language was used in the rough draft (Boyd, *Declaration of Independence* (1943), plate 10 and p. 2 of plate 5).

33. The word "utterly" was added to the rough draft language (ibid.).

34. The phrase "in the Legislature" was added to the rough draft language (ibid.).

35. Locke, *Two Treatises,* p. 408.

36. Ibid., pp. 398–99.

37. The word "only" was added to the rough draft language after "Tyrants" (Boyd, *Declaration of Independence* (1943), plate 10 and p. 2 of plate 5).

38. The same language was used in the rough draft (ibid.).

39. Locke, *Two Treatises,* p. 409.

40. The same language was used in the rough draft (Boyd, *Declaration of Independence* (1943), plate 10 and p. 2 of plate 5).

41. The phrase "long Time, after such Dissolutions" was originally "long space of time" in the rough draft (ibid.).

42. The word "Constitution" was "constitutions" in the rough draft; otherwise, the same language was used (ibid., plate 10 and pp. 2, 4 of plate 5).

43. The rough draft did not contain the words "Acts of" (ibid., plate 10 and p. 2 of plate 5).

44. The same language was used in the rough draft (ibid.).

45. Locke, *Two Treatises,* p. 362.

46. This language is the same as that of the rough draft (Boyd, *Declaration of Independence* (1943), plate 10 and p. 3 of plate 5).

47. Locke, *Two Treatises,* pp. 402, 420.

48. Ibid., pp. 335–36.

49. *Government Commonplace Book,* pp. 22–23.

50. Chinard in ibid., p. 23.

51. This is the same language contained in the rough draft (Boyd, *Declaration of Independence* (1943), plate 10 and p. 4 of plate 5).

52. The words "an unwarrantable" and "us" were inserted in place of "a" and "these our states," respectively, in the rough draft (ibid.).

53. Ibid.

54. This language is the same in the rough draft (ibid.).

55. See Jefferson, *Summary View,* pp. iv, 5.

56. *Government Commonplace Book,* pp. 64–65, 137, 186. Robert Willman mentions Blackstone's view that the source of feudalism was "the German tribal organization" ("Blackstone and the Theoretical Perfection of English Law," p. 45). Caroline Robbins's research led her to conclude that Jefferson's "obsession" with the Saxon myth was partly due to his reading of Obadiah Hulme, *An Historical Essay on the English Constitution* (*The Eighteenth Century Commonwealthman,* pp. 363–64).

57. As one of the revisers of the law of the state of Virginia after the adoption of the Declaration of Independence, Jefferson said of the common law that the revisers "only needed to go over Saxon statutes and found in general [that they] only had to reduce law to its ancient Saxon condition to make it what it should be" (quoted in Dumbauld, *Thomas Jefferson and the Law,* p. 135.

58. Jefferson, *Summary View,* p. v.

59. Ibid., p. 6. Jefferson retained this idea after the Revolution as settlers migrated from the original states across the continent; he believed that "squatter sovereignty" would result in a series of "sister republics," according to Goetsmann, "Savage Enough to Prefer the Woods," p. 109. See also Wiltse, "Thomas Jefferson on the Law of Nations," pp. 69–70.

60. Jefferson, *Summary View,* p. 6.

61. This argument, although specifically applicable to the colonies, falls within the general appeal to the Saxons made by some in the eighteenth century, according to Pocock, *The Ancient Constitution and Feudal Law,* p. 239.

62. Locke, *Two Treatises,* p. 345.

63. Boyd, *Declaration of Independence* (1943), pp. 19–20; *Papers* (Boyd and Cullen), 1:415–16.

64. Jefferson to James Madison, 30 August 1823, in *Writings* (Ford), 10:266.

65. Jefferson to Henry Lee, 8 May 1825, in ibid., p. 343.

66. Jefferson to Thomas Mann Randolph, 30 May 1790, in *Writings*

(Lipscomb and Bergh), 8:31. On Jefferson's "Federalist" reference, see Hamilton, Madison, and Jay, *The Federalist Papers.*

67. Boyd, *Declaration of Independence* (1943), pp. 13, 21. See also Dana, "The Political Principles of the Declaration," pp. 319–43.

68. C. Smith, *James Wilson,* pp. 26, 55; and Hill, *George Mason, Constitutionalist,* p. 140.

69. Becker, *Declaration of Independence,* p. 27; Bailyn, *The Ideological Origins of the American Revolution,* pp. 27, 36; and Dworetz, *The Unvarnished Doctrine,* pp. 65–96. For reservations about the familiarity and influence of the *Second Treatise* in the colonies at the time of the Revolution, see Pocock, "Machiavelli, Harrington, and English Political Ideologies," p. 581; Tate, "The Social Contract in America," pp. 376–78; and Dunn, "The Politics of Locke in England and America," pp. 79–80.

70. In response to Miles King's claim to have had a divine revelation from God, Jefferson expressed a polite skepticism: "Whether the particular revelation you suppose to have been made to yourself were real or imaginary, your reason alone is the competent judge. For dispute as long as we will on religious tenets, our reason at last must ultimately decide, as it is the only oracle which God has given us to determine between what really comes from Him and the phantasms of a disordered or deluded imagination. When He means to make a personal revelation, He carries conviction of its authenticity to the reason He has bestowed as the umpire of truth. You believe you have been favored with such a special communication. Your reason, not mine, is to judge of this; and if it shall be His pleasure to favor me with a like admonition, I shall obey it with the same fidelity with which I would obey His known will in all cases. Hitherto I have been under the guidance of that portion of reason which He has thought proper to deal out to me. I have followed it faithfully in all important cases, to such a degree at least as leaves me without uneasiness; and if on minor occasions I have erred from its dictates, I have trust in Him who made us what we are, and know it was not His plan to make us always unerring" (26 September 1814, in *Writings* (Lipscomb and Bergh), 14:197.

71. *Papers* (Boyd and Cullen), 1:79.

72. Locke, *Of the Conduct of the Understanding,* p. 56 (hereafter cited as *Conduct*).

73. Jefferson to Meeting of the Visitors, University of Virginia, 7 October 1822, in *Writings* (Lipscomb and Bergh), 19:414.

74. Locke, *Conduct,* pp. 59–60.

75. Jefferson to Peter Carr, 10 August 1787, in *Writings* (Lipscomb and Bergh), 6:261, 258.

76. *Literary Commonplace Book* (Wilson), pp. 97, 227.

77. Ibid., pp. 120, 227.

78. Ibid., pp. 71–72, 228. Chinard's edition of the *Literary Commonplace Book* gives a slightly different translation.

79. Locke, *Two Treatises,* pp. 304, 271.

80. Ibid., pp. 269–71, 284.

81. Ibid., pp. 269–71.

82. Ibid., pp. 357–58, 360, 363: "A Man, as has been proved, cannot subject himself to the Arbitrary Power of another; and having in the State of Nature no Arbitrary Power over the Life, Liberty, or Possession of another, but only so much as the Law of Nature gave him for the preservation of himself, and the rest of Mankind; this is all he doth, or can give up to the Common-wealth, and by it to the *Legislative Power,* so that the Legislative can have no more than this. Their Power in the utmost Bounds of it, is *limited to the publick good* of the Society. It is a Power, that hath no other end but preservation, and therefore can never have a right to destroy, en-slave, or designedly to impoverish the Subjects. The Obligations of the Law of Nature, cease not in Society, but only in many Cases are drawn closer, and have by Humane Laws known Penalties annexed to them, to inforce their observation. Thus the Law of Nature stands as an Eternal Rule to all Men, *Legislators* as well as others. The *Rules* that they make for other Mens Actions, must, as well as their own and other Mens Actions, be conformable to the Law of Nature, i.e. to the Will of God, of which that is a Declaration, and the *fundamental Law of Nature* being *the preservation of Mankind,* no Humane Sanction can be good, or valid against it. . . .

"For all the power the Government has, being only for the good of the Society, as it ought not to be *Arbitrary* and at Pleasure, so it ought to be exercised by *established and promulgated Laws:* that both the People may know their Duty, and be safe and secure within the limits of the Law, and the Rulers too kept within their due bounds, and not to be tempted, by the Power they have in their hands, to imploy it to such purposes, and by such mea-sures, as they would not have known, and own not willingly. . . .

"These are the *Bounds* which the trust that is put in them by the Society, and the Law of God and Nature, have *set to the Legislative* Power of every Commonwealth, in all Forms of Government. First, They are to govern by *promulgated established Laws.* . . . Secondly, These *Laws* also ought to be designed *for* no other end ultimately but *the good of the People."*

83. Ibid., pp. 426–27: "Here, 'tis like, the common Question will be made, *Who shall be Judge* whether the Prince or Legislative act contrary to their Trust? This, perhaps, ill affected and factious Men may spread among the People, when the Prince only makes use of his due Prerogative. To this I reply, *The People shall be Judge;* for who shall be *Judge* whether his Trustee or Deputy acts well, and according to the Trust reposed in him, but he who deputes him, and must, by having deputed him have still a Power to discard him, when he fails in his Trust? If this be reasonable in particular Cases of private Men, why should it be otherwise in that of the greatest moment; where the Welfare of Millions is concerned, and also where the evil, if not prevented, is greater, and the Redress very difficult, dear, and dangerous?"

84. Jefferson's rough draft version: "We hold these truths to be sacred and undeniable; that all men are created equal and independent; that from that equal creation they derive rights, inherent & inalienable, among which are the preservation of life, liberty, & the pursuit of happiness; that to secure these ends, governments are instituted among men, deriving their just powers from the consent of the governed; that whenever any form of government becomes destructive of these ends, it is the right of the people to alter or to abolish it, & to institute new government, laying it's foundation on such principles & organising it's powers in such form, as to them shall seem most likely to effect their safety & happiness." Boyd believes that Jefferson himself changed "sacred and undeniable" to "self-evident." With two exceptions, he also made the other changes that appear in the first printing as approved by the Continental Congress, for these changes appeared in the rough draft in Jefferson's handwriting when it was submitted to the Congress, and John Adams in a letter to Timothy Pickering did not attribute any of them to himself, Benjamin Franklin, or the committee to whom Jefferson first submitted his draft. The Congress made the two changes that were not Jefferson's. They replaced the words "inherent and" with "certain" and changed "inalienable" to "unalienable." See Boyd, *Declaration of Independence* (1943), plate 10, p. 1 of plate 5, and pp. 24–26, 32; John Adams, *Works,* 2:514. Jefferson to James Madison, 30 August 1823, attributed a few other changes to Franklin and Adams: "You have seen the original paper [rough draft] now in my hands, with the corrections of Dr. Franklin and Mr. Adams interlined in their own handwritings. Their alterations were two or three only, and merely verbal" (*Writings* [Lipscomb and Bergh], 15:461). For a detailed account of the writing of the Declaration, see also Hazelton, *The Declaration of Independence: Its History,* pp. 141–55.

85. Two references to God in the final paragraph of the Declaration have more orthodox Judeo-Christian connotations: "appealing to the Supreme Judge of the World for the Rectitude of our Intentions" and "with a firm Reliance on the Protection of divine Providence." Neither of these references was written by Jefferson, however. Both were inserted by Congress (Boyd, *Declaration of Independence* (1943), p. 34).

Chapter 4. Kames and the Moral Sense

1. A. Koch, *The Philosophy of Thomas Jefferson,* p. 4.

2. Jefferson to Robert Skipwith, 3 August 1771, in *Papers* (Boyd and Cullen), 1:80.

3. Hume, *Essays and Treatises,* 1:179.

4. Bolingbroke regarded scripture as history and commented on the clerical corruption of scripture in his *Letters on the Study and Use of History* (in *Works,* 2:347–49): "I have said so much concerning the share which divines of all religions have taken in the corruption of history, that I should have anathemas pronounced against me, no doubt, in the east and west, by the

dairo, the mufti, and the pope, if these letters were submitted to ecclesiastical censure; for surely, my Lord, the clergy have a better title, than the sons
of Apollo, to be called 'genus irratabile vatum.' What would it be, if I went
about to shew, how many of the Christian clergy abuse, by misrepresentation and false quotation, the history they can no longer corrupt? And yet this
task would not be, even to me, an hard one. . . . No scholar will dare to deny,
that false history, as well as sham miracles, has been employed to propagate
christianity formerly: and whoever examines the writers of our own age, will
find the same abuse of history continued. Many and many instances of this
abuse might be produced. It is grown into custom, writers copy one another,
and the mistake that was committed, or the falsehood that was invented by
one, is adopted by hundreds." Compare the following anticlerical statement
of Jefferson: "I have contemplated on their order from the Magi of the East
to the Saints on the West, and I have found no difference of Character, but of
more or less caution, in proportion to their information or ignorance of
those on whom their interested duperies were to be plaid off" (*Writings* [Ford],
10:12–13). Jefferson, like Bolingbroke, used *genus irratabile vatum* in describing the clergy in his letters of 15 February 1818 to Albert Gallatin and
19 July 1822 to Benjamin Waterhouse (both in *Writings* [Lipscomb and
Bergh], 14:259, 15:391).

    5. Bolingbroke, *Works,* 4:412–13: "Such is the knavery and such the
folly of mankind, that no example, antient nor modern, pagan nor christian,
can be produced of such an order of men [priests] once established that has
not aimed at acquiring from their institution, and that has not acquired,
sooner or later, immoderate wealth and exorbitant power.

    "Few men are so little acquainted with the history of the christian world
as not to know, that the wealth of this church is equal, at least in many
countries, to that of the egyptian church; that the influence of the antient
could be greater than that of the modern magi over all ranks of men; and
that the bishop of Rome has exercised, even over kings in many countries, a
power which he claimed, in all, of the same nature with that of the ethiopian
church over kings of one country." Compare Jefferson on Christian and Jewish
priestcraft: "I abuse the priests, indeed, who have so much abused the pure
and holy doctrines of their Master, and who have laid me under no obligations of reticence as to the tricks of their trade. The genuine system of Jesus,
and the artificial structures they have erected, to make them the instruments
of wealth, power, and preeminence to themselves, are as distinct things in my
view as light and darkness; and while I have classed them with soothsayers
and necromancers, I place Him among the greatest reformers of morals, and
scourges of priest-craft that have ever existed. . . . But His heresies against
Judaism prevailing in the long run, the priests have tacked about, and rebuilt
upon them the temple which He destroyed, as splendid, as profitable, and as
imposing as that" (to Charles Clay, Esq., 29 January 1815, in *Writings*
[Lipscomb and Bergh], 14:233).

6. Becker, *The Declaration of Independence*, p. 31.

7. Jefferson to Charles Clay, Esq., 29 June 1815, in *Writings* (Lipscomb and Bergh), 14:233–34. For hierarchical aspects of Christian sects other than Catholicism, see Stout, "Religion, Communications, and the Ideological Origins of the American Revolution," pp. 525–26; Willard, "The Character of a Good Ruler," p. 251; and Foster, *Their Solitary Way*, p. 18.

8. Locke, *Two Treatises*, p. 271.

9. See chapter 3, notes 82, 83.

10. Dunn, *The Political Thought of John Locke*, pp. 182–83.

11. Locke, *Two Treatises*, p. 351.

12. Locke, *Human Understanding*, p. 549.

13. Dunn, *The Political Thought of John Locke*, p. 192.

14. Locke, *Works*, 2:532, 535. For a reconciliation of *The Reasonableness of Christianity* and *Human Understanding*, see Ashcraft, "Faith and Knowledge in Locke's Philosophy," pp. 194–223.

15. A meaning of the *Second Treatise* was that most men had to look to those with superior rational capacity for moral knowledge, according to Aarsleff, "The State of Nature and the Nature of Man in Locke," p. 133.

16. *Human Understanding* was on a 1767 reading list of books Jefferson recommended to a law student in his care; see *The Complete Jefferson*, pp. 1043–47. Although the original and Jefferson's first copy of that original list are missing, Jefferson sent another copy to John Minor (30 August 1814, in *Writings* [Ford], 11:480), stating that it was "without change" except that books published later had made it possible "in some of the departments of science to substitute better for less perfect publications which we then possessed."

17. Jefferson briefly paraphrased *Reasonableness* in October or November 1776 (*Papers* [Boyd and Cullen], 1:525, 529, 549–50).

18. See White, *The Philosophy of the American Revolution*, p. 275.

19. *Government Commonplace Book*, pp. 167, 13, 95–135.

20. Chinard in ibid., p. 19.

21. Wills, *Inventing America*, p. 201.

22. Hamowy, "Jefferson and the Scottish Enlightenment," pp. 514, 522.

23. See *The Complete Jefferson*, pp. 1043–47.

24. Kames, *Essays on the Principles of Morality and Natural Religion*, pp. 95–96 (hereafter cited as *Essays*). J. Ferguson, in *The Philosophy of Dr. Samuel Clarke and Its Critics*, pp. 170–75, wrote that Clarke's moral theory was based on the rationally determined "fitness or unfitness of certain kinds of conduct of some persons to other persons which arises from the different relations in which people may stand to one another." Such a rationally made moral determination was similar to Locke's rationally demonstrated law of nature in that it was "as evident as that in mathematics" once deduced by using abstract reason.

25. "The greatest part of mankind want leisure or capacity for Demon-

stration; nor can carry a chain of Proofs, which in that way they must always depend on for Conviction, and cannot be required to assent to till they see the Demonstration" (Locke, *Works*, 2:535).

26. Kames, *Essays*, pp. 60, 99. Cf. Hutcheson, *An Inquiry into the Original of our Ideas of Beauty and Virtue*, pp. xiv–xv: "The weakness of our Reason, and the avocations arising from the Infirmity and Necessitys of our Nature, are so great, that very few Men could ever have form'd those long Deductions of Reason, which shew some Actions to be in the whole *advantageous* to the *Agent* and their Contrarys *pernicious*. The *AUTHOR* of Nature has much better furnish'd us for a virtuous Conduct, than our *Moralists* seem to imagine, by almost as quick and powerful Instructions, as we have for the preservation of our Bodys. He has made *Virtue* a lovely *Form* to excite our pursuit of it; and has given us *strong Affections* to be the Springs of each virtuous Action."

27. It appears on his 1767 list of books recommended to a law student.

28. Kames, *Principles of Equity*, pp. 30–31. Broderick, "Pulpit, Physics, and Politics," p. 58, points out that "introspection" plus "observation of other men" gave the Scots a knowledge of human nature based on what they deemed a crude kind of empiricism.

29. Kames, *Essays*, pp. 76, 88–90.

30. McGuinness, *Henry Home, Lord Kames*, p. 35. Jefferson, it seems, read Hobbes. He took exception to Hobbes's idea (*Leviathan*, p. 89) that "the Desires, and other Passions of man, are in themselves no sin. No more are the Actions, that proceed from those Passions, till they know a Law that forbids them: which till Lawes be made they cannot know: nor can any Law be made, till they have agreed upon the Person that shall make it." Jefferson expressed his disagreement when he said of a proposed work on morals by Destutt Tracy, "I lament to see that he will adopt the principles of Hobbes, or humiliation to human nature; that the sense of justice and injustice is not derived from our natural organization, but founded on convention only" (to Francis W. Gilmer, 7 June 1816, in *Writings* [Lipscomb and Bergh], 15:24–25). Although this comment was made in 1816, it would seem probable that he read Hobbes during the years before 1776 when he was reading extensively, at which time he read Kames. Jefferson's awareness of Kames's assimilation of parts of Hobbes's ideas on man as a result of reading *Essays* may well have been what stimulated his interest in Hobbes.

31. Kames, *Essays*, p. 76.

32. Ibid., p. 63. Cf. Hutcheson, *A System of Moral Philosophy*, 1:61: "This moral sense from its very nature appears to be designed for regulating and controlling all our powers. This dignity and commanding nature we are immediately conscious of, as we are conscious of the power itself. Nor can such matters of immediate feeling be otherwise proved but by appeals to the heart."

33. Kames, *Essays*, p. 123. See Forbes, "Natural Law and the Scottish

Enlightenment," pp. 198–99, for Kames's ideas on determining the laws of nature.

34. Kames, *Essays,* p. 99.

35. Locke, *Works,* 2:535.

36. Kames, *Essays,* pp. 59–60, 61, 63, 64, 66, 71, 128, 68. Kames defined the law of nature as "rules of our conduct and behavior, founded on natural principles, approved of by the moral sense, and enforced by natural rewards and punishments" (p. 122).

37. Ibid., p. 19.

38. Jefferson to Robert Skipwith, 3 August 1771, in *Papers* (Boyd and Cullen), 1:76–79.

39. Kames, *Essays,* p. 67.

40. Jefferson to Peter Carr, 10 August 1787, in *Writings* (Lipscomb and Bergh), 6:257–58. Unlike Jefferson, Locke believed in original sin, according to Spellman, *John Locke and the Problem of Depravity,* pp. 211–14.

41. John Dewey, *The Living Thoughts of Thomas Jefferson,* p. 14, wrote that the basis of Jefferson's political theory was his faith in the moral nature of man.

42. White, *Philosophy of the American Revolution,* pp. 118, 120–21.

43. Ibid., pp. 122–23, 268, 125.

44. *Papers* (Boyd and Cullen), 1:33–34.

45. Jefferson, *Summary View,* p. 12.

46. White, *Philosophy of the American Revolution,* p. 114.

47. Ibid.

48. "We are not left to gather our duty by abstract reasoning, nor indeed by any reasoning. It is engraved upon the table of our hearts. We adapt our actions to the course of nature, by mere instinct, without reasoning, or even experience" (Kames, *Essays,* p. 316).

49. Jefferson, *Summary View,* p. 22.

50. Kames, *Essays,* pp. 58–59.

51. This language from the first printing is identical to Jefferson's in his rough draft (Boyd, *Declaration of Independence* (1943), plate 10 and p. 1 of plate 5).

52. Jefferson to Henry Lee, 8 May 1825, in *Writings* (Ford), 10:343.

53. This language is identical to Jefferson's in his rough draft (Boyd, *Declaration of Independence* (1943), plate 10 and p. 1 of plate 5).

54. Wills, *Inventing America,* pp. 184, 191.

55. A. Smith, *The Theory of Moral Sentiments,* p. 261.

56. Jefferson to Henry Lee, 8 May 1825, in *Writings* (Ford), 10:343.

57. Wills, *Inventing America,* pp. 184, 190–92.

58. Jefferson to Richard Price, 12 July 1789, in *Papers* (Boyd and Cullen), 15:252.

59. "The moral sense, tho' rooted in the nature of man, admits of great refinements by culture and education. It improves gradually like our other

powers and faculties, 'till it comes to be productive of the strongest as well as the most delicate feelings" (Kames, *Essays,* p. 143).

60. Kames, *Elements of Criticism,* 2:492, 485.

61. Kames, *Essays,* pp. 37–38.

62. Jefferson to Thomas Law, 13 June 1814, in *Writings* (Lipscomb and Bergh), 14:142–43.

63. Ibid., 14:144.

64. Kames, *Elements of Criticism,* 2:489, 492.

65. Jefferson to Maria Cosway, 12 October 1786, in Bullock, *My Head and My Heart,* pp. 38–39.

66. Ibid., p. 38.

67. Kames, *Principles of Equity,* p. 32.

68. Jefferson to James Fishbach, 27 September 1809, in *Writings* (Lipscomb and Bergh), 12:315.

69. Jefferson to Thomas Law, 13 June 1814, in ibid., 14:139, 141.

70. Ibid.

71. Jefferson to William Short, 4 August 1820, in ibid., 15:261.

72. Jefferson to William Short, 13 April 1820, in ibid., 15:245.

73. Jefferson to F.A. Van Der Kemp, 25 April 1816, in ibid., 15:3.

74. *Jefferson's Extracts from the Gospels,* p. 14. For the Jefferson-Priestley friendship, see Browne, "Joseph Priestley and the American 'Fathers,'" pp. 142–43. For Priestley's influence, see also Jefferson to his daughter Martha, 23 April 1803, in *Family Letters,* pp. 243–44.

75. Jefferson to John Adams, 13 October 1813, in *Writings* (Lipscomb and Bergh), 13:389–90. For an excellent account of Jefferson's views on Christianity, see Kimball, "Thomas Jefferson and Religion," pp. 161–67.

76. See *Jefferson's Extracts from the Gospels,* p. 3. The work has also been published as *The Jefferson Bible.*

77. Jefferson to Benjamin Rush, 23 September 1800, in *Writings* (Lipscomb and Bergh), 10:174.

78. Jefferson to John Adams, 5 July 1814, in ibid., 14:149.

79. Jefferson to William Short, 13 April 1820, in ibid., 15:245.

80. Jefferson to Elbridge Gerry, 29 March 1801, in ibid., 10:254. For Jefferson's anger at the Christian clergy, see Knoles, "The Religious Ideas of Thomas Jefferson," pp. 250–52.

81. Jefferson to Benjamin Rush, 21 April 1803, in *Writings* (Lipscomb and Bergh), 10:385.

82. Jefferson, *The Life and Morals of Jesus,* in ibid., 20:51.

83. Criminal law punishments were supplemental to those provided by nature to enforce its laws, according to Kames: "The purposes of human punishments are, first to add weight to those which nature has provided" (*Historical Law Tracts,* 1:73–74).

84. Ibid., 1:l–2. Kames's concept of atonement excluded the transfer of punishment to an innocent party. "No maxim has a more solid foundation

than that punishment cannot be transferred from the guilty to the innocent" is a statement Jefferson extracted from Kames's *Historical Law Tracts* (*Government Commonplace Book*, pp. 98, 13).

85. Barker, "Natural Law and the American Revolution," pp. 312–13, pointed out that natural law "proceeding from the nature of the universe—from the Being of God and the reason of man" could be traced from Aristotle and "the Stoic thinkers of the Hellenistic age"; it was "adopted by the Catholic Church" and formed "the general teaching of the schoolmen and the canonists." But Barker believed that the "general theory of the seventeenth century" on natural law, "as we find it in Grotius, Pufendorf, and Locke (and also in Hobbes and Spinoza), is a modern secular theory."

86. Jefferson to Benjamin Rush, 21 April 1803, in *Writings* (Lipscomb and Bergh), 10:384.

87. Jefferson to John Adams, 5 May 1817, in ibid., 15:109.

88. Marshall, *John Locke: Resistance, Religion, and Responsibility*, p. 407.

89. Adams, *Jefferson's Extracts from the Gospels*, p. 41.

90. Priestley, *Theological and Miscellaneous Works*, 5:488–89: "It is acknowledged that, to be a Christian, a man must believe some facts that are of an extraordinary nature, such as we have no opportunity of observing at present. But those facts were so circumstanced, that persons who cannot be denied to have had the best opportunity of examining the evidence of them, and who, if they had not been true, had any motive to pay any regard to them, could not refuse their assent to them; that is, it was such evidence as we ourselves must have been determined by, if we had been in their place; and therefore, if not fully equivalent to the evidence of our own senses at present, is, at least, all the evidence that, at this distance of time, we *can* have in the case. It goes upon the principle that human nature was the same thing then that it is now; and certainly in all other respects it appears to be so.

"That miracles are things in themselves *possible*, must be allowed, so long as it is evident that there is in nature a power equal to the working of them. And certainly the *power, principle*, or *being*, by whatever name it be denominated, which produced the universe, and established the laws of it, is fully equal to any occasional departures from them."

91. Jefferson to Moses Robinson, 23 March 1801, in *Writings* (Lipscomb and Bergh), 10:237.

92. Jesus said unto them (the Jews), "If God were your Father, ye would love me: for I proceeded forth and came from God; neither came I of myself, but he sent me. Why do ye not understand my speech? even because ye cannot hear my word. Ye are of your father the devil, and the lusts of your father ye will do. He was a murderer from the beginning, and abode not in the truth, because there is no truth in him. When he speaketh a lie, he speaketh of his own: for he is a liar, and the father of it. And because I tell you the truth, ye believe me not. Which of you convinceth me of sin? And if I say the

truth, why do ye not believe me? He that is of God heareth God's words: ye therefore hear them not, because ye are not of God."

Chapter 5. Obstacles to Reason

1. See Appleby, "Republicanism in Old and New Contexts," pp. 23–25, for Jefferson's ideas on progress.

2. Jefferson to Benjamin Rush, 16 January 1811, in *Writings* (Lipscomb and Bergh), 13:4.

3. Jefferson had Bacon's writings bound on 28 October 1765, according to Dumas Malone, who believes that Jefferson read all the books he owned at that time of his life (*Jefferson and His Time,* 1:103 n. 17).

4. Bacon, *Novum Organon,* pp. 14, 17, 11.

5. Ibid., pp. xxv (from that part of the outline of the "Instauratio Magna" which relates to the *Novum Organon*), 83, 57. Isaac Kramnick wrote that progress through science became "the theme of the age" during the late Enlightenment ("Religion and Radicalism," pp. 522–24).

6. *Thomas Jefferson's Garden Book,* pp. 1, 7–8, 610–11; *Thomas Jefferson's Farm Book,* pp. 1–5.

7. Ferguson, *Law and Letters in American Culture,* p. 52. The *Novum Organon's* "Great Instauration" was the basis for Jefferson's method of understanding nature, according to C. Miller, *Jefferson and Nature,* p. 11. For other accounts of Bacon's influence on Jefferson, see S. Brown, *Thomas Jefferson,* pp. 188–97; and Hellenbrand, *The Unfinished Revolution;* p. 159.

8. Bedini, *Thomas Jefferson, Statesman of Science,* p. 92; Peden, preface to Jefferson, *Notes,* pp. xiii–xiv.

9. Jefferson, *Notes,* p. 48.

10. Ibid., pp. 50–52, 66–70, 74, 84, 94–95, 103–5, 144–45, 167.

11. Bacon, *Novum Organon,* pp. 19, 41–42.

12. Popkin, *The History of Skepticism from Erasmus to Spinoza,* pp. xiii–xvi.

13. "Any doctrine, which leads to a distrust of our senses, must land in universal scepticism. If natural feelings, whether from internal or external senses, are not admitted as evidence of truth, I cannot see, that we can be certain of any fact whatever. It is clear, from what is now observed, that, upon this sceptical system, we cannot be certain even of our existence" (Kames, *Essays,* pp. 234–35).

14. *Papers* (Boyd and Cullen), 1:79–80.

15. Bayle, *Historical and Critical Dictionary Selections* (Popkin translation), p. xxiv. If Jefferson read dialogue 24 between John Locke and Pierre Bayle in George Lyttelton's *Dialogues of the Dead* (also on the 1771 Skipwith book list), he would have seen (p. 271) that Bayle referred to his own philosophy as "my scepticism."

16. Peter Bayle, *The Dictionary Historical and Critical,* trans. P. Des Maizeau (the English edition recommended by Jefferson, according to Beller

and Lee, editors of *Selections from Bayle's Dictionary,* p. xx), 4:653–54, 656.

17. Ibid., 4:655–56.

18. Ibid., 4:656; Bayle, *Historical and Critical Dictionary Selections,* p. xxv.

19. Kames, *Essays,* pp. 383–84.

20. Reid's commonsense philosophy was foreshadowed in Kames's *Essays,* according to W. Lehmann, *Henry Home, Lord Kames,* p. 166; and Laurie, *Scottish Philosophy in Its National Development,* p. 103. Walker, *The Scottish Jurists,* p. 221, wrote that Kames and Reid knew each other well and that Reid spent summers at Kames's home for years. Jefferson's reading of Blackstone's *Commentaries* as a law student would have placed him in contact with what Boorstin described in *The Mysterious Science of the Law,* pp. 109–19, as a subtle version of commonsense philosophy.

21. Reid was born in 1710, Small in 1734. See Grave, *Scottish Philosophy of Common Sense,* p. 1; and Ganter, "William Small, Jefferson's Beloved Teacher," p. 506.

22. Davie, *The Democratic Intellect,* pp. 10–12.

23. Reid, *An Inquiry into the Human Mind,* pp. 25–26 (hereafter cited as *Inquiry*).

24. Ibid., p. 60.

25. Locke, *Human Understanding,* pp. 47, 563.

26. Ibid., p. 135: "Such *Qualities,* which in truth are nothing in the Objects themselves, but Powers to produce various Sensations in us by their *primary Qualities,* i.e. by the Bulk, Figure, Texture, and Motion of their insensible parts, as Colours, Sounds, Taste, *etc.*"

27. Reid said of Locke's view: "Mr Locke saw clearly, and proved incontestably, that the sensations we have by taste, smell, and hearing, as well as the sensations of colour, heat, and cold, are not resemblances of any thing in bodies; and in this he agrees with DesCartes and Malbranche. Joining this opinion with the hypothesis, it follows necessarily, that three senses of the five are cut off from giving us any intelligence of the material world, as being altogether inept for that office" (*Inquiry,* pp. 209–10).

28. Ibid., pp. 23–24: "His [Berkeley's] arguments are founded upon the principles which were formerly laid down by DesCartes, Malebranche and Locke, and which have been very generally received. And the opinion of the ablest judges seems to be, that they neither have been, nor can be confuted; and that he hath proved by unanswerable arguments what no man in his senses can believe. . . . As the Bishop [Berkeley] undid the whole material world, this author [Hume], upon the same grounds, undoes the world of spirits [minds], and leaves nothing in nature but ideas and impressions, without any subject on which they may be impressed."

29. Grave, *Scottish Philosophy of Common Sense,* p. 53.

30. As Reid put it, "The result of his [Berkeley's] inquiry was, a serious

conviction, that there is no such thing as a material world; nothing in nature but spirits and ideas, and that the belief of material substances, and of abstract ideas, are the chief causes of all our errors in philosophy, and of infidelity and heresy in religion" (*Inquiry*, p. 23). See also Berkeley, *Of the Principles of Human Knowledge*, part 1, *The Age of Enlightment*, pp. 132–33.

31. Reid, *Inquiry*, pp. 61, 57, 65.

32. Hume, *A Treatise of Human Nature* (hereafter, *Treatise*), p. 213: "Suppose two objects to be presented to us, of which the one is the cause and the other the effect; 'tis plain, that from the simple consideration of one, or both these objects we never shall perceive the tie, by which they are united, or be able certainly to pronounce, that there is a connexion betwixt them. "Tis not, therefore, from any one instance, that we arrive at the idea of cause and effect, of a necessary connexion of power, of force, of energy, and of efficacy. Did we never see any but particular conjunctions of objects, entirely different from each other, we should never be able to form any such ideas.

"But again; suppose we observe several instances, in which the same objects are always conjoin'd together, we immediately conceive a connexion betwixt them, and begin to draw an inference from one to another. This multiplicity of resembling instances, therefore, constitutes the very essence of power or connexion, and is the source, from which the idea of it arises." For Locke's view that cause and effect could be determined and his philosophy of science, see Yolton, "The Science of Nature," pp. 183–93.

33. Reid, *Inquiry*, pp. 30–31.

34. Ibid., pp. 504, 205, 3, 28.

35. Locke, *Human Understanding*, p. 525.

36. Reid, *Inquiry*, p. 533.

37. Ibid., pp. 534, 156.

38. Grave, *Scottish Philosophy of Common Sense*, p. 3.

39. Reid, *Inquiry*, pp. 534, 34.

40. Jefferson to John Adams, 14 March 1820, in *Writings* (Lipscomb and Bergh), 15:239; Grave, *Scottish Philosophy of Common Sense*, p. 2.

41. Jefferson to Robert Walsh, 9 January 1818, in Chinard, *Jefferson et les idealogues*, pp. 173–74.

42. Jefferson to John Adams, 15 August 1820, in *Writings* (Lipscomb and Bergh), 15:275–76.

43. Bacon, *Novum Organon*, pp. 70, 37.

44. Jefferson, *Notes*, pp. 159–60.

45. Bacon, *Novum Organon*, p. 37; Chinard, *Thomas Jefferson, the Apostle of Americanism*, p. 512.

46. Jefferson to Charles Clay, 29 January 1815, in *Writings* (Lipscomb and Bergh), 14:233–34.

47. Jefferson to Thomas Seymour, 11 February 1807, in ibid., 11:156.

48. Bolingbroke, *Works*, 4:411–12.

49. Jefferson to Baron von Humboldt, 6 December 1813, and to Horatio

G. Spafford, 17 March 1814, in *Writings* (Lipscomb and Bergh), 14:21, 119.

50. Jefferson to James Smith, 8 December 1822, in ibid., 15:409.

51. *Literary Commonplace Book* (Wilson), pp. 120, 227.

52. Jefferson, *Notes,* p. 159.

53. Jefferson to James Fishbach, 27 September 1809, in *Writings* (Lipscomb and Bergh), 12:315. For Jefferson's value of religious and intellectual pluralism and methods that would enable such pluralism to lead to progress in a democracy, see T. Smith, "Discussion: Thomas Jefferson and the Perfectibility of Mankind," pp. 293–98.

54. *Literary Commonplace Book* (Wilson), pp. 20, 227.

55. *Jefferson's Extracts from the Gospels,* p. 17; Benjamin Rush to Jefferson, 22 August 1800, ibid., p. 318.

56. Jefferson, *Autobiography,* pp. 62–63.

57. Jefferson to Benjamin Rush, 23 September 1800, in *Writings* (Lipscomb and Bergh), 10:175.

58. Jefferson to Thomas Cooper, 10 February 1814, in ibid., 14:85.

59. Jefferson to Thomas Cooper, 2 November 1822, in ibid., 15:405.

60. Jefferson to Joseph Priestley, 21 March 1801, in *The Writings of Thomas Jefferson,* ed. H.A. Washington, 4:373. According to Morgan, *The Meaning of Independence,* p. 73, Jefferson viewed institutionalized Christianity as the "dead hand of the past."

61. Honeywell, *The Educational Work of Thomas Jefferson,* pp. 10–11, 14. No new university was included in the bill, but it made provision for the brightest students in the grammar schools to attend William and Mary at public expense. A separate bill was proposed to liberate William and Mary from the control of the Anglican Church and to expand its curriculum. See also Conant, *Thomas Jefferson and the Development of American Public Education,* pp. 1–19.

62. Jefferson to J.C. Cabell, 28 November 1820, in *Writings* (Lipscomb and Bergh), 15:293.

63. Chinard, *Thomas Jefferson, the Apostle of Americanism,* p. 510; Honeywell, *The Educational Work of Thomas Jefferson,* pp. 108–12; and Commager, *Jefferson, Nationalism, and the Enlightenment,* p. 70.

64. Chinard, *Thomas Jefferson, the Apostle of Americanism,* p. 510.

65. Jefferson to William Roscoe, 27 December 1820, in *Writings* (Lipscomb and Bergh), 15:303. Leonard W. Levy criticizes Jefferson's intention to politicize his university by excluding instruction on the principles of the Federalists and promulgating those of the Republicans (*Jefferson and Civil Liberties,* pp. 153–57).

66. Jefferson to William Short, 13 April 1820, in *Writings* (Lipscomb and Bergh), 15:247, 246.

67. Jefferson to Robert Taylor, 16 May 1820, in ibid., 15:253–55.

68. Locke, *Conduct,* pp. 12–13.

69. John Locke, *On Politics and Education* (New York, 1947), pp. 372–74. Karl Lehmann mentioned Jefferson's preference for "original" authorities to compilers and commentators, which he very likely got from Locke (*Thomas Jefferson, American Humanist,* pp. 87–88). Passmore, "The Malleability of Man in Eighteenth-Century Thought," pp. 21–25, mentions that Locke's theory according to which men can be made virtuous through education, contained in *Some Thoughts concerning Education,* in effect denies original sin.

70. For Jefferson's devotion to reading classical "great masters" and his continual advocacy of their study, see Wright, "Thomas Jefferson and the Classics," pp. 195–217; and Chinard, "Thomas Jefferson as a Classical Scholar," pp. 133–43.

71. Jefferson to Thomas Seymour, 11 February 1807, in *Writings* (Lipscomb and Bergh), 11:156.

72. Jefferson, *Notes,* pp. 147–48.

73. Jefferson expressed this in his "head and heart" letter to Maria Cosway on 12 October 1786: "Morals were too essential to the happiness of man, to be risked on the uncertain combinations of the head [reason]. She [nature] laid their foundation, therefore, in sentiment [heart], not in science [scientific reason]. That [sentiment or moral sense] she gave to all, as necessary to all: this [scientific reason] to a few only, as sufficing with a few" (in Bullock, *My Head and My Heart,* p. 38).

74. Jefferson to Monsieur Correa de Serra, 11 April 1820, Jefferson Papers, S1 R51, L38767.

75. Jefferson to Elbridge Gerry, 26 January 1799, in *Writings* (Lipscomb and Bergh), 10:78.

76. Jefferson to Dupont de Nemours, 24 April 1816, in ibid., 14:491–92. Jefferson's use of "perfection" was consistent with the way it was used by the enlightened of the eighteenth century, who made it a key word in their vocabulary, according to Becker, *The Heavenly City of the Eighteenth-Century Philosophers,* p. 47.

77. Jefferson to George Wythe, 13 August 1786, in *Writings* (Lipscomb and Bergh), 5:397. For Jefferson's ideas on education in relation to freedom, see Bowers, "Jefferson and the Freedom of the Human Spirit," pp. 242–44.

78. "But of all the views of this law none is more important, none more legitimate, than that of rendering the people the safe, as they are the ultimate, guardians of their own liberty. For this purpose the reading in the first stage, where *they* will receive their whole education, is proposed, as has been said, to be chiefly historical. History by apprising them of the past will enable them to judge of the future; it will avail them of the experience of other times and other nations; it will qualify them as judges of the actions and designs of men; it will enable them to know ambition under every disguise it may assume; and knowing it, to defeat its views" (Jefferson, *Notes,* p. 148).

79. The highest level of education was available to exceedingly few poor

students, who had to survive intense competition with other poor students at the lower levels to qualify for free university education in Jefferson's system (ibid., pp. 146–48). Locke's ideas in *Some Thoughts concerning Education* were adapted to those qualified by "birth" and "capacities" to lead the "life of average English gentlemen" (*On Politics and Education*, p. 205).

Chapter 6. Self-Evident Truths

1. Locke, *Two Treatises,* p. 304.

2. This language, used in the first printing of the Declaration, is identical to that of Jefferson's rough draft (Boyd, *Declaration of Independence* (1943), plate 10 and p. 1 of plate 5).

3. This language from the first printing differs from the rough draft, which states "that from that equal creation they derive rights inherent & inalienable, among which are, life, liberty, & the pursuit of Happiness." Jefferson himself made the changes that appear in the first printing with the exception of two: the Continental Congress deleted "inherent and" before "rights" and inserted "certain"; it was also the Congress that changed "inalienable" to "unalienable" (ibid.). For anonymous British ridicule of the Declaration's language, printed in a 1776 issue of *Scott's* magazine, see An Englishman, "The Uncommon Sense of the Americans: Notes on the Declaration," pp. 6–8.

4. Grant, *John Locke's Liberalism,* p. 6. On Locke's meaning of consent, see Dunn, "Consent in the Political Theory of John Locke," pp. 153–82.

5. This language is identical to that in the rough draft (Boyd, *Declaration of Independence* (1943), plate 10 and p.1 of plate 5).

6. In the original rough draft, "self-evident" was "sacred & undeniable" (ibid.).

7. Becker, *The Declaration of Independence,* p. 142. John C. Fitzpatrick also said that Franklin made the alteration (*The Spirit of the Revolution,* pp. 11–12) but offered no reason for his opinion.

8. Boyd, *Declaration of Independence* (1943), p. 24.

9. Ibid., p. 1 of plate 5.

10. See chapter 3, note 84.

11. White, *Philosophy of the American Revolution,* p. 19.

12. Locke, *Human Understanding,* pp. 530–31.

13. Ibid., pp. 531–32.

14. White, *Philosophy of the American Revolution,* pp. 20–22, 268.

15. Hume, *Treatise,* pp. 299–300.

16. Ibid., p. 299.

17. Locke, *Human Understanding,* pp. 335, 618–19.

18. Hume, *Treatise,* pp. 300–301.

19. It should be pointed out that after finishing the *Treatise,* Hume himself was not pleased with his ideas on skepticism, including skepticism of the self, as he stated in the appendix of that work (ibid., pp. 675–78). Kames,

however, did not acknowledge that self-criticism but confined his criticisms to what Hume said in the body of the *Treatise*. Because I present Hume's comments in order to clarify Kames's response to them, I have made no reference to what Hume said in his appendix.

20. Kames, *Essays,* p. 231.

21. Ibid., pp. 231–34.

22. Ibid., p. 234.

23. McGuinness, *Henry Home, Lord Kames,* p. 234.

24. Hume, *Treatise,* p. 300.

25. Hobbes, *Leviathan,* p. 10.

26. Lovejoy, *Essays in the History of Ideas,* pp. 79–80.

27. Kames, *Essays,* p. 234. Jefferson to John Adams, 15 August 1820, in *Writings* (Lipscomb and Bergh), 15:273.

28. Kames, *Essays,* pp. 231–32.

29. Jefferson to John Manners, 12 June 1817, in *Writings* (Lipscomb and Bergh), 15:124.

30. This language is identical to that of the rough draft (Boyd, *Declaration of Independence* (1943), plate 10 and p. 1 of plate 5).

31. See note 3.

32. Jefferson to Judge John Tyler, 17 June 1812, in *Writings* (Lipscomb and Bergh), 13:165.

33. Jefferson to John Cartright, 5 June 1824, in ibid., 16:48.

34. Boyd, *Declaration of Independence* (1943), p. 1 of plate 5.

35. Blackstone, *Commentaries,* p. 129. For Jefferson's criticism of Blackstone and his *Commentaries* for being antirepublican as well as lacking depth of legal knowledge, see Waterman, "Thomas Jefferson and Blackstone's Commentaries," pp. 634–35.

36. For the original version of this passage and the subsequent changes made, see chapter 3, note 84.

37. Kames, *Essays,* pp. 234–35, 317.

38. Jefferson, *Summary View,* p. 135.

39. See Zuckert, *Natural Rights and the New Republicanism,* pp. 8–9; Zuckert, "Thomas Jefferson on Nature and Natural Rights," pp. 137–66.

40. See chapter 3, note 84.

41. See W. Lehmann, *Henry Home, Lord Kames, and the Scottish Enlightment,* p. 166; and Laurie, *Scottish Philosophy in Its National Development,* p. 103.

42. Locke, *Two Treatises,* pp. 285, 278–79, 304. For Lockean ideas on property, see Tully, *A Discourse on Property;* and Strauss, *Natural Right and History,* pp. 234–49.

43. According to Parrington, *Main Currents in American Thought,* 1:350, Jefferson's "substitution of 'pursuit of happiness' for 'property' marks a complete break with the Whiggish doctrine of property rights that Locke had bequeathed to the English middle class."

44. Locke, *Two Treatises,* pp. 285, 287–88.

45. Inaugural Address, 4 March 1801, in *The Portable Thomas Jefferson,* p. 292.

46. Locke, *Two Treatises,* pp. 350–51. Scott, *In Pursuit of Happiness,* p. 29, describes the Lockean end of government.

47. "THE great end of Mens entring into Society, being the enjoyment of their Properties in Peace and Safety, and the great instrument and means of that being the Laws establish'd in that society. . . . But because the Laws, that are at once, and in a short time made, have a constant and lasting force, and need a *perpetual Execution,* or an attendance thereunto: Therefore 'tis necessary there should be a *Power always in being,* which should see to the *Execution* of the Laws that are made, and remain in force" (Locke, *Two Treatises,* pp. 355, 364–65).

48. Dumbauld, *Thomas Jefferson and the Law,* pp. 132, 135–36.

49. *Government Commonplace Book,* pp. 95–135, 13.

50. Kames, *Historical Law Tracts,* 1:148–49. For Kames's ideas on property, see Stein, "The General Notions of Contract and Property in Eighteenth Century Scottish Thought," pp. 9–10.

51. Locke, *Two Treatises,* p. 271.

52. Jefferson to the Republicans of Georgetown, 8 March 1809, in *Writings* (Lipscomb and Bergh), 16:349.

53. Jefferson to Henri Gregoire, 25 February 1809, in *Writings* (Lipscomb and Bergh), 12:255.

54. "I advance it therefore as a suspicion only, that the blacks, whether originally a distinct race, or made distinct by time and circumstances, are inferior to the whites in the endowments both of body and mind" (Jefferson, *Notes,* p. 143).

55. "We find among them numerous instances of the most rigid integrity, and as many as among their better instructed masters, of benevolence, gratitude, and unshaken fidelity" (ibid.).

56. "State a moral case to a ploughman and a professor. The former will decide it as well, and often better than the latter, because he has not been led astray by artificial rules" (Jefferson to Peter Carr, 10 August 1787); "Cultivators of the earth are the most valuable citizens. They are the most vigorous, the most independent, the most virtuous" (Jefferson to John Jay, 23 August 1785, both in *Writings* [Lipscomb and Bergh], 6:257–58, 5:93). See also Query 19 in *Notes,* pp. 164–65, for Jefferson's idea that being dependent upon others for a living corrupted morals, a corruption he deemed prevalent in a manufacturing economy, whereas the ability to support himself and his family independently contributed to a farmer's morality. For a discussion of this query, see Marx, *The Machine in the Garden,* pp. 124–25.

57. "Be assured that no person living wishes more sincerely than I do, to see a complete refutation of the doubts I have myself entertained and expressed on the grade of understanding alloted to them [blacks] by nature, and to find that in this respect they are on a par with ourselves. My doubts were the result of personal observation on the limited sphere of my own

State, where the opportunities for the development of their genius were not favorable, and those of exercising it still less so. I expressed them therefore with great hesitation" (Jefferson to Henri Gregoire, 25 February 1809, in *Writings* [Lipscomb and Bergh], 12:255).

58. The king "has waged cruel war against human nature itself, violating it's most sacred rights of life & liberty in the persons of a distant people who never offended him, captivating & carrying them into slavery in another hemisphere, or to incur miserable death in their transportation thither. this piratical warfare, the opprobrium of *infidel* powers, is the warfare of the *CHRISTIAN* king of Great Britain. determined to keep open a market where MEN should be bought & sold. he has prostituted his negative for suppressing every legislative attempt to prohibit or to restrain this execrable commerce: and that this assemblage of horrors might want no fact of distinguished die, he is now exciting those very people to rise in arms among us, and to purchase that liberty of which *he* has deprived them, by murdering the people upon whom *he* also obtruded them: thus paying off former crimes committed against the *liberties* of one people, with crimes which he urges them to commit against the *lives* of another" (Boyd, *Declaration of Independence* (1943), p. 3 of plate 5). Friedenwald, *The Declaration of Independence,* p. 132, called this subsequently deleted provision "unquestionably one of the most forceful clauses that issued from Jefferson's pen," whereas Commager, "The Declaration of Independence," pp. 179–87, said it was not only "bad history" but "rhetorical without being passionate." For Jefferson's views on slavery and criticism of his actions in their context, see Jordon, *White over Black;* Cohen, "Thomas Jefferson and the Problem of Slavery," pp. 503–26; Diggins, "Slavery, Race, and Equality," pp. 206–28; J. Miller, *The Wolf by the Ears.* For more understanding accounts, see Morgan, "Slavery and Freedom," pp. 5–29; Wills, *Inventing America,* pp. 293–306; and Dabney, *The Jefferson Scandals,* pp. 99–112.

59. Jefferson, *Notes,* p. 163.

60. Ibid., p. 60. See also note 58.

61. See Appleby, "Jefferson and His Complex Legacy," p. 10.

62. Locke, *Two Treatises,* pp. 173–74.

63. Jefferson to Isaac H. Tiffany, 4 April 1819, Jefferson Papers, 38353, S1 R51.

64. Locke, *Two Treatises,* p. 284.

65. Tuck, *Natural Rights Theories,* pp. 5–6.

66. "And that all Men may be restrained from invading others Rights, and from doing hurt to one another, and the Law of Nature be observed, which willeth the Peace and *Preservation of all Mankind,* the *Execution* of the Law on Nature is in that State, put into every Mans hands, whereby every one has a right to punish the transgressors of that Law to such a Degree, as may hinder its Violation. For the *Law of Nature* would, as all other Laws that concern Men in this World, be in vain, if there were no body that in the State of Nature, had a *Power to Execute* that Law, and thereby preserve the innocent and restrain offenders, and if any one in the State of Na-

ture may punish another, for any evil he has done, every one may do so. For in that *State of perfect Equality,* where naturally there is no superiority or jurisdiction of one, over another, what any may do in Prosecution of that Law, every one must needs have a Right to do. . . .

"*Where-ever Law ends, Tyranny begins,* if the Law be transgressed to another's harm. And whosoever in Authority exceeds the Power given him by the Law, and makes use of the Force he has under his Command, to compass that upon the Subject, which the Law allows not, ceases in that to be a Magistrate, and acting without Authority, may be opposed, as any other Man, who by force invades the Right of another" (Locke, *Two Treatises,* pp. 271–72, 400–401).

67. White, *Philosophy of the American Revolution,* pp. 162–63, 180–82.

68. Burlamaqui, *The Principles of Natural Law,* p. 60.

69. This language is identical with that of Jefferson's rough draft except for the words "under absolute Despotism," discussed in chapter 3, note 19 (Boyd, *Declaration of Independence* (1943), plate 10 and p. 1 of plate 5).

70. Locke, *Two Treatises,* pp. 271–72, 400–401.

71. This language is identical with that of the rough draft (Boyd, *Declaration of Independence* (1943), plate 10 and p. 1 of plate 5).

72. Boorstin, *The Lost World of Thomas Jefferson,* p. 237.

73. Jones, *The Pursuit of Happiness,* p. 86. See also Ganter, "Jefferson's 'Pursuit of Happiness' and Some Forgotten Men," pp. 422–34, 558–85 (two installments).

74. Locke, *Human Understanding,* pp. 229–30.

75. Ibid., pp. 258–59.

76. Ibid., pp. 279, 266.

77. Ibid., pp. 236, 250–51, 254.

78. Ibid., pp. 238, 284.

79. Ibid., p. 241.

80. Ibid., pp. 254, 257, 262.

81. Ibid., pp. 263, 273.

82. Mason, *Papers,* p. 287.

83. Schlesinger, "The Lost Meaning of the 'Pursuit of Happiness,'" pp. 325–27.

84. The same language was used in the rough draft (Boyd, *Declaration of Independence* (1943), plate 10 and p. 1 of plate 5).

85. Locke, *Human Understanding,* pp. 256, 270, 273–74, 267.

86. Ibid., p. 268. For the relationship of Locke's idea of freedom to happiness, see Polin, "John Locke's Conception of Freedom," pp. 1–5.

87. Jefferson to John Page, 21 February 1770, in *Papers* (Boyd and Cullen), 1:36. A. Koch mentioned the influence of Locke's chapter "Of Power" on Jefferson's "Pursuit of Happiness" but did not give a reason for her opinion (*Power, Morals, and the Founding Fathers,* pp. 29–31).

88. Jefferson, *Notes,* p. 147.

89. "Man is a complex machine, composed of various principles of mo-

tion, which may be conceived as so many springs and weights counteracting and balancing one another. These being accurately adjusted, the movement of life is beautiful, because regular and uniform. But if some springs or weights be withdrawn, those which remain, acting now without opposition from their antagonist forces, will disorder the balance, and derange the whole machine. Remove those principles of action which operate by reflection, and whose objects are complex and general ideas, and the necessary consequence will be, to double the force of the appetites and passions, pointing at particular objects; which is always the case with those who act by sense, and not reflection. They are tyrannized by passion and appetite, and have no consistent rule of conduct. No wonder, the moral sense is of no sufficient authority to command obedience in such a case. This is the character of savages. We have no reason then to conclude, from the above picture, that even the greatest savages are destitute of the moral sense. Their defect rather lies in the weakness of their general principles of action, which terminate in objects too complex for savages readily to comprehend. This defect is remedied by education and reflection; and then it is, that the moral sense, in concert with these general principles, acquires its full authority, which is openly recognized, and chearfully submitted to" (Kames, *Essays,* pp. 140–42).

90. Wiltse, *The Jeffersonian Tradition in American Democracy,* p. 67.

91. Jefferson to Amos J. Cook, 21 January 1816, in *Writings* (Lipscomb and Bergh), 14:405.

92. Jefferson to M. De Warville, 15 August 1786, in ibid., 5:402.

93. Opinion on Treaty, 28 April 1793, in ibid., 3:239. For further discussion of Jefferson's ideas of virtue in relation to happiness, see Agresto, "Liberty, Virtue, and Republicanism, 1776–1787," pp. 492–94.

94. Locke, *Human Understanding,* pp. 269–70.

95. Jefferson to William Johnson, 12 June 1823, in *Writings* (Lipscomb and Bergh), 15:441. Jefferson's trust in the populace would ultimately lead to the destruction of democracy, according to Macaulay, in "I Cannot Reckon Jefferson among the Benefactors Of Mankind," pp. 260–63.

96. Jefferson to William Johnson, 12 June 1823, in *Writings* (Lipscomb and Bergh), 15:440. Hartz, *The Liberal Tradition in America,* p. 40, wrote that "the Christian concept of sin and salvation" was made into a "pillar of the status quo" by "reactionary church establishments" at the time of the Revolution.

97. Jefferson to Horatio G. Spafford, 17 March 1814, in *Writings* (Lipscomb and Bergh), 14:119.

98. Meeting of the Visitors, 7 October 1822, in ibid., 19:416.

Chapter 7. Religious Freedom

1. Locke, *Treatise and Letter,* pp. 135–36. Jefferson's 1776 paraphrase: "Every church is to itself orthodox, to others erroneous or heretical" (*Papers* [Boyd and Cullen], 1:546).

2. *Papers* (Boyd and Cullen), 1:549.

3. Ibid., 1:544–48.

4. Locke, *Treatise and Letter,* p. 127.

5. *Papers* (Boyd and Cullen), 1:544.

6. Jefferson to Thomas Whittmore, 5 June 1822, in *Writings* (Lipscomb and Bergh), 15:373–74.

7. Jefferson, *Autobiography,* p. 62.

8. Ibid.

9. *Papers* (Boyd and Cullen), 1:530, 535–36; Kelly, *The Athanasian Creed,* pp. 17–20.

10. *Papers* (Boyd and Cullen), 1:535–36.

11. Ibid., 1:555.

12. Jefferson to James Smith, 8 December 1822, in *Writings* (Lipscomb and Bergh), 15:409: "The Athanasian paradox that one is three, and three but one, is so incomprehensible to the human mind, that no candid man can say he has any idea of it, and how can he believe what presents no idea?" The depth of Jefferson's critical biblical scholarship (which included knowledge of the Greek language that enabled him to translate New Testament passages from the Greek text) is seen in an argument against the Trinity from his 11 April 1823 letter to John Adams, in *Writings* (Lipscomb and Bergh), 15:429–30:

His [Jesus'] doctrine of the cosmogony of the world is very clearly laid down in the three first verses of the first chapter of John, in these words: "Ἐν ἀρχῇ ἦν ὁ λόγος, καὶ ὁ λόγος ἦν πρὸς τὸν Θεὸν, καὶ Θεὸς ἦν ὁ λόγος. Οὗτος ἦν ἐν ἀρχῇ πρὸς τὸν Θεόν. Πάντα δι᾽ αὐτοῦ ἐγένετο καὶ χωρὶς αὐτοῦ ἐγένετο οὐδὲ ἕν, ὃ γέγονεν."

Which truly translated means, "In the beginning God existed, and reason [or mind] was with God, and that mind was God. This was in the beginning with God. All things were created by it, and without it was made not one thing which was made." Yet this text, so plainly declaring the doctrine of Jesus, that the world was created by the Supreme, Intelligent Being, has been perverted by modern Christians to build up a second person of their tritheism, by a mistranslation of the word λόγος. One of its legitimate meanings, indeed, is "a word." But in that sense it makes an unmeaning jargon; while the other meaning, "reason," equally legitimate, explains rationally the eternal pre-existence of God, and His creation of the world. Knowing how incomprehensible it was that "a word," the mere action or articulation of the organs of speech could create a world, they undertook to make of this articulation a second pre-existing being, and ascribe to him, and not to God, the creation of the universe. The atheist here plumes himself on the uselessness of such a God, and the simpler hypothesis of a self-existent universe.

13. Jefferson, *Notes,* p. 158. This description is also found in Jefferson's 1776 Notes on Acts of Parliament (*Papers* [Boyd and Cullen], 1:541).

14. Ibid., 1:553.

15. Frend, *The Rise of Christianity,* pp. 492–500.

16. Chadwick, *The Early Church,* p. 130.

17. *Papers* (Boyd and Cullen), 1:553–54. Brackets and ellipses in this extract are Jefferson's.

18. Ibid., 1:536, 529. These brackets were placed by the editors of the collection.

19. Ibid., 1:532–33.

20. *The Portable Thomas Jefferson,* p. 251.

21. Fabian, "Jefferson's Notes on Virginia," p. 125, pointed out that the main part of the section on religion in *Notes* involves a "plea for religious liberty" that contains "the substance of the arguments advanced by Jefferson in 1776 in support of his Resolutions for Disestablishing the Church of England and Repealing Laws Interfering with Freedom of Worship."

22. Jefferson, *Notes,* pp. 157–59. Jefferson used the same language in the rough draft copy (Boyd, *Declaration of Independence* (1943), plate 10 and p. 5 of plate 5).

23. Locke, *Treatise and Letter,* p. 164.

24. Ibid.

25. Cranston, *John Locke,* p. 276.

26. Locke, *Treatise and Letter,* p. 131. Jefferson's paraphrase: "[A church] is a *voluntary* society of men, joining together of their own accord, in order to the [publick] worshipping of god in such a manner as they judge [accept]able to him & effectual to the salvation of their souls. [it is] *voluntary* because no man is *by nature* bound to any church. the hopes of salvation is the cause of his entering into it. if he find any thing wrong in it, he [sh]ould be as free to go out as he was to come in" (*Papers* [Boyd and Cullen], 1:545).

27. Locke, *Treatise and Letter,* p. 128.

28. Ibid., pp. 129, 143. Jefferson's paraphrase: "I may grow rich by art I am compelled to follow, I may recover health by medicines I am compelled to take agt. my own judgmnt. but I cannot be saved by a *worship* I disbelieve & abhor" (*Papers* [Boyd and Cullen], 1:547).

29. Locke, *Treatise and Letter,* pp. 130, 129. This irrationality of using force in religion is discussed in Waldron, "Locke: Toleration and the Rationality of Persecution," pp. 67–69.

30. Locke, *Treatise and Letter,* pp. 125, 131.

31. Ibid., p. 139. Jefferson's paraphrase: "The care of every man's soul belongs to himself" (*Papers* [Boyd and Cullen], 1:546).

32. Locke, *Treatise and Letter,* p. 142. Jefferson's paraphrase: "I cannot give up my guidance to the magistrate; because he knows no more of the way to heaven than I do" (*Papers* [Boyd and Cullen], 1:547).

33. Locke, *Treatise and Letter,* pp. 141–42.

34. This language was deleted by the Virginia assembly when the Statute was passed (*The Portable Thomas Jefferson*, p. 251).

35. The italicized part was deleted by the Virginia assembly (ibid., p. 251).

36. Meeting of the Visitors, 7 October 1822, in *Writings* (Lipscomb and Bergh), 19:416.

37. *The Portable Thomas Jefferson*, p. 251.

38. Ibid.

39. Wills, *Under God*, pp. 68, 359.

40. *Papers* (Boyd and Cullen), 1:537.

41. Ahlstrom, *A Religious History of the American People*, pp. 78, 94.

42. Ibid., pp. 155–56.

43. Jefferson to Benjamin Rush, 23 September 1800, in *Writings* (Lipscomb and Bergh), 10:175.

44. Locke, *Treatise and Letter*, p. 162.

45. *The Portable Thomas Jefferson*, p. 251; *Papers* (Boyd and Cullen), 1:538 (the brackets are mine).

46. Jefferson to Mrs. Harrison Smith, 6 August 1816, in *Writings* (Lipscomb and Bergh), 15:60.

47. *The Portable Thomas Jefferson*, p. 251.

48. For delusion as an aspect of human nature according to eighteenth-century thinkers, see Lovejoy, *Reflections on Human Nature*, pp. 32–34.

49. *The Portable Thomas Jefferson*, pp. 251–52.

50. Wills, *Under God*, p. 366.

51. Jefferson, *Autobiography*, pp. 61–62; Burleigh, *A Church History of Scotland*, p. 254.

52. Wills, *Under God*, p. 369.

53. *Papers* (Boyd and Cullen), 1:537.

54. Jefferson to Miles King, 26 September 1814, in *Writings* (Lipscomb and Bergh), 14:198.

55. Ibid., 14:197.

56. *The Portable Thomas Jefferson*, p. 252.

57. Jefferson, *Notes*, pp. 158–59.

58. *The Portable Thomas Jefferson*, p. 252.

59. Locke, *Treatise and Letter*, p. 153.

60. *The Portable Thomas Jefferson*, p. 253.

61. Jefferson, *Notes*, p. 160; Locke, *Treatise and Letter*, p. 153.

62. *The Portable Thomas Jefferson*, p. 253.

63. Jefferson to Mordecai M. Noah, 28 May 1818, Jefferson Papers, 37988, S1 R50. Jefferson sympathized with the Jews and decried the way institutionalized Christianity had persecuted them; see his comments to Joseph Marx, 8 July 1820: "Thomas Jefferson presents . . . his compliments & thanks for the Transactions of the Paris Sanhedren, which he shall read with great interest, and with the regret he has ever felt at seeing

a sect, the parent and basis of all those of Christendom, singled out by all of them for a persecution and oppression which proved they have profited nothing from the benevolent doctrines of him whom they profess to make the model of their principles and practice" (Jefferson Papers, S1 R52, 38865).

64. *Papers* (Boyd and Cullen), 1:548. For Locke's rationale in excluding Catholics from toleration, see Greene, *Religion and the State*, p. 63.

65. Jefferson, *Autobiography*, p. 71.

66. Locke, *Treatise and Letter*, pp. 136–37.

67. Jefferson to Mordecai M. Noah, 28 May 1818, Jefferson Papers, 37988, S1 R50.

68. *The Portable Thomas Jefferson*, p. 253.

69. See, e.g., Ketcham, *James Madison*, pp. 163–65; and Brant, "Madison," pp. 3–24.

70. Jefferson to James Madison, 20 December 1787, in Thomas Jefferson, *Writings*, ed. Merrill D. Peterson, pp. 915–16 (cited hereafter as *Writings* [Peterson]). Jefferson "converted Madison to the cause of adding the Bill of Rights to the new Federal Constitution," according to Levy, "Jefferson as a Civil Libertarian," p. 190. See also A. Koch, *Jefferson and Madison*, pp. 49, 56; and G. Wood, *The Creation of the American Republic*, pp. 542–43.

71. B. Mitchell and L.P. Mitchell, *A Biography of the Constitution of the United States*, p. 384.

72. Jefferson to the Baptists of Danbury, 1 January 1802, in *Writings* (Lipscomb and Bergh), 16:281–82. Separation of church and state did not weaken religion or morals in America, according to Commager, *The Empire of Reason*, p. 230.

73. See Tulley, "Locke," p. 616.

74. Jefferson was aware that political, like religious, differences could cause bloodshed and therefore espoused tolerance in both, as he stated in his Inaugural address, 4 March 1801: "And let us reflect that having banished from our land that religious intolerance under which mankind so long bled and suffered, we have yet gained little if we countenance a political intolerance as despotic, as wicked, and capable of as bitter and bloody persecutions" (*Writings* [Lipscomb and Bergh], 3:318–19).

75. *The Portable Thomas Jefferson*, p. 253.

76. *Papers* (Boyd and Cullen), 1:548–49.

77. Shaftesbury, *Characteristics of Men, Manners, Opinions, Times*, 1:31–32.

78. Jefferson, *Notes*, p. 161.

79. Ibid., p. 160. For an abbreviated form of this statement, see his 1776 notes for arguments to the Virginia assembly, in *Papers* (Boyd and Cullen), 1:538.

80. *The Portable Thomas Jefferson*, p. 252.

81. Howe, *The Unitarian Conscience*, pp. 216–17.

82. *Papers* (Boyd and Cullen), 1:80; *Writings* (Ford), 11:480–85; Cicero,

Brutus, On the Nature of the Gods, On Divination, On Duties, pp. 410, 426.

83. See Middleton, *History of the Life of Marcus Tullius Cicero;* and Middleton, *A Letter to Dr Waterland,* pp. 48–53. Jefferson obviously did not go along with Middleton's views on state religion, but he acknowledged both Priestley's and Middleton's influence on him as a result of their use of history in religion in a manner reminiscent of Bolingbroke's historical proofs: "You are right in supposing . . . that I had not read much of Priestley's Predestination, his no-soul system, or his controversy with Horsley. But I have read his Corruptions of Christianity, and Early Opinions of Jesus, over and over again; and I rest on them, and on Middleton's writings, especially his letters from Rome, and to Waterland, as the basis of my own faith. These writings have never been answered, nor can be answered by quoting historical proofs, as they have done. For these facts, therefore, I cling to their learning, so much superior to my own" (to John Adams, 22 August 1813, in *Writings* [Lipscomb and Bergh], 13:351–52).

84. Locke, *Treatise and Letter,* p. 163.

85. *Papers* (Boyd and Cullen), 1:538.

86. Jefferson, *Notes,* p. 160.

87. Locke, *Treatise and Letter,* p. 161. These ideas of Locke were based on observation and experience, according to De Beer, in "Locke and English Liberalism," p. 36.

88. Jefferson, *Notes,* pp. 160–61; Jefferson to John Thomas, 18 November 1807, in *Writings* (Lipscomb and Bergh), 16:291.

89. Jefferson to the General Meeting of Correspondence of the Six Baptist Associations, Virginia, 21 November 1808, in ibid., 16:320–21.

90. In 1780 Joseph Galloway wrote in "The View from Outside," p. 21, of the political influence on their followers of various ecclesiastical authorities in the colonies before the Revolutionary War—especially the Presbyterians, in whose synods "all their general affairs, political as well as religious, are debated and decided" and "from hence their orders and decrees are issued throughout America; and to them as ready and implicit obedience is paid as is due the authority of any sovereign power whatever." For the New England clergy's preachments and authority in politics in colonial America, see Buel, "Democracy and the American Revolution," p. 179. Morgan, "The Revolution as an Intellectual Movement," pp. 11–33, wrote that the clergy of all colonial sects never stopped giving instruction in political thought in the 1760s and 1770s. See also Thornton, *The Pulpit of the American Revolution,* pp. 276–77.

91. Jefferson to John Adams, 17 May 1818, in *Writings* (Lipscomb and Bergh), 15:170.

92. Jefferson, *Autobiography,* pp. 61–62.

93. Jefferson to Thomas Cooper, 2 November 1822, in *Writings* (Peterson), p. 1464. Natural religion such as Jefferson's, which rejected both revelation and the divinity of Christ, logically anticipated Unitarianism, according to Savelle, *The Seeds of Liberty,* p. 31. Bottorff, *Thomas Jefferson,*

p. 87, points out that the "Unitarian sentiments" expressed in Jefferson's letters sometimes "meant the Unitarian sect" and sometimes "a theistic belief in one God, not a god of three persons."

94. Geffen, *Philadelphia Unitarianism,* pp. 17–18, 144–45, 238; Howe, *Unitarian Conscience,* p. 16.

95. Geffen, *Philadelphia Unitarianism,* p. 8.

96. *Jefferson's Exracts from the Gospels,* p. 14. See also Jefferson to his daughter Martha, 23 April 1803, in *Family Letters,* pp. 243–44.

97. Gibbs, *Joseph Priestley,* p. 25; Geffen, *Philadelphia Unitarianism,* pp. 50, 239. See Jefferson's outline of Unitarian principles in his letter to Benjamin Waterhouse, 26 June 1822, in *Writings* (Lipscomb and Bergh), 15:383–85.

98. Ibid.

99. Jefferson to Francis Hopkinson, 13 March 1789, in ibid., 7:300.

100. Jefferson to Benjamin Waterhouse, 26 June 1822, in ibid., 15:385. Wood, "Ideology and the Origins of Liberal America," p. 638, wrote that this statement of Jefferson's indicates his belief that "the rise of the people ought to mean that society would come to think more like him."

101. Howe, *Unitarian Conscience,* pp. 5–6. For Jefferson's liberal Enlightenment religious views, see Schneider, "The Enlightenment in Thomas Jefferson," pp. 246–52.

102. Sanford, *The Religious Life of Thomas Jefferson,* p. 66.

Conclusion

1. Jefferson to James Monroe, 20 May 1782, in *The Portable Thomas Jefferson,* p. 365.

2. Jefferson to Francis W. Gilmer, 7 June 1816, in *Writings* (Lipscomb and Bergh), 15:25. Despite Jefferson's use of syllogistic reasoning here, he seems to have been aware of its limitations, having read Locke's statement (*Human Understanding,* pp. 671–72): "And I readily own, that all right reasoning may be reduced to his [Aristotle's] Forms of Syllogism. But yet I think without any diminuation to him I may truly say, that they are not the only, nor the best way of reasoning, for the leading of those into Truth who are willing to find it, and desire to make the best use they may of their Reason, for the attainment of Knowledge."

3. Pangle, *The Spirit of Modern Republicanism,* p. 211.

4. Jefferson to David Hartley, 2 July 1787, in *Writings* (Lipscomb and Bergh), 6:151.

5. Randall, *The Life of Thomas Jefferson,* 3:563.

6. Jefferson to Roger C. Weightman, 24 June 1826, in *Writings* (Lipscomb and Bergh), 16:181–82.

Bibliography

Primary Sources

Adams, John. *The Works of John Adams*. Ed. Charles Francis Adams. Boston: Little, Brown, 1850.

Aquinas, Thomas. *Basic Writings of Saint Thomas Aquinas*. Vol. 1. Ed. Anton C. Pegis. New York: Random, 1945.

———. *The Summa Theologica of St. Thomas Aquinas*. 2d ed. Trans. Fathers of the English Dominican Province. Vol. 7. London: Burns, Cates, and Washbourne, 1927.

Augustine, Aurelius. *The Enchiridion*. Trans. J.F. Shaw; ed. Marcus Dods. In *The Works of Aurelius Augustine, Bishop of Hippo*, vol. 9. Edinburgh: T. and T. Clark, 1873.

———. *The Fathers of the Church: Saint Augustine Treatises on Various Subjects*. Vol. 16. Ed. Roy J. DeFarrari; trans. Mary Sarah Muldowney, Harold B. Jaffee, Mary Frances McDonald, Luanne Meagher, M. Clement Eagan, and Mary E. DeFerrari. New York: Fathers of the Church, 1952.

———. *The Works of Aurelius Augustine, Bishop of Hippo*. Vols. 1 and 2. Ed. and trans. Marcus Dods. Edinburgh: T. and T. Clark, 1871.

Bacon, Francis. *The Novum Organon*. Trans. G.W. Kitchin. Oxford: Typographed Academico, 1855.

Bayle, Peter. *The Dictionary Historical and Critical*. Trans. P. Des Maizeau. 5 vols. 2d ed. London: J.J. and P. Knapton, 1734–38.

———. *Pierre Bayle: Historical and Critical Dictionary Selections*. Trans. Richard L. Popkin. New York: Bobbs-Merrill, 1965.

———. *Selections from Bayle's Dictionary*. Ed. E.A. Beller and M. duP. Lee Jr. Princeton: Princeton Univ. Press, 1952.

Berkeley, George. *Of the Principles of Human Knowledge*. Part 1, *The Age of Enlightenment: The 18th Century Philosophers*. Ed. Isaiah Berlin. New York: Mentor/New American Library, 1956.

Blackstone, William. *Commentaries on the Laws of England*. Notes and additions by Edward Christian. 4 vols. London: Thomas Tegg, 1830.

Bolingbroke, Henry St. John, Lord Viscount. *The Works of Henry St. John, Lord Viscount Bolingbroke*. 5 vols. London: David Mallet Esq., 1754.

Burlamaqui, J.J. *The Principles of Natural Law.* Trans. Mr. Nugent. Dublin: J. Sheppard and G. Cecil, 1769.

Calvin, John. *Institutes of the Christian Religion in Two Volumes.* Ed. John T. McNeill; trans. Ford Lewis Battles. Library of Christian Classics, vols. 20–21. London: S.C.M. Press, 1961.

Cicero, Marcus Tullius. *Brutus, On the Nature of the Gods, On Divination, On Duties.* Trans. Hubert M. Poteat. Chicago: Univ. of Chicago Press, 1950.

Dodsley, Robert. *The Oeconomy of Human Life.* Dublin: G. Faulkner, 1761.

Englishman, An. "The Uncommon Sense of the Americans: Notes on the Declaration." In *A Casebook on the Declaration of Independence,* ed. Robert Ginsberg, pp. 6–8. New York: Crowell, 1967.

Hamilton, Alexander, James Madison, and John Jay. *The Federalist Papers.* Ed. Clinton Rossiter. New York: Mentor/New American Library, 1961.

Hobbes, Thomas. *Leviathan.* Ed. Richard Tuck. Cambridge: Cambridge Univ. Press, 1991.

Hume, David. *Essays and Treatises on Several Subjects.* 4 vols. Edinburgh: A. Kincaid and Donaldson, 1753–54.

———. *A Treatise of Human Nature.* Ed. Ernest Mosner. London: Penguin, 1969.

Hutcheson, Francis. *An Inquiry into the Original of Our Ideas of Beauty and Virtue.* London: A. Bettesworth, F. Fayram, 1726.

———. *A System of Moral Philosophy.* 2 vols. Glasgow: his son Francis Hutcheson, 1755.

Jefferson, Thomas. *Autobiography of Thomas Jefferson.* Ed. Paul Leicester Ford. New York: Putnam's, 1914.

———. *The Commonplace Book of Thomas Jefferson: A Repository of His Ideas on Government.* Ed. Gilbert Chinard. Baltimore, Md.: Johns Hopkins Press, 1926.

———. *The Complete Jefferson.* Ed. Saul K. Padover. New York: Duell, Sloan, and Pearce, 1943.

———. *The Family Letters of Thomas Jefferson.* Ed. Edwin Morris Betts and James Adam Bear Jr. Columbia: Univ. of Missouri Press, 1966.

———. *The Jefferson Bible.* New York: Grosset and Dunlap, 1940.

———. *Jefferson's Extracts from the Gospels.* Ed. Dickinson W. Adams. Papers of Thomas Jefferson, 2d series. Princeton: Princeton Univ. Press, 1983.

———. *Jefferson's Literary Commonplace Book.* Ed. Douglas L. Wilson. Papers of Thomas Jefferson, 2d series. Princeton: Princeton Univ. Press, 1989.

———. *The Literary Bible of Thomas Jefferson: His Commonplace Book of Philosphers and Poets.* Ed. Gilbert Chinard. Baltimore, Md.: Johns Hopkins Press, 1928.

———. *Notes on the State of Virginia.* Ed. William Peden. New York: Norton, 1972.

————. Papers. Series 1. Library of Congress, Washington, D.C.

————. *The Papers of Thomas Jefferson.* Ed. Jullian P. Boyd and Charles T. Cullen. 26 vols. Princeton: Princeton Univ. Press, 1950.

————. *The Portable Thomas Jefferson.* Ed. Merrill D. Peterson. Kingsport, Tenn.: Penguin, 1981.

————. *A Summary View of the Rights of British America.* Ed. Thomas P. Abernethy. New York: Scholars Facsimiles and Reprints, 1943.

————. *Thomas Jefferson's Farm Book.* Ed. Edwin Morris Betts. Princeton: Princeton Univ. Press, 1953.

————. *Thomas Jefferson's Garden Book.* Ed. Edwin Morris Betts. Philadelphia: American Philosophical Society, 1944.

————. *Thomas Jefferson: Writings.* Ed. Merrill D. Peterson. Kingsport, Tenn.: Viking Press, 1984.

————. *The Writings of Thomas Jefferson.* 11 vols. Ed. Paul Leicester Ford. New York: Putnam's, 1892.

————. *The Writings of Thomas Jefferson.* 20 vols. Ed. Andrew A. Lipscomb and Albert Ellery Bergh. Washington, D.C.: Thomas Jefferson Memorial Association, 1903.

————. *The Writings of Thomas Jefferson.* 9 vols. Ed. H.A. Washington. New York: J.C. Riker, 1857.

Jefferson, Thomas, Abigail Adams, and John Adams. *The Adams-Jefferson Letters: The Complete Correspondence between Thomas Jefferson and Abigail and John Adams.* Ed. Lester J. Cappon. 2 vols. Chapel Hill: Univ. of North Carolina Press, 1959.

Kames, Henry Home, Lord. *Elements of Criticism.* 3d ed. 2 vols. Edinburgh: A. Kincaid and J. Bell, 1765.

————. *Essays on the Principles of Morality and Natural Religion.* Edinburgh: A. Kincaid and A. Donaldson, 1751.

————. *Historical Law Tracts.* 2 vols. Edinburgh: A. Kincaid and J. Bell, 1758.

————. *Principles of Equity.* 2d ed. Edinburgh: A. Kincaid and J. Bell, 1767.

Letters of Members of the Continental Congress. Ed. Edmund C. Burnett. 7 vols. Washington, D.C.: Carnegie Institution of Washington, 1921.

Locke, John, *An Essay concerning Human Understanding.* Ed. Peter H. Nidditch. Oxford: Clarendon Press, 1984.

————. *Of the Conduct of the Understanding.* Ed. Bolton Corney. London: Bell and Daldy, 1859.

————. *On Politics and Education.* Roslyn, N.Y.: Walter J. Black, 1947.

————. *The Second Treatise of Government and A Letter concerning Toleration.* Ed. J.W. Gough. 3d ed. Oxford: Basil Blackwell, 1976.

————. *Two Treatises of Government.* Ed. Peter Laslett. Cambridge: Cambridge Univ. Press, 1988.

————. *The Works of John Locke Esq.* 3 vols. London: John Churchill and Samuel Manship, 1714.

Loyola, Ignatius of. "Spiritual Exercises." In *Powers of Imagining Ignatius de Loyola: A Philosophical Hermeneutic of Imagining through the Collected Works of Ignatius de Loyola.* Albany: State Univ. of New York Press, 1986.

————. "Spiritual Exercises of Saint Ignatius of Loyola." Trans. Charles Seager. In *Classics of Western Thought, Middle Ages, Renaissance and Reformation,* 3d ed., ed. Karl F. Thompson, vol. 2. New York: Harcourt Bruce Jovanovich, 1980.

Luther, Martin. *Luther's Works.* Ed. Hilton C. Osward. Vol. 25. Saint Louis, Mo.: Concordia, 1972.

Maimonides, Moses. "Epistle to Yemen." Trans. Boaz Cohen. In *Introduction to Contemporary Civilization in the West,* 3d ed., ed. Columbia College Staff, vol. 1. New York: Columbia Univ. Press, 1960.

————. *The Guide of the Perplexed.* Trans. Chaim Rabin; intro. Julius Guttmann. London: East and West Library, 1952.

Mason, George. *The Papers of George Mason.* 3 vols. Ed. Robert A. Rutland. Chapel Hill: Univ. of North Carolina Press, 1970.

Middleton, Conyers. *A Letter to Dr Waterland.* London: J. Peele, 1731.

Priestley, Joseph. *The Theological and Miscellaneous Works of Joseph Priestley.* 25 vols. Ed. John Towill Rutt. Hackney: George Smallfield, 1817–32.

Reid, Thomas. *An Inquiry into the Human Mind.* Edinburgh: A. Kincaid and J. Bell, 1764.

Shaftesbury, Anthony Ashley Cooper, Third Earl of. *Characteristics of Men, Manners, Opinions, Times.* 3 vols. London: J. Darby, 1737–38.

Smith, Adam. *The Theory of Moral Sentiments.* London: A. Millar, 1759.

Spinoza, Benedict. *A Theologico-Politico Treatise and a Political Treatise.* Trans. R.H.M. Elwes. Reproduction of London 1883 edition. New York: Dover, 1951.

Toland, John. *Christianity Not Mysterious.* London, 1696. Facsimile rpt., Stuttgaart-Bad Cannstatt, 1964.

Toulmin, Joshua A.M. *Memoirs of the Life, Character, Sentiments, and Writings of Faustus Socinus.* London: J. Brown, 1777.

Willard, Samuel. "The Character of a Good Ruler." In *The Puritans,* ed. Perry Miller and Thomas H. Johnson, pp. 250–56. New York: American Book, 1938.

Zwingli, Huldreich. *The Latin Works of Huldreich Zwingli.* Vol. 2. Ed. Samuel Jackson Macauley; trans. Henry Preble, Walter Lichtenstein, and Lawrence A. McLouth. Philadelphia: American Society of Church History, 1922.

Secondary Sources

Aarsleff, Hans. "The State of Nature and the Nature of Man in Locke." In *John Locke: Problems and Perspectives,* ed. John Yolton, pp. 45–80. Cambridge: Cambridge Univ. Press, 1969.

Adair, Douglas. "The Jefferson Scandals." In *Fame and the Founding Fathers,* ed. Trevor Colbourne, pp. 160–91. New York: Norton, 1974.

Agresto, John T. "Liberty, Virtue, and Republicanism, 1776–1787." *Review of Politics* 39 (1977): 473–504.

Ahlstrom, Sydney E. *A Religious History of the American People.* London: Yale Univ. Press, 1972.

Appleby, Joyce. "Commercial Farming and the 'Agrarian Myth' in the Early Republic." *Journal of American History* 68 (1982): 833–49.

———. "Jefferson and His Complex Legacy." In *Jeffersonian Legacies,* ed. Peter S. Onuf, pp. 1–16. Charlottesville, Va., 1993.

———. "Republicanism in Old and New Contexts." *William and Mary Quarterly,* 3d ser., 43 (1986): 20–34.

———. "What Is Still American in the Political Philosophy of Thomas Jefferson." *William and Mary Quarterly,* 3d ser., 39 (1982): 287–309.

Ashcraft, Richard. "Faith and Knowledge in Locke's Philosophy," In *John Locke: Problems and Perspectives,* ed. John W. Yolton, pp. 194–223. Cambridge: Cambridge Univ. Press, 1969.

Bailyn, Bernard. *The Ideological Origins of the American Revolution.* Cambridge, Mass.: Belknap Press of Harvard Univ. Press, 1976.

Banning, Lance. *The Jeffersonian Persuasion: Evolution of a Party Ideology.* Ithaca, N.Y.: Cornell Univ. Press, 1978.

Barker, Sir Ernest. "Natural Law and the American Revolution." In *Traditions of Civility: Eight Essays,* pp. 263–355. Cambridge: Cambridge Univ. Press, 1948.

Becker, Carl L. *The Declaration of Independence: A Study in the History of Political Ideas.* New York: Vintage, 1958.

———. *The Heavenly City of the Eighteenth-Century Philosophers.* New Haven, Conn.: Yale Univ. Press, 1952.

———. "What Is Still Living in the Political Philosophy of Thomas Jefferson?" In *Thomas Jefferson: A Profile,* ed. Merrill D. Peterson, pp. 41–60. New York: Hill and Wang, 1969.

Bedini, Silvio A. *Thomas Jefferson, Statesman of Science.* New York: Macmillan, 1990.

Benson, C. Randolph. *Thomas Jefferson as Social Scientist.* Rutherford, N.J.: Fairleigh Dickenson Univ. Press, 1971.

Bicknell, E.J. *A Theological Introduction to the Thirty-Nine Articles of the Church of England.* Rev. H.J. Carpenter. 3d ed. London: Longmans, Green, 1955.

Blackburn, Joyce. *George Wythe of Williamsburg.* New York: Harper and Row, 1975.

Bolton, H.C., and R.V. Wells. *The Lunar Society of Birmingham.* Birmingham: Society of the Chemical Industry, 1955.

Boorstin, Daniel. *The Lost World of Thomas Jefferson.* New York: H. Holt, 1948.

———. *The Mysterious Science of the Law: An Essay on Blackstone's "Commentaries."* Cambridge: Harvard Univ. Press, 1941.

———. "The Myth of an American Enlightenment." In *America and the Image of Europe*, pp. 65–78. New York: World Publishing, 1960.

Bottorff, William K. *Thomas Jefferson*. Twayne's United States Authors' Series, ed. Sylvia E. Bowman. Boston: Twayne, 1979.

Bowers, Clauge G. "Jefferson and the Freedom of the Human Spirit." *Ethics: An International Journal of Social, Political, and Legal Philosophy* 53 (1942–43): 237–45.

Boyd, Julian P. *The Declaration of Independence: The Evolution of the Text.* Washington, D.C.: Library of Congress, 1943.

———. *The Declaration of Independence: The Evolution of the Text.* Princeton: Princeton Univ. Press, 1945.

Brant, Irving. "Madison: On the Separation of Church and State." *William and Mary Quarterly*, 3d ser., 8 (1951): 3–24.

Broderick, Francis L. "Pulpit, Physics, and Politics: The Curriculum of the College of New Jersey, 1746–1794." *William and Mary Quarterly*, 3d ser., 6 (1949): 42–68.

Brodie, Fawn M. *Thomas Jefferson: An Intimate History.* New York: Norton, 1974.

Brown, Roland W. "Jefferson's Contribution to Paleontology." *Journal of the Washington Academy of Sciences* 33 (1943): 257–59.

Brown, Stuart Gerry. "The Mind of Thomas Jefferson." *Ethics: An International Journal of Social, Political, and Legal Philosophy* 73 (1963): 79–99.

———. *Thomas Jefferson*. Great American Thinkers Series, ed. Thomas S. Knight and Arthur W. Brown. New York: Square Press, 1963.

Browne, Charles Albert. "Joseph Priestley and the American 'Fathers.'" *American Scholar* 4 (1935): 133–47.

Buel, Richard, Jr. "Democracy and the American Revolution: A Frame of Reference." *William and Mary Quarterly*, 3d ser., 21 (1964): 165–90.

Bullock, Helen Duprey. *My Head and My Heart: A Little History of Thomas Jefferson and Maria Cosway.* New York: Putnam's, 1945.

Burleigh, J.H.S. *A Church History of Scotland.* Oxford: Oxford Univ. Press, 1960.

Burns, James MacGregor. *The Vineyard of Liberty.* Vintage Books edn. New York: Vintage Books, 1983.

Caldwell, L.K. "The Jurisprudence of Thomas Jefferson." *Indiana Law Journal* 18 (1942–43): 193–213.

Cant, Ronald G. "Origins of the Enlightenment in Scotland: The Universities." In *The Origins and Nature of the Scottish Enlightenment*, ed. R.H. Campbell and Andrew S. Skinner, pp. 42–64. Edinburgh, 1982.

Cassirer, Ernst. *The Philosophy of the Enlightenment.* Trans. Fritz C.A. Koelln and James P. Pettegrove. Princeton: Princeton Univ. Press, 1951.

Chadwick, Henry. *The Early Church.* London: Penguin, 1987.

Chinard, Gilbert. "Jefferson among the Philosophers." *Ethics: An International Journal of Social, Political, and Legal Philosophy* 53 (1942–43): 255–68.

———. *Jefferson et les idealogues.* Baltimore: Johns Hopkins Press, 1925.

———. *Thomas Jefferson, the Apostle of Americanism.* Ann Arbor: Univ. of Michigan Press, 1957.

———. "Thomas Jefferson as a Classical Scholar." *American Scholar* 1 (1932): 133–43.

Chitwood, Oliver Perry. *Richard Henry Lee: Statesman of the Revolution.* Morgantown: West Virginia Univ. Library, 1967.

Clark, Austin H. "Thomas Jefferson and Science." *Journal of the Washington Academy of Sciences* 33 (1943): 193–203.

Cohen, William. "Thomas Jefferson and the Problem of Slavery." *Journal of American History* 56 (1969–70): 503–26.

Colbourn, H. Trevor. "Thomas Jefferson's Use of the Past." *William and Mary Quarterly,* 3d ser., 15 (1958): 56–70.

Commager, Henry Steele. "The Declaration of Independence." In *Thomas Jefferson: The Man, His World, His Influence,* ed. Lally Weymouth, pp. 179–87. London: Weidenfeld and Nicolson, 1973.

———. *The Empire of Reason: How Europe Imagined and America Realized the Enlightenment.* New York: Anchor Books, 1978.

———. *Jefferson, Nationalism, and the Enlightenment.* New York: George Braziller, 1975.

Conant, James B. *Thomas Jefferson and the Development of American Public Education.* Berkeley: Univ. of California Press, 1962.

Conkin, Paul K. "The Religious Pilgrimage of Thomas Jefferson." In *Jefferson Legacies,* ed. Peter S. Onuf, pp. 19–49. Charlottesville: Univ. Press of Virginia, 1993.

Cranston, Maurice. *John Locke.* Oxford: Oxford Univ. Press, 1985.

Curti, Merle. *Human Nature in American Thought: A History.* Madison: Univ. of Wisconsin Press, 1980.

Dabney, Virginius. *The Jefferson Scandals: A Rebuttal.* New York: Dodd, Mead, 1981.

Dana, William F. "The Political Principles of the Declaration." *Harvard Law Review* 13 (1900): 319–43.

Davie, George Elder. *The Democratic Intellect: Scotland and Her Universities in the Nineteenth Century.* Edinburgh: Edinburgh Univ. Press, 1961.

Davis, Henry. *Moral and Pastoral Theology: A Summary.* London: Sheed and Ward, 1952.

Davis, John W. "Thomas Jefferson, Attorney at Law." In *Jefferson Reader: A Treasury of Writings about Thomas Jefferson,* ed. Francis Coleman Rosenberger, pp. 117–30. New York: Dutton, 1953.

De Beer, Esmond S. "Locke and English Liberalism." In *John Locke: Prob-*

lems and Perspectives, ed. John W. Yolton, pp. 34–44. Cambridge: Cambridge Univ. Press, 1969.

Dewey, John. *The Living Thoughts of Thomas Jefferson.* Living Thoughts Library, ed. Alfred O. Mendel, Philadelphia: D. McKay, 1940.

Dickenson, H.T. *Bolingbroke.* London: Constable, 1970.

Diggins, John Patrick. *The Lost Soul of American Politics: Virtue, Self-Interest, and the Foundations of Liberalism.* New York: Basic Books, 1984.

———. "Slavery and Equality." *American Quarterly* 28 (1976): 206–28.

Dillenberger, John, and Claude Welch. *Protestant Christianity.* 2d ed. New York: Macmillan, 1988.

Dos Passos, John. *The Head and Heart of Thomas Jefferson.* London: Robert Hale, 1955.

Duff, Stella F. "The Case against the King: The Virginia Gazettes Indict George III." *William and Mary Quarterly,* 3d ser., 6 (1949): 383–97.

Dumbauld, Edward. *The Declaration of Independence and What It Means Today.* Norman: Univ. of Oklahoma Press, 1950.

———. *Thomas Jefferson and the Law.* Norman: Univ. of Oklahoma Press, 1978.

Dunn, John. "Consent in the Political Theory of John Locke." *Historical Journal* 10 (1967): 153–82.

———. *The Political Thought of John Locke.* Paperback edn. Cambridge: Cambridge Univ. Press, 1988.

———. "The Politics of Locke in England and America in the Eighteenth Century." In *John Locke: Problems and Perspectives,* ed. John W. Yolton, pp. 45–80. Cambridge: Cambridge Univ. Press, 1969.

Dworetz, Steven. *The Unvarnished Doctrine: Locke, Liberalism, and the American Revolution.* Durham: Duke Univ. Press, 1988.

Fabian, Bernard. "Jefferson's Notes on Virginia: The Genesis of Query XVII, The different religions received into the state?" *William and Mary Quarterly,* 3d ser., 12 (1955): 124–38.

Ferguson, James P. *The Philosophy of Dr. Samuel Clarke and Its Critics.* New York: Vantage, 1974.

Ferguson, Robert A. *Law and Letters in American Culture.* Cambridge: Harvard Univ. Press, 1984.

Fisher, Sydney George. "The Accusations." In *A Casebook on the Declaration of Independence,* ed. Robert Ginsberg, pp. 127–35. New York: Crowell, 1967.

Fitzpatrick, John C. *The Spirit of the Revolution: New Light from Some of the Original Sources of American History.* Boston: Houghton Mifflin, 1924.

Forbes, Duncan. "Natural Law and the Scottish Enlightenment." In *The Origins and Nature of the Scottish Enlightenment,* eds. R.H. Campbell and Andrew S. Skinner, pp. 186–204. Edinburgh: J. Donald, 1982.

Foster, Stephen. *Their Solitary Way: The Puritan Social Ethic in the First*

Century of Settlement in New England. New Haven: Yale Univ. Press, 1971.

Frend, W.H.C. *The Rise of Christianity.* London: Darton, Longman and Todd, 1986.

Friedenwald, Herbert. *The Declaration of Independence: An Interpretation and an Analysis.* New York: Macmillan, 1904.

Galloway, Joseph. "'The View from Outside': Historical and Political Reflections on the Rise and Progress of the American Revolution, London 1780." In *The Ambiguity of the American Revolution,* ed. Jack P. Greene, pp. 16–28. New York: Harper and Row, 1968.

Ganter, Herbert Lawrence. "Jefferson's 'Pursuit of Happiness' and Some Forgotten Men." *William and Mary Quarterly,* 2d ser., 16 (1936): 422–34, 558–85.

————. "William Small, Jefferson's Beloved Teacher." *William and Mary Quarterly,* 3d ser., 4 (1947): 505–11.

Gaustad, Edwin Scott. *The Great Awakening in New England.* New York: Harper and Brothers, 1957.

Gay, Peter. *The Enlightenment: An Interpretation.* London: Weidenfeld and Nicolson, 1966.

Geffen, Elizebeth M. *Philadelphia Unitarianism, 1791–1861.* Philadelphia: Univ. of Pennsylvania Press, 1961.

Gibbs, F.W. *Joseph Priestley: Adventurer in Science and Champion of Truth.* London: Thomas Nelson and Sons, 1965.

Goetsmann, William. "Savage Enough to Prefer the Woods: The Cosmopolite and the West." In *Thomas Jefferson: The Man, His World, His Influence,* ed. Lally Weymouth, pp. 107–25. London: Weidenfeld and Nicolson, 1973.

Goldie, Mark. "The Reception of Hobbes." In *The Cambridge History of Political Thought: 1450–1700,* ed. J.H. Burns and Mark Goldie, pp. 589–615. Cambridge: Cambridge Univ. Press, 1991.

Grant, Ruth W. *John Locke's Liberalism.* Chicago: Univ. of Chicago Press, 1987.

Grave, S.A. *The Scottish Philosophy of Common Sense.* Oxford: Clarendon Press, 1960.

Greene, Evarts B. *Religion and the State: The Making and Testing of an American Tradition.* New York: New York Univ. Press, 1941.

Hamowy, Ronald. "Jefferson and the Scottish Enlightment: A Critique of Garry Wills' *Inventing America: Jefferson's Declaration of Independence.*" *William and Mary Quarterly,* 3d ser., 36 (1979): 503–23.

Harris, Ian. *The Mind of John Locke: A Study of Political Theory in Its Intellectual Setting.* Cambridge: Cambridge Univ. Press, 1994.

Hart, Jeffrey. *Viscount Bolingbroke: Tory Humanist.* London: Routledge and K. Paul, 1965.

Hartz, Louis. *The Liberal Tradition in America: An Interpretation of American Political Thought since the Revolution.* New York: Harcourt, Brace, 1955.

Hawke, David. *A Transaction of Free Men: The Birth and Course of the Declaration of Independence.* New York: Scribner, 1964.

Hazelton, John H. *The Declaration of Independence: Its History.* New York: Dodd, Mead, 1906.

Hellenbrand, Harold. *The Unfinished Revolution: Education and Politics in the Thought of Thomas Jefferson.* Cranbury, N.J.: Associated Univ. Presses, 1990.

Hill, Helen. *George Mason, Constitutionalist.* Cambridge: Harvard Univ. Press, 1938.

Honeywell, Roy J. *The Educational Work of Thomas Jefferson.* Cambridge: Harvard Univ. Press, 1931.

Howe, Daniel Walker. *The Unitarian Conscience: Harvard Moral Philosophy, 1805–1861.* Cambridge: Harvard Univ. Press, 1970.

Jones, Howard Mumford. *The Pursuit of Happiness.* Cambridge: Harvard Univ. Press, 1953.

Jordon, Winthrop D. *White over Black: American Attitudes toward the Negro, 1552–1812.* Chapel Hill: Univ. of North Carolina Press, 1968.

Kelly, J.D.N. *The Athanasian Creed: The Paddock Lectures for 1962–3.* London: Adam and Charles Black, 1964.

———. *Early Christian Doctrines.* 4th ed. London: Adam and Charles Black, 1968.

Kenny, Courtney. "The Evolution of the Law of Blasphemy." *Cambridge Law Journal* 1 (1922): 127–42.

Ketcham, Ralph. *James Madison: A Biography.* New York: Macmillan, 1971.

Kimball, Marie. "Thomas Jefferson and Religion." In *Jefferson Reader: A Treasury of Writings about Thomas Jefferson,* ed. Francis Coleman Rosenberger, pp. 117–30. New York: Dutton, 1953.

Knoles, George Harmon. "The Religious Ideas of Thomas Jefferson." In *Thomas Jefferson: A Profile,* ed. Merrill D. Peterson, pp. 243–60. New York: Hill and Wang, 1969.

Koch, Adrienne. *Jefferson and Madison: The Great Collaboration.* New York: Oxford Univ. Press, 1964.

———. *The Philosophy of Thomas Jefferson.* New York: Columbia Univ. Press, 1943.

———. *Power, Morals, and the Founding Fathers: Essays in the Interpretation of the American Enlightenment.* Ithaca, N.Y.: Cornell Univ. Press, 1961.

Koch, G. Adolph. *Republican Religion: The American Revoution and the Cult of Reason.* New York: H. Holt, 1933.

Kramnick, Isaac. Preface to *Lord Bolingbroke: Historical Writings.* Chicago: Univ. of Chicago Press, 1972.

———. "Religion and Radicalism: English Political Theory in the Age of Revolution." *Political Theory* 5 (1977): 505–34.

———. *Republicanism and Bourgeois Radicalism: Political Ideology in Late Eighteenth-Century England and America.* Ithaca, N.Y.: Cornell Univ. Press, 1990.

———. "Republican Revisionism Revisited." *American Historical Review* 87 (1982): 629–64.

Laurie, Henry. *Scottish Philosophy in Its National Development.* Glasgow: James Maclehose and Sons, 1902.

Lehmann, Karl. *Thomas Jefferson, American Humanist.* Phoenix edn. Chicago: Univ. of Chicago Press, 1965.

Lehmann, William C. *Henry Home, Lord Kames, and the Scottish Enlightenment.* The Hague: Martinus Nijhoff, 1971.

Levy, Leonard. *Jefferson and Civil Liberties: The Darker Side.* Cambridge: Belknap Press of Harvard Univ. Press, 1963.

———. "Jefferson as a Civil Libertarian." In *Thomas Jefferson: The Man, His World, His Influence,* ed. Lally Weymouth, pp. 189–215. London: Weidenfeld and Nicolson, 1973.

Lieberman, David. *The Province of Legislation Determined.* Cambridge: Cambridge Univ. Press, 1989.

Lienesch, Michael. *New Order of the Ages.* Princeton: Princeton Univ. Press, 1988.

Lind, John. "An Answer to the Declaration." In *A Casebook on the Declaration of Independence,* ed. Robert Ginsberg, pp. 9–17. New York: Crowell, 1966.

Lovejoy, Arthur O. *Essays in the History of Ideas.* Baltimore: Johns Hopkins Univ. Press, 1955.

———. *The Great Chain of Being: A Study of the History of an Idea.* Cambridge: Harvard Univ. Press, 1936.

———. *Reflections on Human Nature.* Baltimore: Johns Hopkins Univ. Press, 1961.

Lyttleton, George. *Dialogues of the Dead.* Dublin: n.p., 1760.

Macaulay, Thomas Babington. "I Cannot Reckon Jefferson among the Benefactors of Mankind." In *Jefferson Reader: A Treasury of Writings about Thomas Jefferson,* ed. Francis Coleman Rosenberger, pp. 260–63. New York: Dutton, 1953.

Macpherson, C.B. *Democratic Theory: Essays in Retrieval.* Oxford: Clarendon Press, 1973.

———. *The Political Theory of Possessive Individualism: Hobbes to Locke.* Oxford: Clarendon Press, 1962.

Malone, Dumas. *Jefferson and His Time.* 6 vols. Boston: Little, Brown, 1948–81.

———. "Jefferson Goes to School in Williamsburg." *Virginia Quarterly* 81 (1957): 481–96.

Marshall, John. *John Locke: Resistance, Religion, and Responsibility.* Cambridge: Cambridge Univ. Press, 1994.

Martin, Edwin T. *Thomas Jefferson, Scientist.* New York: Henry Schuman, 1952.

Marx, Leo. *The Machine in the Garden: Technology and the Pastoral Ideal in America.* New York: Oxford Univ. Press, 1970.

Mathews, Richard. *The Radical Politics of Thomas Jefferson.* Lawrence, Kans.: Univ. Press of Kansas, 1984.

McDonald, Forrest. *The Presidency of Thomas Jefferson.* Lawrence: Univ. Press of Kansas, 1976.

McGuinness, Arthur E. *Henry Home, Lord Kames.* New York: Twayne, 1970.

Middleton, Conyers. *The History of the Life of Marcus Tullius Cicero.* 2 vols. London: Richard Manby and Henry Shute Cox, 1757.

Miller, Charles A. *Jefferson and Nature: An Interpretation.* Baltimore: Johns Hopkins Univ. Press, 1988.

Miller, John C. *The Origins of the American Revolution.* Boston: Little, Brown, 1943.

——. *The Wolf by the Ears: Thomas Jefferson and Slavery.* New York: Free Press, 1977.

Miller, Perry. "Covenant to Revival." In *Religion in American Life: The Shaping of American Religion,* vol. 1, pp. 322–68. Princeton: Princeton Univ. Press, 1961.

——. *Errand into the Wilderness.* Cambridge: Belknap Press of Harvard Univ. Press, 1956.

Mitchell, Broadus, and Louise Pearson Mitchell. *A Biography of the Constitution of the United States.* New York: Oxford Univ. Press, 1975.

Morgan, Edmund S. *The Meaning of Independence: John Adams, George Washington, Thomas Jefferson.* Charlottesville: Univ. Press of Virginia, 1975.

——. "The Revolution as an Intellectual Movement." In *Paths of American Thought,* ed. Arthur M. Schlesinger Jr. and Morton White, pp. 11–33. London: Chatto and Windus, 1964.

——. "Slavery and Freedom: The American Paradox." *Journal of American History* 59 (1972–73): 5–29.

Mourret, Fernand. *A History of the Catholic Church.* Vol. 6. Trans. Newton Thompson. Saint Louis, Mo.: B. Hearder, 1947.

Murrin, John M. "The Great Inversion, or Court versus Country: A Comparison of the Revolution Settlements in England (1688–1721) and America (1776–1816)." In *Three British Revolutions: 1642, 1688, 1776,* ed. J.G.A. Pocock, pp. 368–453. Princeton: Princeton Univ. Press, 1980.

O'Brien, Conor Cruise. *The Long Affair: Thomas Jefferson and the French Revolution, 1785–1800.* Chicago: Univ. of Chicago Press, 1996.

Pangle, Thomas L. *The Spirit of Modern Republicanism.* Paperback edn. Chicago: Univ. of Chicago Press, 1990.

Parrington, Vernon Louis. *Main Currents in American Thought.* Vol. 1, *1620–1800: The Colonial Mind.* New York: Harcourt, Brace, 1954.

Passmore, J.A. "The Malleability of Man in Eighteenth-Century Thought." In *Aspects of the Eighteenth Century,* ed. Earl R. Wasserman, pp. 21–46. Baltimore: Johns Hopkins Press, 1965.

Perry, Ralph Barton. *Puritanism and Democracy.* New York: Vanguard, 1944.

Pocock, J.G.A. *The Ancient Constitution and Feudal Law: A Study of En-*

glish Historical Thought in the Seventeenth Century. Portway Bath: Cedric Chivers, 1974.

———. "Cambridge Paradigims and Scottish Philosophers: A Study of the Relations between the Civic Humanist and Civil Jurisprudential Interpretation of Eighteenth-Century Social Thought." In *Wealth and Virtue,* ed. Istvan Hont and Michael Ignatieff, pp. 235–52. Cambridge: Cambridge Univ. Press, 1983.

———. "Machiavelli, Harrington, and English Political Ideologies in the Eighteenth Century." *William and Mary Quarterly,* 3d ser., 22 (1965): 549–83.

———. *The Machiavellian Moment: Florentine Political Thought and the Atlantic Republican Tradition.* Princeton: Princeton Univ. Press, 1975.

———. "The Myth of John Locke and the Obsession with Liberalism." In *John Locke: Papers Read at a Clark Library Seminar,* pp. 1–24. Los Angeles: William Andrews Clark Memorial Library, 1980.

———. *Virtue, Commerce, and History: Essays on Political Thought and History, Chiefly in the Eighteenth Century.* Cambridge, 1985.

———. "Virtue and Commerce in the Eighteenth Century." *Journal of Interdisciplinary History* 3 (1972): 119–34.

Polin, Raymond. "John Locke's Conception of Freedom." In *John Locke: Problems and Perspectives,* ed. John W. Yolton, pp. 1–18. Cambridge: Cambridge Univ. Press, 1969.

Pollock, John. *George Whitefield and the Great Awakening.* London: Hodder and Stoughton, 1973.

Popkin, Richard H. *The History of Skepticism from Erasmus to Spinoza.* Berkeley: Univ. of California Press, 1979.

Randall, Henry S. *The Life of Thomas Jefferson.* 3 vols. New York: Derby and Jackson, 1858.

Robbins, Caroline. *The Eighteenth-Century Commonwealthman: Studies in the Transmission, Development, and Circumstances of English Liberal Thought from the Restoration of Charles II until the War with the Thirteen Colonies.* Cambridge: Harvard Univ. Press, 1959.

Rossiter, Clinton. *Seedtime of the Republic: The Origin of the American Tradition of Political Liberty.* New York: Harcourt, Brace, 1953.

Sanford, Charles B. *The Religious Life of Thomas Jefferson.* Charlottesville: Univ. Press of Virginia, 1984.

Savelle, Max. *Seeds of Liberty: The Genesis of the American Mind.* Seattle: Univ. of Washington Press, 1965.

Schachner, Nathan. *Thomas Jefferson: A Biography.* New York: Appleton-Century-Crofts, 1957.

Schlesinger, Arthur M. "The Lost Meaning of 'The Pursuit of Happiness.'" *William and Mary Quarterly,* 3d ser., 21 (1964): 325–27.

Schneider, Herbert W. "The Enlightenment in Thomas Jefferson." *Ethics: An International Journal of Social, Political, and Legal Philosophy* 54 (1942–43): 246–54.

Schofield, Robert E. *The Lunar Society of Birmingham.* London: Clarendon Press, 1963.

Scott, William B. *In Pursuit of Happiness: American Conceptions of Property from the Seventeenth to the Twentieth Century.* Bloomington: Indiana Univ. Press, 1977.

Shain, Barry Alan. *The Myth of American Individualism: The Protestant Origins of American Political Thought.* Princeton: Princeton Univ. Press, 1994.

Sheldon, Garrett Ward. *The Political Philosophy of Thomas Jefferson.* Baltimore: Johns Hopkins Univ. Press, 1991.

Skinner, Quentin. "The Principles and Practice of Opposition: The Case of Bolingbroke versus Walpole." In *Historical Perspectives,* ed. Neil McKendrick, pp. 93–128. London: Europa Publications, 1974.

Smith, Charles Page. *James Wilson.* Chapel Hill: Univ. of North Carolina Press, 1956.

Smith, T.V. "Discussion: Thomas Jefferson and the Perfectibility of Mankind." *Ethics: An International Journal of Social, Political, and Legal Philosophy* 53 (1942–43): 293–310.

Sowerby, Millicent E. *Catalogue of the Library of Thomas Jefferson.* Charlottesville: Univ. Press of Virginia, 1983.

Spellman, W.M. *John Locke and the Problem of Depravity.* Oxford: Clarendon Press, 1988.

Spragens, Thomas A., Jr. "Communitarianism and the Liberal Tradition." Paper delivered at American Political Science Association meeting, New York, 1994.

Stein, Peter. "The General Notions of Contract and Property in Eighteenth Century Scottish Thought." *Juridical Review: The Law Journal of the Scottish Universities* 1963–64, pp. 1–13.

Stout, Harry S. "Religion, Communications, and the Ideological Origins of the American Revolution." *William and Mary Quarterly,* 3d ser., 34 (1977): 525–26.

Strauss, Leo. *Natural Right and History.* Chicago: Univ. of Chicago Press, 1953.

Tate, Thad W. "The Social Contract in America, 1774–1787: Revolutionary Theory as a Conservative Instrument." *William and Mary Quarterly,* 3d. ser., 22 (1965): 375–91.

Thornton, John Wingate, ed. *The Pulpit of the American Revolution; or, The Political Sermons of the Period of 1776.* New York: Da Capo Press, 1970.

Tracy, Joseph. *The Great Awakening.* London: Banner of Truth Trust, 1976.

Tuck, Richard. *Natural Rights Theories: Their Origin and Development.* Paperback edn. Cambridge: Cambridge Univ. Press, 1981.

Tully, James. *A Discourse on Property: John Locke and His Adversaries.* Cambridge: Cambridge Univ. Press, 1980.

———. "Locke." In *The Cambridge History of Political Thought: 1450–*

1700, ed. J.H. Burns and Mark Goldie. Cambridge: Cambridge Univ. Press, 1991.

Waldron, Jeremy. "Locke: Toleration and the Rationality of Persecution." In *Justifying Toleration: Conceptual and Historical Perspectives,* ed. Susan Mendus, pp. 61–86. Cambridge: Cambridge Univ. Press, 1988.

Walker, David M. *The Scottish Jurists.* Edinburgh: W. Green and Son, 1985.

Waterman, Julian S. "Thomas Jefferson and Blackstone's Commentaries." *Illinois Law Review* 27 (1933): 629–59.

White, Morton. *The Philosophy of the American Revolution.* New York: Oxford Univ. Press, 1978.

Willman, Robert. "Blackstone and the Theoretical Perfection of English Law in the Reign of Charles II." *Historical Journal* 26 (1983): 39–70.

Wills, Garry. *Inventing America: Jefferson's Declaration of Independence.* New York: Vintage Books, 1979.

————. *Under God: Religion and American Politics.* New York: Simon and Schuster, 1990.

Wiltse, Charles M. *The Jeffersonian Tradition in American Democracy.* Chapel Hill: Univ. of North Carolina Press, 1935.

————. "Thomas Jefferson and the Law of Nations." *American Journal of International Law* 29 (1935): 66–81.

Winslow, Ola Elizabeth. *Jonathan Edwards.* New York: Macmillan, 1940.

Wishy, Bernard. "John Locke and the Spirit of 76." *Political Science Quarterly* 73 (1958): 413–25.

Wood, Forrest G. *The Arrogance of Faith.* New York: Alfred A. Knopf, 1990.

Wood, Gordon S. *The Creation of the American Republic, 1776–1787.* Chapel Hill: Univ. of North Carolina Press, 1969.

————. "Ideology and the Origins of Liberal America." *William and Mary Quarterly,* 3d ser., 44 (1977): 628–40.

Wright, Louis B. "Thomas Jefferson and the Classics." In *Thomas Jefferson: A Profile,* ed. Merrill D. Peterson, pp. 195–217. New York: Hill and Wang, 1969.

Yolton, John W. *John Locke and the Way of Ideas.* London: Oxford Univ. Press, 1956.

————. "The Science of Nature." In *John Locke: Problems and Perspectives,* ed. John W. Yolton, pp. 183–93. Cambridge: Cambridge Univ. Press, 1969.

Zuckert, Michael P. *Natural Rights and the New Republicanism.* Princeton: Princeton Univ. Press, 1994.

————. "Thomas Jefferson on Nature and Natural Rights." In *The Framers and Fundamental Rights,* ed. Robert A. Licht, pp. 137–66. Washington, D.C.: AEI Press, 1991.

Index of Persons

Index of Subjects